Managerial Economics: Problems and Exercises

Managerial Economics: Problems and Exercises

by

Edwin Mansfield
University of Pennsylvania

W.W. Norton & Company
New York London

Copyright © 1990 by W.W. Norton & Company, Inc.
Printed in the United States of America.

ALL RIGHTS RESERVED

ISBN 0-393-95730-6

W.W. Norton & Company, Inc., 500 Fifth Avenue, New York, NY 10110
W.W. Norton & Company Ltd., 37 Great Russell Street, London WC1B 3NU

1 2 3 4 5 6 7 8 9 0

Contents

Preface		vii
Chapter 1	Introduction to Managerial Economics	1
Chapter 2	Optimization Techniques	5
Chapter 3	Demand Theory	15
Chapter 4	Estimating Demand Functions	27
Chapter 5	Business and Economic Forecasting	40
Chapter 6	Production Theory	50
Chapter 7	Technological Change and Industrial Innovation	62
Chapter 8	The Analysis of Costs	71
Chapter 9	Linear Programming	88
Chapter 10	Perfect Competition, Monopoly, and Monopolistic Competition	104
Chatper 11	Oligopoly and Strategic Behavior	118
Chapter 12	Pricing Techniques	130
Chapter 13	Risk Analysis	137
Chapter 14	Capital Budgeting	148
Chapter 15	Government and Business	158
Brief Answers to Even-Numbered End-of-Chapter Questions and Problems in the Text		167

Preface

This *Study Guide to Managerial Economics* is designed to supplement my text *Managerial Economics*. Each chapter of this book parallels closely the contents of the corresponding chapter of my text. In order to provide comprehensive and varied exercises and problems, a four-pronged approach has been adopted:

1. *Chapter profiles* highlight and summarize the principal points of the chapter in the text.
2. Limbering-up exercises in the form of *completion questions* open the way to systematic review of each chapter.
3. Self-tests in the form of *true or false* and *multiple choice* questions are provided.
4. A considerable number of *problems* are taken up. These problems often simulate real-world situations and require the student to work with actual data in tabular and diagrammatic form.

Answers to all the questions and problems are contained at the end of each chapter. In addition, answers to the even-numbered questions and problems in the text are included. (The answers to the odd-numbered questions and problems are provided at the end of the text *Managerial Economics*.)

This book contains over 500 questions and problems, enough to provide the student with a thorough review. Since a study guide should be a flexible learning tool, I have sought to supply not only a large number of questions but also a wide range in terms of difficulty. Each chapter begins at a relatively easy level, increasing gradually in rigor as students build confidence along with competence. The more demanding an economic concept, the more extensive the amount of review material given to it. Some of the problems at the end of chapters are hard enough so that the typical student should not expect to answer them all. Even the best students should be challenged by some of them.

E.M.

October 1989

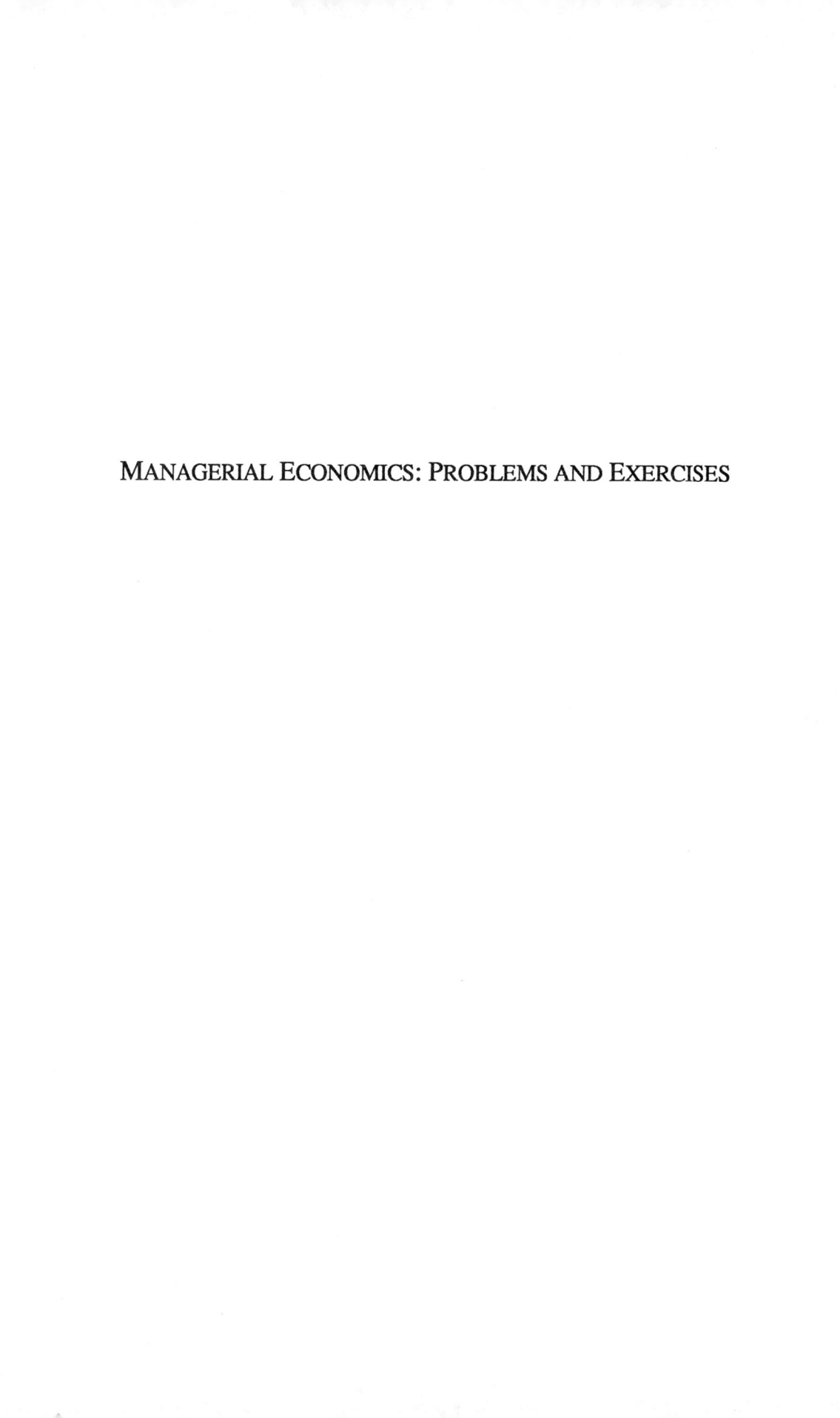

MANAGERIAL ECONOMICS: PROBLEMS AND EXERCISES

CHAPTER 1

Introduction to Managerial Economics

Chapter Profile

Managerial economics draws heavily on economics (particularly microeconomics) and the decision sciences. In contrast to microeconomics, which is largely descriptive, managerial economics is prescriptive. Courses in managerial economics provide fundamental analytical tools, as well as play a major integrating role. Managerial economics is at the core of the management of nonbusiness organizations like government agencies, as well as the management of firms.

Both for nonbusiness organizations and firms, the process of decision making can be divided into the following five basic steps. (1) Establish or identify the organization's objectives. (2) Define the problem. (3) Identify possible solutions. (4) Select the best possible solution. (5) Implement the decision.

To apply managerial economics to business management, we need a theory of the firm. According to the theory accepted by most managerial economists, the firm tries to maximize its value, defined as the present value of its expected future cash flows (which for now are equated with profits). However, this maximization occurs subject to constraints, since the firm has limited inputs, particularly in the very short run, and must act in accord with a variety of laws and contracts.

Managerial economists define profits somewhat differently than do accountants. When economists speak of profit, they mean profit over and above what the owners' labor and capital employed in the business could earn elsewhere. To a considerable extent, the differences between the concept of profit used by the accountant and that used by the economist reflect the difference in their functions.

Three important reasons for the existence of profits are innovation, risk, and monopoly power. Profits and losses are the mainsprings of a free-enterprise economy. They are signals that indicate where resources are needed and where they are too abundant. They are important incentives for innovation and risk taking. They are society's reward for efficiency.

Although managerial economists generally assume that firms want to maximize profit (and hence their value), this assumption is not universally adopted. Some have suggested that the firm "satisfices" rather than maximizes profit. That is, firms aim at a satisfactory rate of profit rather than the maximum figure. Others have suggested that firms attempt to maximize sales subject to the constraint that profits be at least a minimum amount. These models can be useful, but profit maximization remains the standard assumption in managerial economics.

CHAPTER ONE

The field of managerial economics is intimately related to a prominent problem facing the United States and Canada (and a number of other countries)—the fact that many of our firms are being challenged more seriously by foreign rivals. In the business environment of the 1990s, there is little room for managers who fail to understand the principles and techniques of managerial economics.

Cases for Analysis

Because this is an introductory chapter, we do not present the full range of questions that will be included in subsequent chapters of this study guide. Instead, we take up four cases, our purpose being to introduce the student to various kinds of problems facing American firms in the 1990s. Each of these cases comes from the National Research Council's *Toward a New Era in U.S. Manufacturing*.[1]

Case 1: A Period of Change in the U.S. Auto Industry

"Through improved management, changed work rules, large investments in automation, and a variety of other measures, the three major U.S. automobile manufacturers have reduced their break-even volume for domestic production by more than 30 percent since 1980. Despite this dramatic improvement, estimates of the cost advantage of Japanese producers have grown from $1,000–$2,000 per car in 1979–80 to $2,000–$2,600 in 1985. Based on consumer surveys, U.S. cars also have lagged behind Japanese makes in quality. U.S. producers have launched new projects—General Motors' Saturn, Chrysler's Liberty, and Ford's Alpha—to eliminate these gaps by rethinking management concepts, employee relations and compensation, and technology. All three companies also are aggressively pursuing joint ventures with foreign producers . . . to offset the cost disadvantage of domestic production. The companies' approaches differ, but these programs clearly indicate that senior managers in the U.S. automobile industry recognize both the shortcomings of traditional practices and the opportunities that new technologies and new management approaches will provide."

1. Why do Japanese auto manufacturers have a cost advantage over American auto manufacturers?

2. What can American auto manufacturers do to improve their position?

3. Why are American auto producers "aggressively pursuing joint ventures with foreign producers"?

Case 2: Black and Decker versus Makita Electric Works

"Black and Decker Corporation has devoted significant effort to reducing costs and increasing efficiency by pursuing new investments, increasing automation, reducing its work force, and standardizing parts and product lines across its international operations.

---

[1] National Research Council, *Toward a New Era in U.S. Manufacturing* (Washington, D.C.: National Academy Press, 1986), pp. 17–19.

Despite these long-term efforts, the company faced growing competition in the world power tool market from Makita Electric Works, Ltd., of Japan and lost a significant part of its market share. Since 1980, Black and Decker has spend $80 million on plant modernization, cut its work force by 40 percent, and adopted new manufacturing practices. The company has regained a 20 percent share of the world market in power tools at the cost of reduced profits resulting from price pressures from the Japanese company."

1. Why should Black and Decker want to achieve a 20 percent market share if it is at the cost of reduced profits?
2. Does this mean that Black and Decker is not interested in maximizing profit? Why or why not?
3. Does it mean that Black and Decker is attempting to maximize sales? Why or why not?

Case 3: American Producers of Floppy Disk Drives: A Vanished Breed

"Floppy disk drives are used in lower-end home computers and personal computers, whereas rigid disk drives are used most often in advanced personal computers and engineering work station products. The disk drive industry was created by U.S. electronics firms from technology developed by International Business Machines and Control Data Corporation. Several smaller firms entered the field in the mid-1970s and quickly grew to substantial size. In recent years, however, the status of U.S. disk drive manufacturers has changed considerably. The leading U.S. maker of Floppy disk drives in 1980 was Shugart Associates. Xerox Corporation, the owner of Shugart, has since announced the closing of the unit as a disk drive manufacturer. In 1984, more than 20 Japanese firms manufactured floppy disk drives; no U.S. manufacturers did so. While the United States retains a strong position in rigid disk drives, the Japanese are likely to dominate the next-generation technology, optical disk drives."

1. What would be the value of Shugart Associates?
2. Why do you think that Xerox closed it as a disk drive manufacturer?
3. What constraints limited what Xerox could do to increase the value of Shugart Associates?

Case 4: Chaparral Steel: A Vigorous Competitor

"Chaparral Steel Company, a minimill operation based in Midlothian, Texas, figures that if it can produce steel at a labor cost per ton no higher than the per-ton cost of shipping steel to this country from Korea, it can beat Korean producers. In achieving this goal, the company has invested in some of the most modern steel plants in the world and can produce steel using 1.8 man-hours per ton, compared with 2.3 for the Koreans and 6+ for integrated U.S. producers. Although its capacity and range of product are more focused than those of large integrated producers, Chaparral illustrates two important aspects of the new manufacturing environment. First, the company's experience (and that

CHAPTER ONE

of other minimill operations, such as Nucor Corporation) has shown that U.S. producers can be world leaders and can pose more of a threat to traditional U.S. manufacturers, albeit in a relatively narrow product line, than foreign competitors. Second, traditional competitive targets, such as matching the production costs of competitors, may not be enough to ensure long-term competitiveness; other targets, such as the shipping costs used by Chaparral, may need to be considered."

1. Are Chaparral Steel's profits in part a reward for successful innovation?
2. Are they a signal indicating where resources are needed?
3. Are they a reward for efficiency?

Answers

Case 1

1. Because of higher productivity as well as lower prices of some inputs.
2. American auto manufacturers can learn from their Japanese (and other) rivals how to improve their productivity.
3. American producers can learn from foreign producers and can obtain low-cost inputs and products.

Case 2

1. Black and Decker many feel that if it holds on to a 20 percent market share, it will be more profitable in the long run than it would if the company did not do so.
2. No.
3. No.

Case 3

1. The present value of its profits.
2. Because the present value of its profits was less as a disk drive manufacturer than it would have been if it had produced something else (or had been sold).
3. Many of Shugart's assets were relatively specialized. Many of its employees and suppliers may have had contracts with the firm that could not be changed readily. Xerox also was constrained by the limits of existing technological knowledge, and the nature and extent of competition from other firms.

Case 4

1. Yes.
2. Yes.
3. Yes.

CHAPTER 2

Optimization Techniques

Chapter Profile

Functional relationships can be represented by tables, graphs, or equations The marginal value of a dependent variable is defined as the change in this variable associated with a one-unit change in a particular independent variable. The dependent variable achieves a maximum when its marginal value shifts from positive to negative.

The derivative of Y with respect to X, denoted by dY/dX, is the limit of the ratio $\Delta Y/\Delta X$ as ΔX approaches zero. Geometrically, it is the slope of the curve showing Y (on the vertical axis) as a function of X (on the horizontal axis). We have provided rules that enable us to find the value of this derivative.

To find the value of X that maximizes or minimizes Y, we determine the value of X where dY/dX equals zero. To tell whether this is a maximum or a minimum, we find the second derivative of Y with respect to X, denoted by d^2Y/dX^2, which is the derivative of dY/dX. If this second derivative is negative, we have found a maximum; if it is positive, we have found a minimum.

A dependent variable often depends on a number of independent variables, not just one. To find the value of each of the independent variables that maximizes the dependent variable, we determine the partial derivative of Y with respect to each of the independent variables, denoted by $\delta Y/\delta X$, and set it equal to zero. To obtain the partial derivative of Y with respect to X, we apply the ordinary rules for finding a derivative; however, all independent variables other than X are treated as constants.

Managers of firms and other organizations generally face constraints that limit the options available to them. In relatively simple cases where there is only one constraint, we can use this constraint to express one of the decision variables as a function of the other decision variables, and we can apply the techniques for unconstrained optimization.

In more complex cases, constrained optimization problems can be solved by the method of Lagrangian multipliers. The Lagrangian function combines the function to be maximized or minimized with the constraints. To solve the constrained optimization problem, we optimize the Lagrangian function.

CHAPTER TWO

Questions

Completion

1. The derivative of Y with respect to X is defined as the limit of _____ as ΔX approaches _____.
2. If Y equals a constant, $\frac{dY}{dX}$ equals _____.
3. If Y equals AX^b, $\frac{dY}{dX}$ equals _____.
4. If $Y = U + W$, $\frac{dY}{dX}$ equals _____.
5. In the graph below, the slope of the curve equals _____ when Y is a maximum.

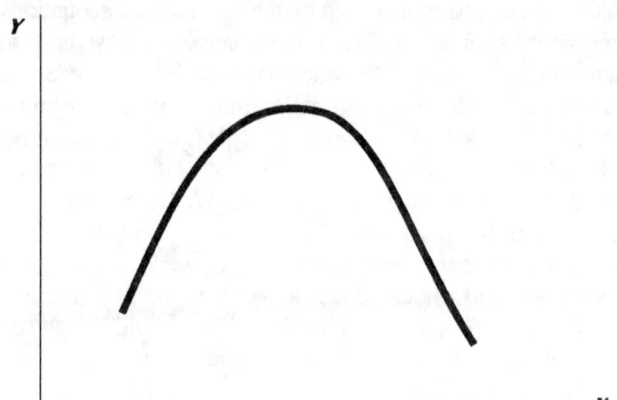

6. In the previous question, the value of d^2Y/dX^2 is (positive, negative, zero) _____ at the point where Y is a maximum.
7. If TR equals total revenue and Q equals output, $\frac{dTR}{dQ}$ equals _____.
8. The partial derivative of Y with respect to X_1 shows the effect of X_1 on _____ when other independent variables are _____ _____.
9. The Lagrangian multiplier λ, measures the change in the variable to be maximized or minimized if the constraint is relaxed by _____ unit(s).

True or False

_____ 1. The marginal value of a dependent variable is always positive or zero.

_____ 2. At any point where $\frac{d^2Y}{dX^2}$ is negative, Y is a maximum.

_____ 3. To find the value of $\delta Y/\delta X_1$, all independent variable other than X_1 are treated as constants.

_____ 4. If $Y = 3X^4, \frac{dY}{dX} = 12X^2$.

_____ 5. If $Y = 2X + X^3, \frac{dY}{dX} = 2 + 3X^2$.

_____ 6. If $Y = 3X_1 + 4X_2, \frac{\delta Y}{\delta X_1} = 4$.

_____ 7. If $Y = 3X_1 + 6X_2$, it is impossible to find a value of X_1 and X_2 where $\frac{\delta Y}{\delta X_1}$ and $\frac{\delta Y}{\delta X_2}$ equal zero.

_____ 8. If $Y = 4X(2 - X^2), \frac{dY}{dX} = 8 - 12X^2$.

_____ 9. If $Y = 5X_1^{.2} X_2^{.8}, \frac{\delta Y}{\delta X_1} = .2(5X_1^{-.8} X_2^{.8})$.

_____ 10. If $Y = f(W)$ and $W = g(X), \frac{dY}{dX} = \frac{dY}{dW} \cdot \frac{dW}{dX}$.

Multiple Choice

1. If $Y = -30 + 20X - 10X^2$, the value of X that maximizes Y equals

   a. 1.
   b. 2.
   c. 3.
   d. 4.
   e. none of the above.

2. In question 1, the maximum value of Y equals

   a. −20.
   b. −30.
   c. −10.
   d. 20.
   e. none of the above.

3. If $Y = 40 - 5X + 10X^2$, the value of X that minimizes Y equals

   a. .15.
   b. .20.
   c. .25.
   d. .30.
   e. none of the above.

CHAPTER TWO

4. In question 3, the minimum value of Y equals

   a. $39\,5/8$.
   b. $40\,3/8$.
   c. $40\,5/8$.
   d. $39\,3/8$.
   e. none of the above.

5. In question 3, the value of d^2Y/dX^2 at the minimum value of Y is

   a. 5.
   b. –5.
   c. 20.
   d. 10.
   e. none of the above.

6. If $Y = 100 + 2X - \frac{3}{2}X^2 + \frac{X^3}{3}$, the values of X that result in $\frac{dY}{dX}$ equaling zero are

   a. 1 and 2.
   b. 1 and 3.
   c. 2 and 3.
   d. 2 and 4.
   e. none of the above.

7. In question 6, if $X = 1$, the value of $\frac{d^2Y}{dX^2}$ is

   a. –8.
   b. –6.
   c. –4.
   d. –1.
   e. none of the above.

8. In question 6, Y is a maximum when X equals

   a. 0.
   b. 1.
   c. 2.
   d. 3.
   e. none of the above.

9. If $Y = 100 + 20X_1 + 14X_2 - 2X_2^2$, the value of $\frac{\delta Y}{\delta X_1}$

   a. does not vary with the value of X_1.
   b. does not vary with the value of X_2.
   c. equals 20.
   d. all of the above.
   e. none of the above.

8

CHAPTER TWO

10. In question 9, the value of $\dfrac{\delta Y}{\delta X_2}$

    a. equals $14 - 4X_2$.
    b. equals zero when $X_2 = 3.5$.
    c. decreases as X_2 increases.
    d. all of the above.
    e. none of the above.

Problems

1. The total cost function at the Tate Company is $TC = 200 + 3Q + 7Q^2$, where TC is total cost, and Q is output.

    a. What is marginal cost when $Q = 1$?
    b. What is marginal cost when $Q = 5$?
    c. What is marginal cost when $Q = 10$?

2. For the Algonquin Company, the relationship between profit and output is as follows:

Output (number of units per day)	Profit (thousands of dollars per day)
0	–8
1	–4
2	0
3	4
4	8
5	11
6	13
7	12
8	11

    a. What is the marginal profit when output is between 1 and 2 units per day? When output is between 4 and 5 units per day?
    b. At what output is profit a maximum?
    c. At what output is average profit a maximum? Should the Algonquin Company produce this output? Why or why not?

3. Determine the first derivative of the following functions:

    a. $Y = 4$.
    b. $Y = 4X$.
    c. $Y = 4X^2 + 6$.
    d. $Y = 4X^3 + 6X$.
    e. $Y = 4X^3 + 6X + 10$.

CHAPTER TWO

4. The Phoenix Corporation's chief executive officer believes that the relationship between its profit (π) and its output (Q) is as follows:

$$\pi = -20 - 5Q + 10Q^2 - 2Q^3.$$

   a. Should this firm set $Q = 5$? Why or why not?
   b. Should it set $Q = 10$? Why or why not?
   c. Should it set $Q = 20$? Why or why not?

5. Find the partial derivative of Y with respect to X in each of the following cases:

   a. $Y = 8 + 4X + 6Z$.
   b. $Y = 8X + 4X^2 + 6Z$.
   c. $Y = 8X + 4X^3 + 6Z + 2Z^2$.
   d. $Y = X \div Z$.

6. At the Peoria Company, the relationship between profit (π) and output (Q) is as follows:

$$\pi = -40 + 20Q - 2Q^2.$$

   a. At what value of Q does $\dfrac{d\pi}{dQ} = 0$?
   b. Is π minimized or maximized at this value of Q?
   c. What is the second derivative of π with respect to Q at this value of Q?

7. Determine the second derivative of Y with respect to X in each of the following cases:

   a. $Y = 7X$.
   b. $Y = 7 \div X$.
   c. $Y = 7X^2$.
   d. $Y = 7X(2 + X^2)$.

8. The Cornell Corporation makes two products, chairs and tables. The relationship between π, the firm's annual profit (in thousands of dollars), and its output of each good is

$$\pi = -80 + 30Q_1 + 25Q_2 - 4Q_1^2 - 3Q_2^2 - 2Q_1Q_2,$$

where Q_1 is the firm's hourly output of chairs, and Q_2 is the firm's hourly output of tables. (Neither Q_1 nor Q_2 needs to be an integer.)

   a. Find the output of chairs and the output of tables that will maximize the firm's profit.
   b. What is the maximum profit that the firm can earn per year?

9. For the Knowland Corporation, the relationship between profit and output is the following:

Output (number of units per day)	Profit (thousands of dollars per day)
0	−30
1	−24
2	−15
3	0
4	6
5	21
6	36
7	63
8	66
9	69
10	60

   a. What is the marginal profit when output is between 3 and 4 units per day? When output is between 8 and 9 units per day?
   b. At what output is average profit a maximum?
   c. Should the Knowland Corporation produce 7 units per day? Why or why not?

10. The total cost function at the Driftwood Company is $TC = 300 + 2Q + 3Q^2$, where TC is total cost and Q is output.

   a. What is marginal cost when output is 8?
   b. What is marginal cost when output is 10?
   c. What is marginal cost when output is 12?

11. The Secane Company's profit is related in the following way to its output:

   $\pi = -80 + 30Q - 4Q^2$, where π is total profit and Q is output.

   a. If the firm's output equals 5, what is its marginal profit?
   b. Derive an equation relating the firm's marginal profit to its output.
   c. What output will maximize the firm's profit?

12. The Lone Star Corporation makes two products, lumber and paper. The relationship between π, the firm's annual profit (in thousands of dollars), and its output of each good is

   $$\pi = -100 + 80Q_1 + 60Q_2 - 10Q_1^2 - 8Q_2^2 - 5Q_1Q_2,$$

   where Q_1 is the firm's annual output of lumber (in tons), and Q_2 is the firm's annual output of paper (in tons). Find the output of each good that the Lone Star Corporation should produce if it wants to maximize profit.

CHAPTER TWO

13. A firm produces two goods. Its total cost per day (in dollars) equals

$$TC = 14X_1^2 + 18X_2^2 - 3X_1X_2,$$

where X_1 is the number of units of the first good produced per day, and X_2 is the number of units of the second good produced per day. Because of commitments to customers, the firm must produce a total of 20 units of the two goods per day. If the firm's managers want to minimize its costs (without violating the commitment to its customers), how many units of each good should it produce per day?

Answers

Completion

1. $\Delta Y/\Delta X$, zero 2. zero 3. bAX^{b-1} 4. $\dfrac{dU}{dX} + \dfrac{dW}{dX}$ 5. zero 6. negative 7. marginal revenue 8. Y, held constant 9. one

True or False

1. False 2. False 3. True 4. False 5. True 6. False 7. True 8. True 9. True 10. True

Multiple Choice

1. a 2. a 3. c 4. d 5. c 6. a 7. d 8. b 9. d 10. d

Problems

1. Marginal cost equals dTC/dQ. When $Q = 1$, marginal cost equals
   a. $3 + 14(1) = 17$.
   b. $3 + 14(5) = 73$.
   c. $3 + 14(10) = 143$.

2. a. 4 thousand dollars, 3 thousand dollars.
   b. 6 units per day.
   c. 5 units per day. If the firm wants to maximize profit, it obviously should not produce this output.

3. a. Zero.
   b. 4.
   c. $8X$.
   d. $12X^2 + 6$.
   e. $12X^2 + 6$.

4. a. No. Since $d\pi/dQ$ is not equal to zero when $Q = 5$, π is not a maximum.
   b. No. Since $d\pi/dQ$ is not equal to zero when $Q = 10$, π is not a maximum.
   c. No. Since $d\pi/dQ$ is not equal to zero when $Q = 20$, π is not a maximum.

CHAPTER TWO

5. a. 4.
   b. $8 + 8X$.
   c. $8 + 12X^2$.
   d. $\dfrac{1}{Z}$.

6. a. 5.
   b. Q is maximized.
   c. -4.

7. a. Zero.
   b. $14/X^3$.
   c. 14.
   d. $42X$.

8. a. $\dfrac{\delta \pi}{\delta Q_1} = 30 - 8Q_1 - 2Q_2 = 0$

   $\dfrac{\delta \pi}{\delta Q_2} = 25 - 6Q_2 - 2Q_1 = 0.$

   Since $Q_2 = 15 - 4Q_1$, it follows that
   $$25 - 6(15 - 4Q_1) - 2Q_1 = 0$$
   $$22Q_1 = 65$$
   $$Q_1 = 65/22.$$
   Thus, $Q_2 = 15 - 4(65/22) = 15 - 4(2.95) = 15 - 11.8 = 3.2$.

   b. $\pi = -80 + 30(2.95) + 25(3.2) - 4(2.95)^2 - 3(3.2)^2 - 2(2.95)(3.2)$
   $= -80 + 88.5 + 80 - 34.81 - 30.72 - 18.88$
   $= 4.09$.

9. a. 6 thousand dollars, 3 thousand dollars.
   b. 7 units per day.
   c. Not if it wants to maximize profit.

10. Marginal cost equals dTC/dQ. When $Q = 8$, marginal cost equals
    a. $2 + 6(8) = 50$.
    b. $2 + 6(10) = 62$.
    c. $2 + 6(12) = 74$.

11. a. $\dfrac{d\pi}{dQ} = 30 - 8Q = 30 - 8(5) = -10.$
    b. Marginal profit $= 30 - 8Q$.
    c. $Q = 30/8$.

12. $\dfrac{\delta \pi}{\delta Q_1} = 80 - 20Q_1 - 5Q_2 = 0$

    $\dfrac{\delta \pi}{\delta Q_2} = 60 - 16Q_2 - 5Q_1 = 0.$

CHAPTER TWO

Since $Q_2 = 16 - 4Q_1$,
$$60 - 16(16 - 4Q_1) - 5Q_1 = 0$$
$$59Q_1 = 196$$
$$Q_1 = 3.32.$$

Thus, $Q_2 = 16 - 4(3.32) = 2.72$. In other words, Lone Star should produce 3.32 tons of lumber and 2.72 tons of paper.

13. Because $X_1 = 20 - X_2$,
$$TC = 14(20 - X_2)^2 + 18X_2^2 - 3(20 - X_2)(X_2)$$
$$= 5{,}600 - 560X_2 + 14X_2^2 + 18X_2^2 - 60X_2 + 3X_2^2$$
$$= 5{,}600 - 620X_2 + 35X_2^2$$
$$\frac{dTC}{dX_2} = -620 + 70X_2 = 0$$
$$X_2 = \frac{620}{70} = 8.86.$$

Since $X_1 = 20 - X_2$, it follows that $X_1 = 11.14$. In other words, the firm should produce 11.14 units of the first good and 8.86 units of the second good per day.

CHAPTER 3

Demand Theory

Chapter Profile

The market demand curve for a good shows how much of the good will be demanded at each price. The market demand curve shifts in response to changes in tastes, incomes, and the prices of other goods, as well as a host of other factors.

The market demand function for a good is an equation showing how the quantity demanded depends on the good's price, the incomes of consumers, the prices of other goods, advertising expenditure, and other factors. Holding all factors other than the good's price constant, one can derive the market demand curve for the good from the market demand function. Market demand functions can be formulated for individual firms as well as for entire industries.

The price elasticity of demand is the percentage change in quantity demanded resulting from a 1 percent change in price; more precisely, it equal $-(\delta Q_D/\delta P)(P/Q_D)$. Whether a price increase (or decrease) results in an increase in the total amount spent by consumers on a product depends on the price elasticity of demand.

Marginal revenue is the change in total revenue resulting from a 1-unit increase in quantity; that is, it equals the derivative of total revenue with respect to quantity. Marginal revenue equal $P\left(1 - \frac{1}{\eta}\right)$, where P is price, and η is the price elasticity of demand.

The price elasticity of demand for a good tends to be high if it has a large number of close substitutes. Also, for non-durable goods, it tends to be higher in the long run than in the short run. It is sometimes asserted that the demand for a product is relatively price inelastic if the product accounts for a very small percentage of the typical consumer's budget, but this need not be the case.

The income elasticity of demand is the percentage change in quantity demanded resulting from a 1 percent increase in consumer income; that is, it equals $(\delta Q/\delta I)(I/Q)$, where I is the aggregate money income of consumers. The income elasticity of demand may be positive or negative. Like the price elasticity of demand, it is of major importance in forecasting the long-term growth of the quantity demanded for many major products.

The cross elasticity of demand is the percentage change in the quantity demanded of product X resulting from a 1 percent increase in the price of product Y; in other words, it equals $(\delta Q_X/\delta P_Y)(P_Y/Q_X)$. If X and Y are substitutes, it is positive; if they are complements, it is negative. This elasticity is important to managers because they must try to understand and forecast the effects of changes in other firms' prices on their own firm's sales.

The optimal price for a product depends on its price elasticity of demand as well as on its marginal cost. To maximize profit, a firm should set its price equal to $MC\left(\frac{1}{1 - 1/\eta}\right)$, where MC is marginal cost, and η is the price elasticity of demand.

Questions

Completion

1. If the cross elasticity of demand between goods X and Y is positive, these goods are classified as ~~complementary~~ *substitutes*.
2. The income elasticity of demand is the percentage change in quantity demanded resulting from a *percentage* change in money income.
3. Luxury goods are generally assumed to have a ~~positive~~ *high* income elasticity of demand.
4. If a commodity has many close substitutes, its demand is likely to be *price* elastic.
5. The price elasticity of demand equals $\frac{dQ}{dP} \cdot \frac{P}{Q}$.
6. The demand curve for the individual firm under perfect competition is ~~elastic~~ *horizontal*.
7. The price elasticity of demand is generally *higher* in the long run than in the short run (for non-durable goods).
8. The total amount of money spent by consumers on a commodity equals the industry's _____. *total revenue*
9. The __MR__ curve shows marginal revenue at various quantities of output.
10. If the industry is not perfectly competitive, the firm's demand curve will not be _____. *horizontal*

True or False

__T__ 1. The demand for open-heart surgery is likely to be less price elastic than the demand for aspirin.

F __T__ 2. If a good's income elasticity exceeds 1, a decrease in the price of the good will increase the total amount spent on it.

F __T__ 3. The demand curve for an individual firm under perfect competition is downward sloping, its slope being −1.

$I > 1$ elast.

CHAPTER THREE

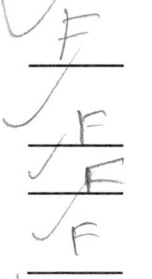

___F___ 4. The market demand curve for a product under perfect competition is horizontal.

___F___ 5. The demand for salt and pepper is likely to be price elastic.

___F___ 6. In general, demand is likely to be more inelastic in the long run than in the short run (for non-durable goods).

___F___ 7. The income elasticity of demand for food is very high.

_____ 8. It is always true that $\eta_{xy} = \eta_{yx}$.

___F___ 9. The direct approach of simply asking people how much they would buy of a particular commodity is the best way to estimate the demand curve.

___F___ 10. The income elasticity of demand will always have the same sign regardless of the level of income at which it is measured.

___T___ 11. Marginal revenue is the ratio of the value of sales to the amount sold.

___F___ 12. When the demand curve is linear, the slope of the marginal revenue curve is twice (in absolute value) the slope of the demand curve.

Multiple Choice

1. The president of a leading producer of tantalum says that an increase in the price of tantalum would have no effect on the total amount spend on tantalum. if this is true, the price elasticity of demand for tantalum is

   a. less than zero.
   b. 1.
   c. 2.
   d. more than 1.
   e. none of the above.

2. The demand for a good is price inelastic if

   a. the price elasticity is 1.
   b. the price elasticity is less than 1.
   c. the price elasticity is greater than 1.
   d. all of the above.
   e. none of the above.

3. The relationship between marginal revenue and the price elasticity of demand is

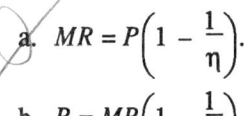

   a. $MR = P\left(1 - \dfrac{1}{\eta}\right)$.
   b. $P = MR\left(1 - \dfrac{1}{\eta}\right)$.
   c. $P = MR(1 + \eta)$.
   d. $MR = P(1 + \eta)$.
   e. none of the above.

17

CHAPTER THREE

4. A demand curve with unitary elasticity at all points is
   a. a straight line.
   b. a parabola.
   c. a hyperbola.
   d. all of the above.
   e. none of the above.

5. Suppose we are concerned with the relationships between the quantity of food demanded and aggregate income. It seems most likely that this relationship will look like
   a. curve A below.
   b. curve B below.
   c. curve C below.
   d. the vertical axis.
   e. the horizontal axis.

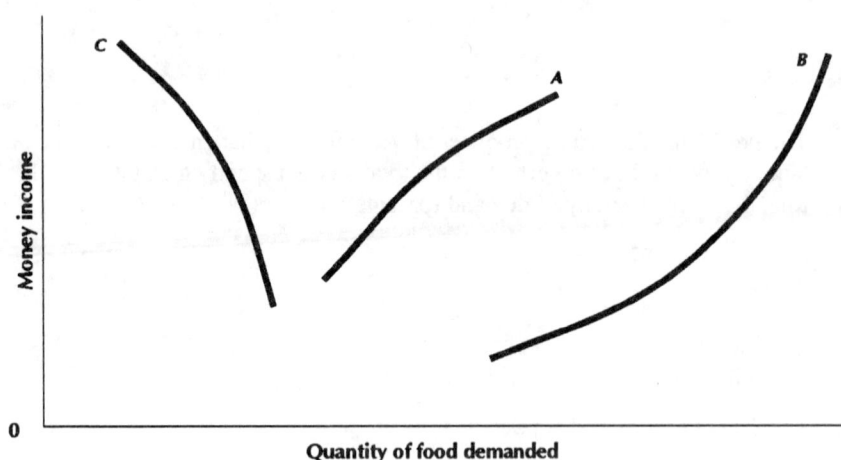

6. If goods X and Y are substitutes, the relationship between the quantity demanded of good X and the price of good Y should be like

   a. curve A below.
   b. curve B below.
   c. the vertical axis.
   d. the horizontal axis.
   e. none of the above.

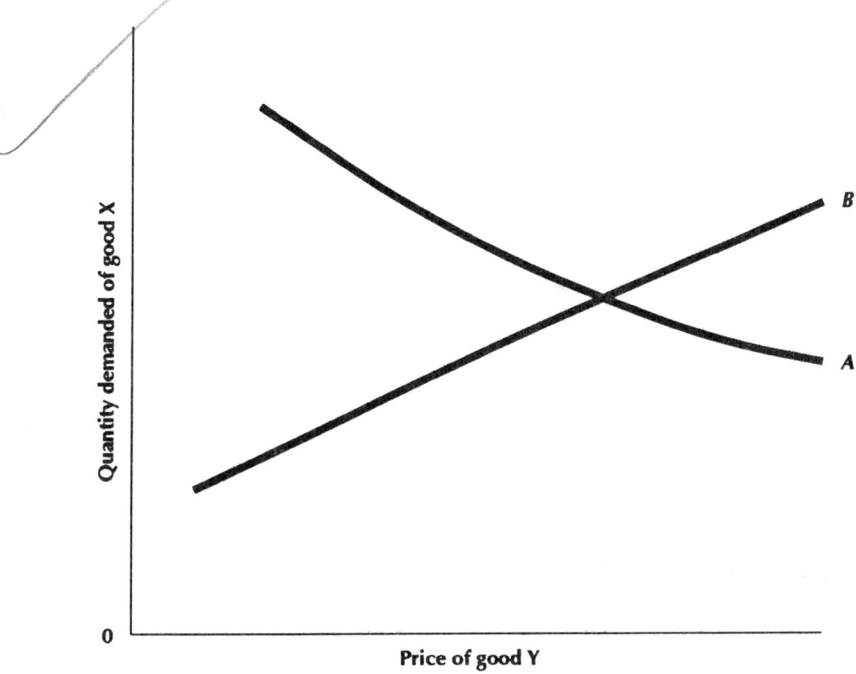

Problems

1. The Economic Research Service of the U.S. Department of Agriculture has reported the results of a study of the effects of the price of various types of oranges on the rate at which they were purchased.[1] In particular, three types of oranges were studied: (1) Florida Indian River, (2) Florida Interior, and (3) California. In nine test stores in Grand Rapids, Michigan, the researchers varied the price of each of these types of oranges for a month. The effect of a 1 percent increase in the price of each type of orange on the rate of purchase of this and each of the other types of oranges is shown below. For example, a 1 percent increase in the price of Florida Indian River oranges (holding other prices constant) seemed to result in a 3.1 percent decrease in the rate of purchase of Florida Indian River oranges, a 1.6 percent

---

[1]M. Godwin, W. Chapman, an W. Manley, *Competition between Florida and California Valencia Oranges in the Fresh Market* (Department of Agriculture, December 1965). This paper is also summarized in G. Stokes, *Managerial Economics: A Casebook* (New York: Random House, 1969). I have changed the numbers slightly.

increase in the rate of purchase of Florida Interior oranges, and a 0.01 increase in the rate of purchase of California oranges.

	Results in the following percentage change in the rate of purchase of:		
A 1 percent increase in the price of:	Florida Indian River	Florida Interior	California
Florida Indian River	−3.1	+1.6	+0.01
Florida Interior	+1.2	−3.0	+0.1
California	+0.2	+0.1	−2.8

a. What seems to be the price elasticity of demand for each type of orange?
b. What seems to be the cross elasticity of demand for each pair of types of oranges?
c. Which types of oranges seem to be the closest substitutes?
d. Of what use might these results be to orange producers?
e. How accurate do you think this study was? What improvements would you make in it?

2. a. The price elasticity of demand for a particular kind of screwdriver is 2, and marginal revenue is $2. What is the price of this screwdriver?
  b. The demand curve for screwdrivers shifts from D_1 in 1990 to D_2 in 1991. Use calculus to prove that the price elasticity of demand at any price less than $10 will be the same as it was before the shift in the demand curve.

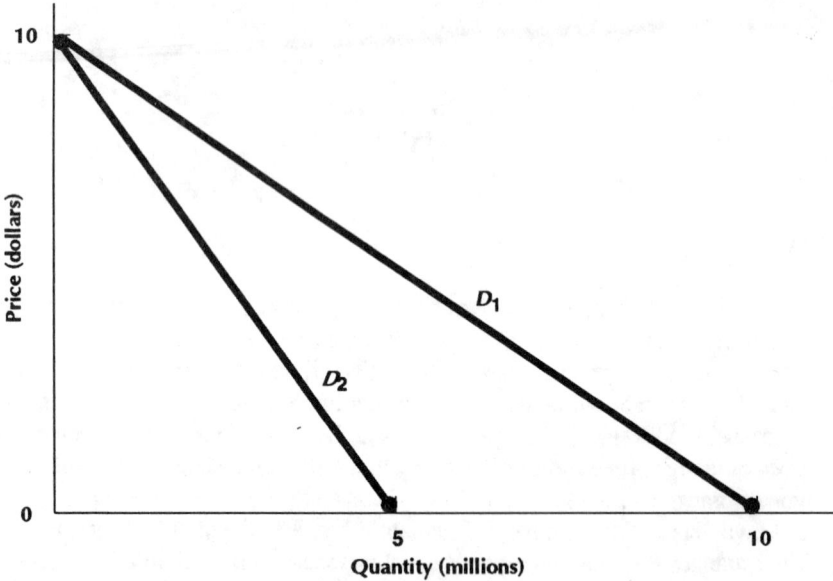

3. The president of your firm claims that the price elasticity of demand is the same as the slope of the demand curve. You (quite correctly) argue that this is not true. To buttress your point, you draw a linear demand curve (from B to A on the grid on p. 21) and point out that although the slope is the same at all points along the demand curve, the price elasticity of demand differs from point to point. (Thus, the

slope and the price elasticity of demand cannot be the same.) The president of your firm asks you to identify those points (on the demand curve you have drawn) where the demand for the product is price elastic, those points where it is price inelastic, and those points where it is of unitary elasticity. Respond to his request.

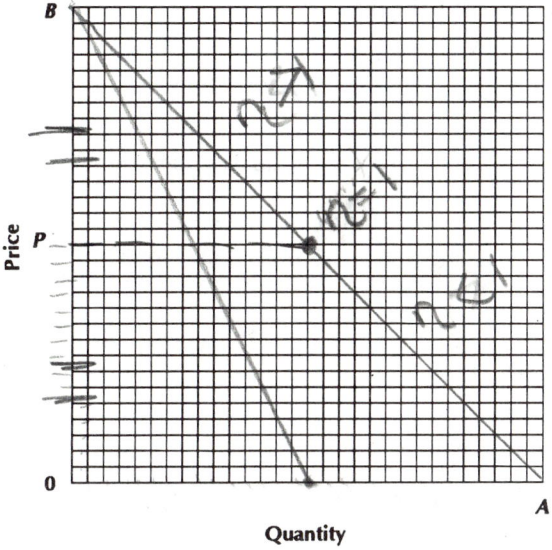

4. a. According to the president of Bethlehem Steel, the demand for steel is price inelastic because steel generally constitutes a very small percentage of the total cost of the product that includes it as a raw material. If this is the case, will a price increase result in an increase or decrease in the amount of money spent on steel?

   b. Suppose you are a business consultant and you become convinced that the U.S. steel industry underestimates the price elasticity of demand for steel. In what way might this information be useful to the steel companies? To the public?

5. a. According to Gregory Chow of Princeton University, the price elasticity of demand for automobiles in the United States is 1.2, and the income elasticity of demand for automobiles is 3. What would be the effect of a 3 percent decline in auto prices on the quantity of autos demanded, assuming Chow's estimates are right?

   b. What would be the effect of a 2 percent increase in income?

6. a. According to the Swedish economist Herman Wold's estimates, the income elasticity of demand for liquor is about 1. If you were an executive for a liquor firm, of what use might this fact be to you in forecasting sales?

   b. According to Rex Daly of the Department of Agriculture, the price elasticity of demand for coffee is about 0.25 to 0.30, and the income elasticity of demand is about 0.23. Suppose you were an economist for the coffee industry. How could you use this information to help forecast coffee sales in the United States?

CHAPTER THREE

7. The Rosenberg Corporation, a maker of machine tools, determines that the demand curve for its product is as follows:

$$P = 1{,}000 - 40Q,$$

where P is the price (in dollars) of a machine tool, and Q is the number of machine tools sold per month.

   a. What is the price elasticity of demand if price equals $500?
   b. At what price, if any, will the demand for Rosenberg's product be of unitary elasticity?

8. The David Company's demand curve for the company's product is

$$P = 2{,}000 - 20Q,$$

where P is the price, and Q is the number sold per month.

   a. Derive the marginal revenue curve for the firm.
   b. At what outputs is the demand for the firm's product price elastic?
   c. If the firm wants to maximize its dollar sales volume, what price should it charge?

9. The Byron Company's marketing vice president concludes that the demand function for its product is

$$Q = 50P^{-1.3}I^{0.9}A^{0.2},$$

where Q is the quantity demanded per month, P is the product's price (in dollars), I is disposable income (in dollars), and A is the firm's advertising expenditures (in thousands of dollars).

   a. What is the price elasticity of demand?
   b. Will increases in price result in increases or decreases in the amount spent on Byron's product?
   c. What is the income elasticity of demand?
   d. What is the advertising elasticity of demand?

10. The Keats Corporation estimates that its demand function is as follows:

$$Q = 200 - 2P + 3I + .5A,$$

where Q is the quantity demanded per month, P is the product's price (in dollars), I is per capita disposable income (in thousands of dollars), and A is the firm's advertising expenditures (in thousands of dollars per month).

   a. During the next decade, per capita disposable income is expected to increase by about $3,000. What effect will this have on the firm's sales?
   b. If Keats wants to raise its price enough to offset the effect of the increase in per capita disposable income, by how much must it raise its price?
   c. If Keats raises its price by this amount, will it increase or decrease the price elasticity of demand? Explain. (In all parts of this problem, population is assumed to remain constant.)

11. The president of the Malibu Corporation estimates that the demand function for the firm's product is

$$Q = 30P^{-2.5}I^{0.8},$$

where Q is the quantity demanded, P is the product's price, and I is disposable income. The marginal cost of the firm's product is estimated to be $40.

   a. Malibu's price for its product is $60. Is this the optimal price? Why or why not?
   b. If it is not the optimal price, write a brief memorandum indicating what price might be better, and why.

12. Harnischfeger, a leading machinery producer, tried to make major changes in the rough-terrain crane industry. It redesigned its cranes for easy manufacture and service through the use of modularized components and reduced material content. It established a conveyorized assembly line and ordered parts in large volumes. The firm's strategy was to become a low-cost producer in the industry. Based on its cost reductions, the firm was able to offer a product of acceptable quality, and cut price by 15 percent, the result being that its market share increased from 15 to 25 percent.[2] Did the demand for its product seem to be price elastic? Explain. (Assume that the total quantity demanded in the market was the same before and after this price cut.)

Answers

Completion

1. substitutes 2. 1 percent 3. high 4. price elastic 5. $-\dfrac{\delta Q_D}{\delta P} \cdot \dfrac{P}{Q_D}$
6. horizontal 7. higher 8. total revenue 9. marginal revenue
10. horizontal

True or False

1. True 2. False 3. False 4. False 5. False 6. False 7. False
8. False 9. False 10. False 11. False 12. True

---

[2]M. Porter, *Competitive Strategy* (New York: Free Press, 1980), p. 37.

CHAPTER THREE

Multiple Choice
1. b 2. b 3. a 4. c 5. b 6. b

Problems

1. a. The price elasticity of demand for Florida Indian River oranges seems to be 3.1; the price elasticity of demand for Florida Interior oranges seems to be 3.0; and the price elasticity of demand for California oranges seems to be 2.8.

   b. The cross elasticities (η_{xy}) are as follows:

   | | X | | |
Y	Florida Indian River	Florida Interior	California
Florida Indian River	—	1.6	0.01
Florida Interior	1.2	—	0.1
California	0.2	0.1	—

   c. Clearly, Florida Indian River and Florida Interior oranges are closer substitutes than the Florida and California oranges.
   d. The fact presented in part c is of obvious use to orange growers in both parts of the country.
   e. The study is limited, of course, by the fact that it pertains to only one city at only one relatively short period of time.

2. a. Since $MR = P\left(1 - \dfrac{1}{\eta}\right)$, it follows that $P = MR \div \left(1 - \dfrac{1}{\eta}\right)$. In this case, $MR = \$2$ and $\eta = 2$; thus, $P = \$2 \div \left(1 - \dfrac{1}{2}\right)$, or $\$4$. ($MR$ equals marginal revenue, P equals price, and η equals the price elasticity of demand.)

   b. The price elasticity of demand is $-\dfrac{dQ}{dP} \cdot \dfrac{P}{Q}$. If the demand curve is D_1, $\dfrac{dQ}{dP} = -1$; thus, $-\dfrac{dQ}{dP} \cdot \dfrac{P}{Q} = \dfrac{P}{Q} = \dfrac{P}{10 - P}$. If the demand curve is D_2, $\dfrac{dQ}{dP} = \dfrac{-1}{2}$; thus, $-\dfrac{dQ}{dP} \cdot \dfrac{P}{Q} = \dfrac{P}{2Q} = \dfrac{P}{10 - P}$. Since the price elasticity of demand equals $\dfrac{P}{10 - P}$ in each case, it must be the same for both demand curves if the price is the same. (Note that if the demand curve is D_1, $Q = 10 - P$, and if it is D_2, $Q = 5 - \dfrac{1}{2}P$. This is clear from the diagram in the question.)

3. The demand curve you have drawn is *BA*.

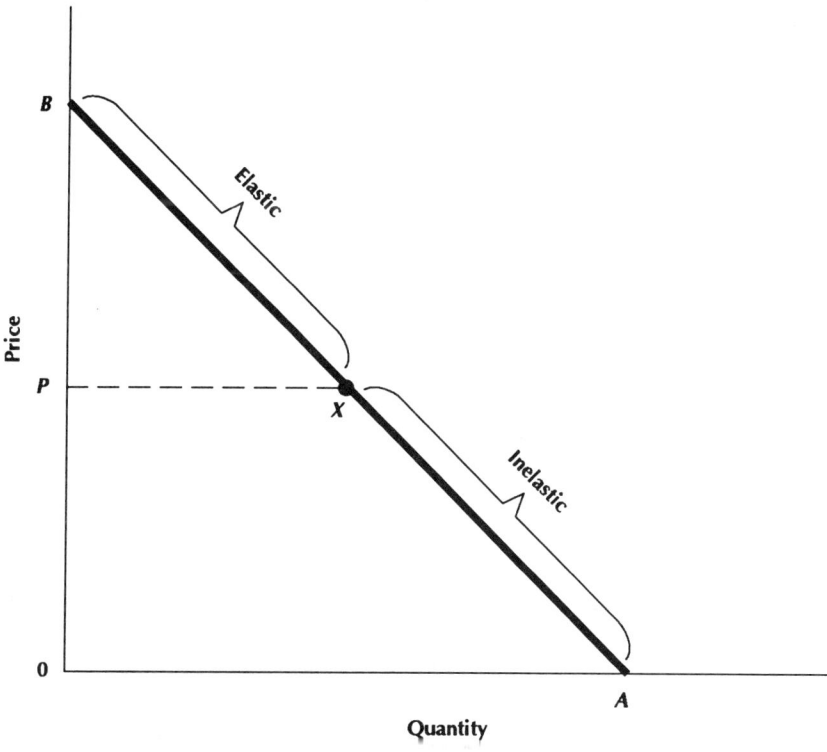

Point *X* is midway between points *B* and *A*.

4. a. It will result in an increase in the amount of money spent on steel.
   b. It might indicate that both the companies and the public might be better off if steel prices were lowered somewhat, since the quantity demanded might expand more than heretofore expected.

5. a. There would be about a 3.6 percent increase in quantity demanded.
   b. There would be about a 6 percent increase in quantity demanded.

6. a. All other things equal, you could expect that a 1 percent increase in income would result in about a 1 percent increase in the total quantity of liquor demanded.

CHAPTER THREE

b. A 1 percent change in price would be expected to result in about a 0.28 percent change in quantity demanded. A 1 percent increase in income would be expected to increase the quantity demanded by about 0.23 percent.

7. a. Since $P = 1,000 - 40Q$, it follows that

$$Q = 25 - .025P.$$

Thus, $\frac{dQ}{dP} = -.025$. If $P = 500$, $Q = 12.5$. Therefore,

$$-\frac{dQ}{dP} \cdot \frac{P}{Q} = \frac{.025(500)}{12.5} = 1.$$

Thus, the price elasticity of demand equals one.

b. $500.

8. a. $MR = 2,000 - 40Q$.
b. If the demand is price elastic, marginal revenue is positive. Thus, the demand is price elastic if

$$MR = 2,000 - 40Q > 0,$$

which is true if $Q < 50$.

c. To maximize its dollar sales volume, the firm should set $\frac{dTR}{dQ} = 0$, where TR equals total revenue. Since $\frac{dTR}{dQ}$ equals marginal revenue, this means that it should set marginal revenue equal to zero. Since $MR = 0$ when $Q = 50$, it follows that the price should be set at $1,000.

9. a. 1.3.
b. Decreases.
c. 0.9.
d. 0.2.

10. a. It will increase the quantity demanded per month by about 9.
b. 4.5 dollars.
c. It will increase it.

11. a. To maximize profit, price should equal

$$\$40\left(\frac{1}{1 - 1/2.5}\right),$$

since the price elasticity of demand equals 2.5. Thus, price should be $40 ÷ 0.6 = $66.67.
b. See part a.

12. Yes. Let Q be the total quantity demanded in the market (which we assume to be constant), and let P be the original price charged by the firm. The arc price elasticity of demand equals

$$\left(\frac{.25Q - .15Q}{.20Q}\right) \div \left(\frac{.85P - P}{.925P}\right) = 3.1.$$

CHAPTER 4

Estimating Demand Functions

Chapter Profile

An identification problem is likely to occur if price in various periods is plotted against quantity, and the resulting relationship is used to estimate the demand curve. Because nonprice variables are not held constant, the demand curve is likely to have shifted from one period to another. Sophisticated econometric methods often permit the estimation of the demand curve under these circumstances.

Market experiments and consumer interviews frequently are used to obtain information concerning the demand curve for products. For example, firms vary price from one city or region to another, and see what the effects are on quantity demanded. An actual illustration in the textbook was the evaluation of the four promotion alternatives by L'eggs Products.

Regression analysis is useful in estimating demand functions and other economic relationships. The **regression line** shows the average relationship between the dependent variable and the independent variable. The method of least squares is the standard technique used to fit a regression line to a set of data. If the regression line is $\hat{Y} = a + bX$, and if a and b are calculated by least squares,

$$b = \frac{\sum_{i=1}^{n}(X_i - \bar{X})(Y_i - \bar{Y})}{\sum_{i=1}^{n}(X_i - \bar{X})^2}$$

$$a = \bar{Y} - b\bar{X}.$$

This value of b is often called the **estimated regression coefficient**.

Whereas a **simple regression** includes only one independent variable, a **multiple regression** includes more than one independent variable. An advantage of multiple regression over simple regression is that one frequently can predict the dependent variable more accurately if more than one independent variable is used. Also, if the dependent variable is influenced by more than one independent variable, a simple regression of the dependent variable on a single independent variable may result in a biased estimate of the effect of this independent variable on the dependent variable.

The first step in **multiple regression analysis** is to identify the independent variables, and then to specify the mathematical form of the equation relating the mean value of the dependent variable to the independent variables. For example, if Y is the

CHAPTER FOUR

dependent variable and X and Z are identified as the independent variables, one might specify that

$$Y_i = A + B_1 X_i + B_2 Z_i + e_i,$$

where e_i is the difference between Y_i and the mean value of Y (given the values of X_i and Z_i). To estimate B_1 and B_2 (called the **true regression coefficients** of X and Z) as well as A (the intercept of this true regression equation), we use the values that minimize the sum of squared deviations of Y_i from $\hat{Y}_i$, the value of the dependent variable predicted by the estimated regression equation.

In a simple regression, the coefficient of determination, r^2, is used to measure the closeness of fit of the regression line. The coefficient of determination equals the proportion of the total variation in the dependent variable that is explained by the regression line. In a multiple regression, the multiple coefficient of determination, R^2, plays the same role. The closer R^2 is to zero, the poorer the fit; the closer it is to 1, the better the fit.

The F-statistic can be used to test whether any of the independent variables has any effect on the dependent variable. The standard error of estimate can help to indicate how well a regression model can predict the dependent variable. The t-statistic for the regression coefficient of each independent variable can be used to test whether this independent variable has any effect on the dependent variable. A confidence interval can be used to estimate each independent variable's true regression coefficient.

A difficult problem that can occur in multiple regression is multicollinearity, a situation where two or more of the independent variables are highly correlated. If multicollinearity exists, it may be impossible to estimate accurately the effect of particular independent variables on the dependent variable. Another frequently encountered problem arises when the error terms in a regression are serially correlated. The Durbin-Watson test can be carried out to determine whether this problem exists.

In performing and interpreting regression and correlation analyses, it is important to bear in mind that a high correlation between two variables does not necessarily mean that the variables are causally related. (And even if they are causally related, the direction of causation may be different from that presumed in the analysis.)

Questions

Completion

1. Regression analysis assumes that the mean value of Y, given the value of X, is a linear function of _____.
2. Regression analysis assumes that the mean value of Y, given the value of X, falls on the population ___regression___ line.
3. The ___estimated___ regression line is an estimate of the population regression line.

CHAPTER FOUR

4. The estimated regression coefficient is an estimate of the ___accuracy___ [slope] of the population regression line.
5. The correlation coefficient is the ___square root___ of the coefficient of determination.
6. Whereas a simple regression includes one independent variable, a multiple regression includes ___2 or more___ independent variables.
7. The unknown constants in the true regression equation are estimated by the method of ___least squares___.
8. If the value of F is (large, small) ___large___, this tends to imply that at least one of the independent variables has an effect on the dependent variable.
9. The value of $(b - B)/s_b$ has the ___t___ distribution with ___n-1___ degrees of freedom.
10. ___Multicollinearity___ is a situation where two or more independent variables are very highly correlated.

True or False

___T___ 1. If each error term is correlated with the subsequent error term, this is a case of serial correlation.

___T___ 2. Even if an observed correlation is due to a causal relationship, the direction of causation may be the reverse of that implied by the regression.

___F / T___ 3. The Y intercept of the regression line measures the change in the predicted value of Y associated with a 1-unit increase in X.

___F___ 4. The higher the coefficient of determination, the worse the fit of the regression line.

___T___ 5. The standard error of estimate is a measure of the amount of scatter of individual observations about the regression line.

Multiple Choice

1. Suppose that $Y = 1$ when $X = 0$, that $Y = 2$ when $X = 1$, and that $Y = 3$ when $X = 2$. In this case, the least-squares estimate of B is
   a. 0.
   b. .05.
   c. 1.
   d. 1.5.
   e. none of the above.

CHAPTER FOUR

2. Based on the data in the previous question, the least-squares estimate of A is

    a. −1.
    b. 0.
    c. 1.
    d. 2.
    e. none of the above.

3. Based on the data in question 1, the standard error of estimate is

    a. 0.
    b. 1.
    c. 2.
    d. 3.
    e. none of the above.

4. Based on the data in question 1, the sample correlation coefficient is

    a. −1.
    b. 0.
    c. .5.
    d. 1.
    e. none of the above.

5. If the sample coefficient of determination is 0.25, this means that

    a. none of the variation in the dependent variable is explained by the regression.
    b. 25 percent of the variation in the dependent variable is explained by the regression.
    c. 50 percent of the variation in the dependent variable is explained by the regression.
    d. 75 percent of the variation in the dependent variable is explained by the regression.
    e. none of the above are true.

6. If the sample coefficient of determination is 0.16, this means that

    a. the dependent variable is inversely related to the independent variable.
    b. the dependent variable increases at an increasing rate with increases in the independent variable.
    c. the dependent variable increases at a decreasing rate with increases in the independent variable.
    d. about 5/6 of the variation in the dependent variable cannot be explained by the regression.
    e. the dependent variable is directly related (in the population) to the independent variable.

7. A multiple regression is calculated with output of wheat (in tons per year) as the dependent variable, and with input of land (in acres) and of labor (in years) as the independent variables. If the regression coefficient of the labor variable is 10.1, this indicates that

a. the annual output of wheat per year of labor equals 10.1.
   b. the number of years of labor required, on the average, to produce a ton of wheat is 10.1.
   c. an extra year of labor is associated with an extra 10.1 tons of wheat per year. ✓
   d. an extra ton of wheat per month is associated with an extra input of 10.1 years of labor.
   e. none of the above is true.

Problems

1. Robert Klitgaard, in his book *Data Analysis for Development* (Oxford: Oxford University Press, 1985), estimated the following correlation coefficients, based on data for 71 countries:

	Per capita gross national product	Calories	Population density	Urban population (percentage)
Life expectancy	0.71	0.55	0.32	0.76
Per capita gross national product		0.53	0.25	0.74
Calories			0.18	0.61
Population density				0.47

   Interpret his results.

2. According to the *Statistical Abstract of the United States*, the retail value of shipments of major kitchen appliances in the United States in 1983 and 1984 (in millions of dollars) was:

Appliance	1983	1984
Refrigerators	3,607	4,001
Microwave ovens	2,586	3,362
Ranges, electric	1,299	1,477
Dishwashers	1,205	1,368
Freezers	568	545
Ranges, gas	695	785
Disposers	395	466

   Regress the 1984 value of shipments of an appliance on its 1983 value of shipments. Interpret your results.

3. A manager is interested in the relationship between a firm's expenditure on typewriters and its expenditure on paper clips. To correct for the fact that some firms are much bigger than others, he divides both a firm's expenditure on typewriters and its expenditure on paper clips by its sales. Having done this, he finds that there is a fairly close direct relationship between a firm's expenditure on typewriters (divided by its sales) and its expenditure on paper clips (divided by its sales). Comment on this procedure.

CHAPTER FOUR

4. A retail outlet for air conditioners believes that its weekly sales are dependant upon the average temperature during the week. It picks at random 12 weeks in 1990 and finds that its sales are related to the average temperature in these weeks as follows:

Mean temperature (degrees)	Sales (number of air conditioners)
72	3
77	4
82	7
43	1
31	0
28	0
81	8
83	5
76	5
60	4
50	4
55	5

a. Plot these data in the graph below.

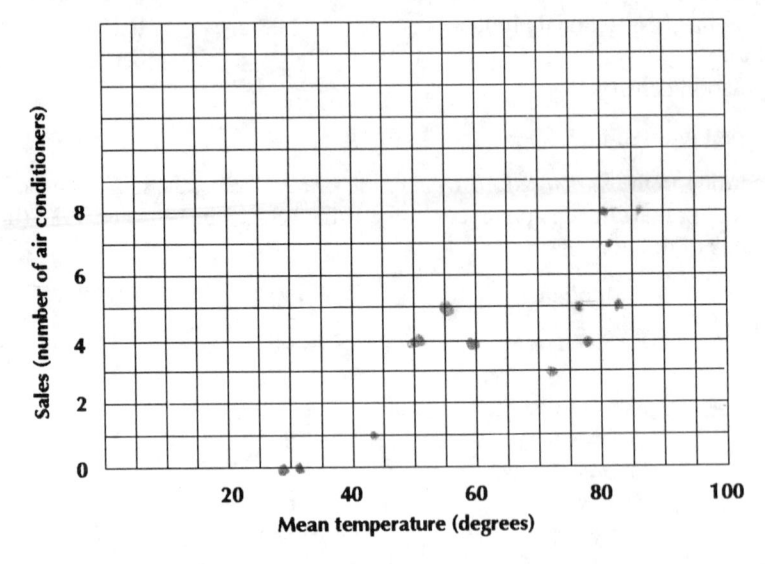

b. Calculate the intercept and slope of the sample regression line, where sales is the dependent variable and temperature is the independent variable.
c. Compute the standard error of estimate.
d. Assume that (holding temperature constant) sales are normally distributed, and calculate a 90 percent confidence interval for the slope of the population regression line.
e. Weather forecasts indicate that next week's mean temperature will be 80°; the retail outlet uses the regression to forecast its sales next week. What will be its forecast? Compute a 90 percent confidence interval for the outlet's sales next week.

f. Calculate the coefficient of determination between the mean temperature and the retail outlet's sales.

5. Suppose that a firm calculates a multiple regression where the dependent variable is the firm's monthly sales (in millions of dollars) and the independent variables are (1) the firm's expenditures on advertising during the relevant month (in millions of dollars) and (2) the amount spent by its competitor on advertising during that month (in millions of dollars). The firm's marketing manager, when he receives the computer printout of the results of the multiple regression, finds that the value of the Durbin-Watson statistic is 1.25.

   a. If the regression is based on 50 observations, what are the implications of this result?
   b. The computer printout shows that the coefficient of determination between this firm's monthly advertising expenditures and its competitor's monthly advertising expenditures equals 0.96. What are the implications of this result?
   c. The marketing manager instructs his staff to obtain data concerning each variable that they think may be correlated with the firm's sales, and includes them all in a regression, regardless of whether there is any theoretical justification for their inclusion. What dangers may exist in this procedure?

*6. Suppose the retail outlet in problem 4 suspects that its sales depend on the price of its air conditoners as well as on the mean temperature. For the randomly chosen 12 weeks, it obtains data regarding the price of an air conditioner as well as the mean temperature and its sales. The results are as follows:

Mean temperature (degrees)	Price of air conditioner (hundreds of dollars)	Sales (number of air conditioners)
72	2	3
77	2	4
82	1	7
43	2	1
31	2	0
28	2	0
81	1	8
83	2	5
76	2	5
60	1	4
50	1	4
55	1	5

   a. Estimate the constants in the population regression equation, where temperature and price are both independent variables.
   b. How much of an increase in weekly sales can be expected if the mean temperature goes up by 1° and the price of an air conditioner is held constant?

---

* This problem is for students who have experience in calculating multiple regressions.

CHAPTER FOUR

c. How much of an increase in weekly sales can be expected if the price of an air conditioner goes down by $1 and the mean temperature remains constant?

d. Suppose the retail outlet is convinced that the price elasticity of demand for its air conditioners is constant when the price of an air conditioner is between $100 and $300. If this is true, is this regression equation of the right mathematical form? If not, what alternative form would you suggest?

7. The Crown Corporation's marketing department, using regression analysis, estimates the firm's demand function, the result being

$$Q = -51 - 1.4P + 2.9I + 1.2 A + 1.3Z,$$
$$(20) \quad (1.8) \quad (3.0) \quad (0.01) \quad (0.4)$$

where Q is the quantity demanded of the firm's product (in tons), P is the price of the firm's product (in dollars per ton), I is per capita income (in dollars), A is the firm's advertising expenditure (in thousands of dollars), and Z is the price (in dollars) of a competing product. The standard error of each regression coefficient is shown in parentheses below the regression coefficient. The regression is based on 100 observations. The value of R^2 is .70. (Population is constant.)

a. Can we be reasonably sure that the coefficient of P is less than minus one?
b. Can we be reasonably sure that the coefficient of A exceeds one?
c. What proportion of the variation in the quantity demanded is *not* explained by this regression?

8. The Strunk Company hires a consultant to estimate the demand function for its product. Using regression analysis, the consultant estimates the demand function to be

$$\log Q = 1.48 - 0.16 \log P + 0.43 \log Z,$$

where Q is the quantity demanded (in tons) of Strunk's product, P is the price (in dollars per ton) of Strunk's product, and Z is the price (in dollars per ton) of a rival product.

a. Calculate the price elasticity of demand for Strunk's product.
b. Calculate the cross elasticity of demand between Strunk's product and the rival product.
c. According to the consultant, $\bar{R}^2 = .95$, the standard error of estimate is .001, and the t-statistics for both regression coefficients exceed 6. If the number of observations is 89, comment on the goodness of fit of the regression.

9. Barbetta's Pizza conducts an experiment in which it raises price by 45 percent during May 1990. This large price increase results in a decrease in the firm's revenues.

a. What problems exist in carrying out an experiment of this sort?
b. Taken at face value, does the price elasticity of demand seem to be greater than or less than 1?

CHAPTER FOUR

10. Because of a shift in consumer tastes, the market demand curve for tortellini has shifted steadily to the right. If one were to plot price against quantity sold, would the resulting relationship approximate the market demand curve?

11. The Fenton Company uses regression analysis to obtain the following estimate of the demand function for its product:

$$\log Q = 3 - 2.6 \log P + 2.7 \log I,$$

where Q is the quantity demanded, P is price, and I is disposable income.

a. Fenton's president is considering a 2 percent price reduction. He argues that these results indicate that it will result in a 9 percent increase in the number of units sold by the firm. Do you agree? Why or why not?
b. The firm's chairman points out that the t-statistic for the regression coefficient of $\log P$ equals -0.8. He says that the estimate of the price elasticity is unreliable. Do you agree? Why or why not?

Answers

Completion
1. X 2. regression 3. sample 4. slope 5. square root 6. 2 or more
7. least squares 8. large 9. $t, n - k - 1$ 10. multicollinearity

True or False
1. True 2. True 3. False 4. False 5. True

Multiple Choice
1. c 2. c 3. a 4. d 5. b 6. d 7. c

Problems

1. There seems to be a direct relationship between all pairs of these variables. The highest correlation (about .75) is between life expectancy and per capita GNP, life expectancy and percentage of population that is urban, and per capita GNP and percent of population that is urban. Of course, correlations of this sort do not indicate the lines of causation.

2. The regression equation is $\hat{Y} = -25 + 1.18X$, where Y is the 1984 sales of an appliance, and X is its 1983 sales. To estimate an appliance's sales, one can use this equation. Since r^2 is about 0.985, this equation seems to fit very well.

3. One possible problem with this procedure is that one can create a spurious correlation by dividing both the independent an dependent variables by the same quantity (in this case, the firm's sales).

35

CHAPTER FOUR

4. a.

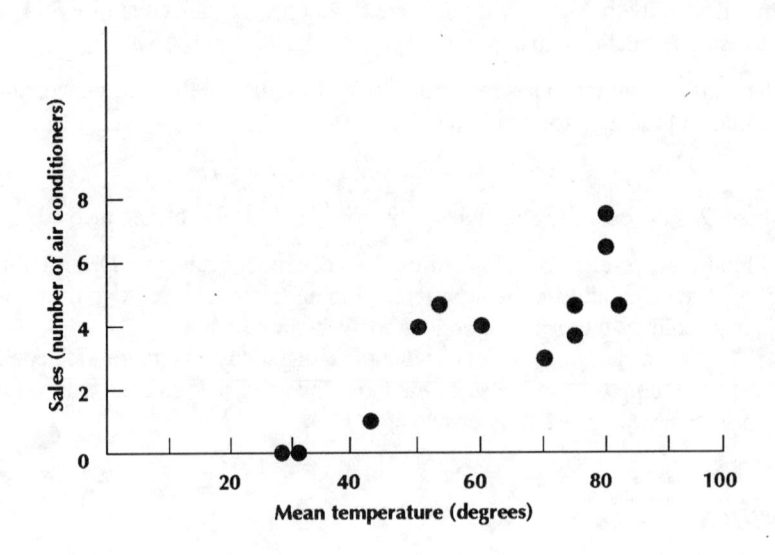

[Scatter plot: Sales (number of air conditioners) vs Mean temperature (degrees)]

b.

	X	Y	X^2	Y^2	XY
	72	3	5,184	9	216
	77	4	5,929	16	308
	82	7	6,724	49	574
	43	1	1,849	1	43
	31	0	961	0	0
	28	0	784	0	0
	81	8	6,561	64	648
	83	5	6,889	25	415
	76	5	5,776	25	380
	60	4	3,600	16	240
	50	4	2,500	16	200
	55	5	3,025	25	275
Sum	738	46	49,782	246	3,299
Mean	61.5	3.8333			

$$b = \frac{12(3,299) - (738)(46)}{12(49,782) - 738^2} = \frac{39,588 - 33,948}{597,384 - 544,644} = \frac{5,640}{52,740} = 0.1069$$

$a = 3.8333 - (.1069)(61.5) = 3.8333 - 6.5743 = -2.741$.
Thus, the sample regression is $\hat{Y} = -2.741 + .1069X$.

c. $s_e = \sqrt{\dfrac{246 + (2.741)(46) - (.1069)(3,299)}{10}}$

$= \sqrt{\dfrac{246 + 126.086 - 352.663}{10}}$

$= \sqrt{1.9423} = 1.39.$

Thus, the standard error of estimate equals 1.39 air conditioners.

d. To begin with, we calculate s_b, the standard error of b.

$$s_b = s_e \sqrt{\frac{1}{\Sigma X_i^2 - (\Sigma X_i)^2/n}}$$

$$= 1.39 \sqrt{\frac{1}{4,395}} = 1.39\left(\frac{1}{66.29}\right) = .021.$$

Since there are 10 degrees of freedom, $t_{.05} = 1.812$. Thus, the 90 percent confidence interval is

$$.1069 \pm (1.812)(.021),$$

or

$$.1069 \pm .0381.$$

That is, the confidence interval is .0688 to .1450.

e. Its forecast is

$$-2.741 + .1069(80) = -2.741 + 8.552 = 5.811.$$

The 90 percent confidence interval is

$$5.811 \pm t_{.05}(1.39) \sqrt{\frac{13}{12} + \frac{(80 - 61.5)^2}{4,395}}$$

$$= 5.811 \pm (1.812)(1.39) \sqrt{\frac{13}{12} + \frac{342.25}{4,395}}$$

$$= 5.811 \pm 2.5187\sqrt{1.0833 + .0779}.$$

Thus, the confidence interval is 5.811 ± 2.714.
In other words, the interval is 3.097 to 8.525.

f. $r^2 = \frac{[12(3,299) - (46)(738)]^2}{[12(49,782) - 738^2][12(246) - 46^2]}$

$$= \frac{[39,588 - 33,948]^2}{[597,384 - 544,644][2,952 - 2,116]}$$

$$= \frac{5,640^2}{(52,740)(836)} = \frac{31,809,600}{44,090,640} = .7214.$$

5. a. Since there are 50 observations and 2 independent variables, $n = 50$ and $k = 2$. If we set $\alpha = .05$ and use a two-tailed test, we should reject the hypothesis of zero serial correlation of the error terms in the regression if the Durbin-Watson statistic is less than 1.38 or greater than 2.62. (See Appendix Table 7 of the text.) Since the observed value of this statistic is 1.25, there is evidence of serial correlation in the error terms.

b. This result indicates that there exists considerable multicollinearity, and that it may be difficult to sort out the effects of the individual independent variables.

c. It is important that the manager have good *a priori* reasons for including each of the independent variables. With enough trial and error, it is not very

CHAPTER FOUR

difficult to find some set of independent variables that "explain" much of the variation in practically any dependent variable, even if these independent variables really have little or no effect on the dependent variable—but only happen to be correlated with it in the sample.

6. a. Let X_1 be temperature and X_2 be price. From problem 4, we know that

$$\Sigma(X_{1i} - \bar{X})^2 = 49{,}782 - (738)(61.5) = 4{,}395$$

$$\Sigma(Y_i - \bar{Y})^2 = 246 - (46)(3.8333) = 69.6682$$

$$\Sigma(X_{1i} - \bar{X})(Y_i - \bar{Y}) = 3{,}299 - (46)(61.5) = 470.$$

If the calculations are to be done by hand, the following additional computations must be made:

X_1	X_2	Y	$X_1 X_2$	X_2^2	$X_2 Y$
72	2	3	144	4	6
77	2	4	154	4	8
82	1	7	82	1	7
43	2	1	86	4	2
31	2	0	62	4	0
28	2	0	56	4	0
81	1	8	81	1	8
83	2	5	166	4	10
76	2	5	152	4	10
60	1	4	60	1	4
50	1	4	50	1	4
55	1	5	55	1	5
Sum 738	19	46	1,148	33	64
Mean 61.5	1.5833	3.8333			

Thus,

$$\Sigma(X_{2i} - \bar{X}_2)^2 = 33 - 19(1.5838) = 33 - 30.0827 = 2.9173$$

$$\Sigma(X_{2i} - \bar{X}_2)(Y_i - \bar{Y}) = 64 - 46(1.5833) = 64 - 72.8318 = -8.8318$$

$$\Sigma(X_{1i} - \bar{X}_1)(X_{2i} - \bar{X}_2) = 1{,}148 - 19(61.5) = 1{,}148 - 1{,}168.5 = -20.5.$$

$$b_1 = \frac{(2.9173)(470) - (-20.5)(-8.8318)}{(4{,}395)(2.9173) - (-20.5)^2} = \frac{1{,}371.131 - 181.052}{12{,}821.53 - 420.25}$$

$$= \frac{1{,}190.079}{12{,}401.28} = 0.0960.$$

$$b_2 = \frac{4{,}395(-8.8318) - (-20.5)(470)}{(4{,}395)(2.9173) - (-20.5)^2} = \frac{-38{,}815.76 + 9{,}635}{12{,}821.53 - 420.25}$$

$$= \frac{-29{,}180.76}{12{,}401.28} = -2.353.$$

$$a = 3.8333 - .096(61.5) - (-2.353)(1.5833)$$
$$= 3.833 - 5.9040 + 3.7255 = 1.6548.$$

Consequently, the multiple regression equation is

$$\hat{Y} = 1.655 + 0.096\, X_1 - 2.353\, X_2.$$

As pointed out in the textbook, multiple regressions ordinarily are calculated on a computer, which prints out this equation. The foregoing calculations are provided here for those readers who are interested in seeing how this equation can be calculated by hand. The general formulas used to obtain b_1, b_2, and a are provided in most statistics books. Students with access to computers should be encouraged to calculate this multiple regression on the computer.

- b. A sales increase of 0.096 air conditioners.
- c. A sales increase of 0.0235 air conditioners. (Recall that X_2 is measured in hundreds of dollars.)
- d. No. If the price elasticity of demand is constant, it may be better to assume that

$$\log Y_i = A + B_1 \log X_{1i} + B_2 \log X_{2i} + e_i.$$

7. a. No.
   b. Yes.
   c. Thirty percent.

8. a. .16.
   b. +.43.
   c. The regression seems to fit well.

9. a. For one thing, such a big price increase may drive away customers.
   b. Greater than one.

10. Not necessarily. In fact, if the supply curve has remained fixed, the resulting relationship would approximate the supply curve, not the demand curve.

11. a. Since the price elasticity of demand is estimated to be 2.6, it will result in about a 5.2 percent increase in the number of units sold.
    b. Certainly, the estimate is subject to large errors. The standard error of this regression coefficient is $\frac{2.6}{0.8} = 3.25$.

CHAPTER 5

Business and Economic Forecasting

Chapter Profile

Although surveys are of considerable use, most major firms seem to base their forecasts in large part on the quantitative analysis of economic time series. The classical approach to business forecasting assumes that an economic time series can be decomposed into four components: trend, seasonal variation, cyclical variation, and irregular movements. If the trend in a time series is **linear**, simple regression may be used to estimate an equation representing the trend. If it seems to be **nonlinear**, a quadratic equation may be estimated by multiple regression, or an exponential trend may be fitted.

The seasonal variation in a particular time series is described by a figure for each month (the seasonal index) that shows the extent to which that month's value typically departs from what would be expected on the basis of trend and cyclical variation. Such seasonal indexes can be used to **deseasonalize** a time series, that is, to remove the seasonal element from the data.

Many business and economic time series go up and down with the fluctuations of the economy as a whole. This cyclical variation, as well as trend and seasonal variation, is reflected in many time series. It is customary to divide business fluctuations into four phases: **trough, expansion, peak,** and **recession**. Variables that go down before the peak and up before the trough are called **leading series**. Some important leading series are new orders for durable goods, average work week, building contracts, stock prices, certain wholesale prices, and claims for unemployement insurance.

Economists sometimes use leading series, which are often called **leading indicators**, to forecast whether a turning point is about to occur. If a large number of leading indicators turn downward, this is viewed as a sign of a coming peak. If a large number turn upward, this is thought to signal an impending trough. Although these indicators are not very reliable, they are watched closely and are used to supplement other, more sophisticated forecasting techniques.

The simplest kind of forecasting method is a straightforward extrapolation of a trend. To allow for seasonal variation, such an extrapolation can be multiplied by the seasonal index (divided by 100) for the month to which the forecast applies. This entire procedure is simply a mechanical extrapolation of the time series into the future.

In recent years, managerial economists have tended to base their forecasts less on simple extrapolations and more on equations (or systems of equations) showing the effects of various independent variables on the variable (or variables) one wants to forecast. These equations (or systems of equations) are called **econometric models**.

CHAPTER FIVE

Questions

Completion

1. A trend is a relatively smooth __long-term__ movement of a time series.
2. Besides a linear trend, one can estimate a __quadratic__ or __exponential__ trend.
*3. __Exponential__ smoothing is one way to calculate a trend.
4. The __seasonal__ index shows the way in which a particular month tends to depart from what would be expected on the basis of the trend and cyclical variation in the time series.
5. The __trough__ is the point where national output is lowest relative to its full-employment level.
6. One simple way to forecast the annual sales of a firm is an __extrapolation__ of the trend in sales into the future.
7. __Leading indicators__ are economic series that typically go down or up before gross national product does.
*8. When used for forecasting, the basic equation for __exponential smoothing__ is $\theta A(t-1) + (1-\theta)F_{t-1}$.
*9. In the previous question if θ is close to 1, past values of the time series are given relatively (little, large) __little__ weight (compared with recent values) in determining the forecast.
10. The trend value of a time series is the value of the variable that would result if only the __trend__ were at work.

True or False

__F__ 1. An exponential trend seems to fit many business and economic time series, including the capital-labor ratio and the savings-income ratio of the American economy.

__T__ *2. Using exponential smoothing, the trend value at time t is a weighted average of all available previous values where the weights decline geometrically as one goes backward in time.

__T__ *3. To calculate the value of an exponentially smoothed time series at time t, all we need is the value of the smoothed time series at time $t-1$.

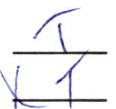

__T__ 4. If a peak occurs in October 1992, a recession must begin then.

__T__ 5. Coincident series like employment and industrial production are useful in forecasting peaks and troughs.

---

* This question pertains to the appendix of Chapter 5.

CHAPTER FIVE

__T__ 6. Leading indicators have sometimes turned down when the economy has not turned down subsequently.

Multiple Choice

1. A market researcher calculates a least-squares linear trend based on data for 1958 to 1990. He lets $t' = -16$ for 1958, ..., $t' = 0$ for 1974, ..., $t' = 16$ for 1990. He computes the mean value of the time series (for 1958 to 1990), and finds that it is 12. For 1974, the trend value of the time series is

   a. 0.
   b. −16.
   c. 16.
   d. 12.
   e. none of the above.

2. The White Corporation calculates a seasonal index for its sales. For September, this index equals 90. If the firm's actual sales for September of this year are $90 million, the "deseasonalized" value of its sales—the value when the seasonal element is removed—is

   a. $81 million.
   b. $100 million.
   c. $90 million.
   d. $109 million.
   e. none of the above.

3. In the case of the White Corporation, the sum of the 12 seasonal indexes for the months of the year is

   a. 100.
   b. 120.
   c. 1,000.
   d. 1,200.
   e. none of the above.

4. The Blue Corporation's marketing vice president estimates a least-squares regression of the firm's annual sales on time, the result being $S = 25 + 3t$, where S is the firm's sales (in millions of dollars), and t is the year minus 1985.

   Based on the extrapolation of this regression, the firm's sales (in millions of dollars) in 1995 are forecasted to be

   a. 30.
   b. 25.
   c. 55.
   d. 60.
   e. none of the above.

5. Leading indicators
   a. include stock prices.
   b. include the average work week.
   c. turn downward in some cases, whereas the economy does not do so subsequently.
   d. do both a and b.
   e. do all of the above.

6. A firm extraplates a quadratic trend of its sales to October 1993, the result being $80 million. The firm knows from past experience that its sales are subject to seasonal variations, and that the seasonal index for October is 104. The firm's forecast of its October 1993 sales is

   a. $80 million + 104.
   b. $80 million × 104.
   c. $80 million + 1.04.
   d. $80 million × 1.04.
   e. none of the above.

Problems

1. A retail store has sales of $2.8 million in November and $3.1 million in December. For this firm's sales, the seasonal index is 95 in November and 110 in December. A local newspaper runs a story saying that the store's sales were depressed in November because of a recession, but that they bounced back in December, thus indicating that a recovery was under way. Do you agree? Why or why not?

2. The Morse Corporation, a hypothetical producer of landing gear, had the following monthly sales:

   | | Sales (millions of dollars) | | |
Month	1987	1988	1989
January	2	3	3
February	3	4	5
March	4	5	4
April	5	6	6
May	6	7	7
June	7	8	8
July	8	8	9
August	7	7	8
September	6	6	7
October	5	5	6
November	4	3	5
December	3	4	3

   a. Is there evidence of seasonal variation in this firm's sales?
   b. How would you characterize this seasonal variation, if it exists?
   c. In 1990, the Morse Corporation's sales increased from $7 million in April to $8 million in May. The seasonal index is 123.0 for May and 106.3 for April.

Allowing for the seasonal variation, do you think that sales increased from April to May? Why or why not?

3. Suppose the Acme Corporation finds that a linear trend for its sales is

$$S = 5 + 0.1t,$$

where S is the firm's monthly sales (in millions of dollars), and t is measured in months from January 1984.

   a. Based on this trend alone, what are the forecasted sales for the firm in February 1992?
   b. Using past experience, the Acme Corporation estimates that the seasonal index for February is 109. How can this information be used to modify the forecast in a? What assumptions underlie this modification? Once this modification is made, what is the forecast of the Acme Corporation's sales in February 1992?

4. During 1974–1985, the sales of the Xerox Corporation were as follows:

Year	Sales (billions of dollars)	Year	Sales (billions of dollars)
1974	3.5	1980	8.0
1975	4.1	1981	8.5
1976	4.4	1982	8.5
1977	5.1	1983	8.3
1978	5.9	1984	8.6
1979	6.9	1985	9.0

   a. Calculate a least-squares linear trend line for the firm's sales.
   b. Plot both the sales data and the trend line in the graph below.
   c. Use this trend line to forecast the Xerox Corporation's sales in 1990.

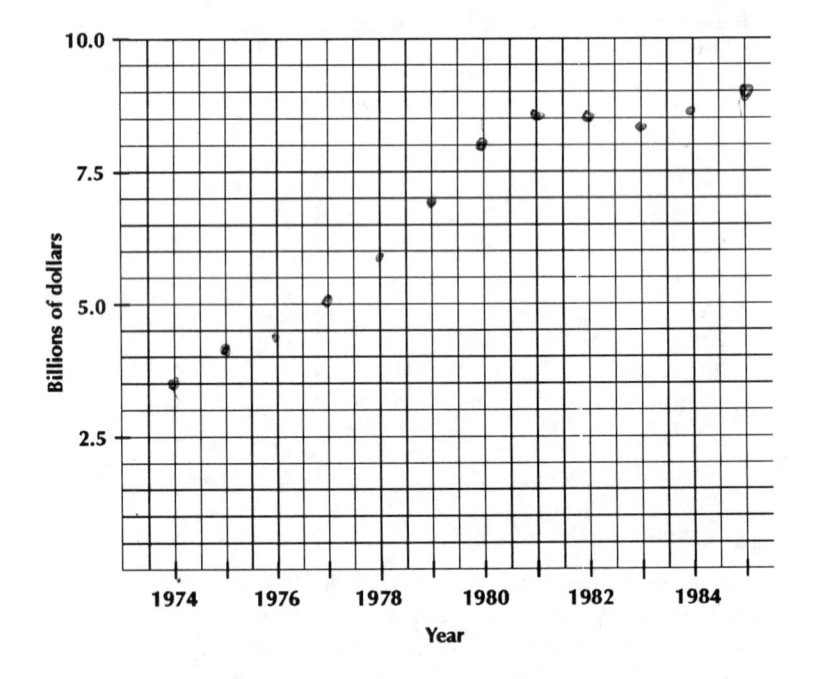

CHAPTER FIVE

* 5. The Dickson Company's sales this year are $32 million, and its sales forecast for this year was $30 million. If the firm uses exponential smoothing to forecast sales and if the smoothing constant equals .15, what will be the firm's sales forecast for next year?

6. During 1974–85, the net income of the Rohm and Haas Corporation, the Philadelphia-based chemical producer, was as follows:

Year	Net income (millions of dollars)	Year	Net income (millions of dollars)
1974	74	1980	94
1975	25	1981	93
1976	−12	1982	86
1977	38	1983	138
1978	55	1984	172
1979	103	1985	141

   a. Calculate a least-squares linear trend line for the firm's net income.
   b. Plot both the net income data and the trend line in the graph below.
   c. Use this trend line to forecast the Rohm and Haas Corporation's net income in 1991.
   d. Do you think this forecast will be very accurate? Why or why not?

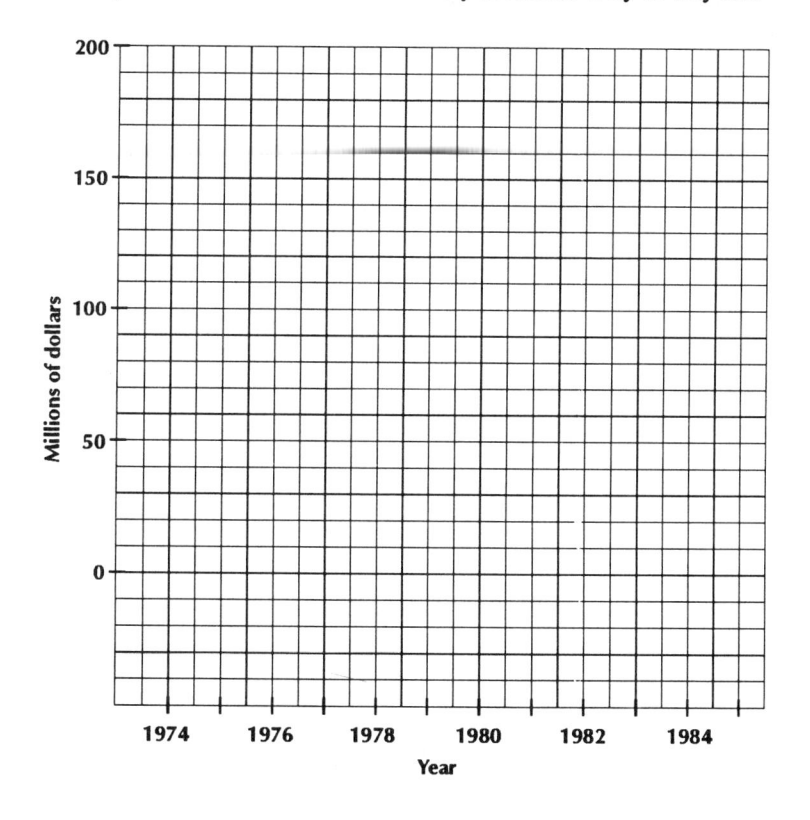

---

* This question pertains to the appendix of Chapter 5.

CHAPTER FIVE

7. The Moss Company's controller calculates a seasonal index for the firm's sales, the results being shown in the second column below. The firm's monthly 1990 sales are shown in the third column.

Month	Seasonal index	1990 sales (millions of dollars)
January	97	3.2
February	96	3.4
March	97	3.6
April	98	4.0
May	99	4.7
June	100	5.0
July	101	5.6
August	103	6.2
September	103	7.0
October	103	7.7
November	102	8.5
December	101	9.0

a. If one divides each month's sales figure by its seasonal index (divided by 100), it is said to be "deseasonalized," that is, the seasonal element is removed from the data. Calculate deseasonalized sales figures for 1990.

b. Why would the managers of the Moss Company want deseasonalized sales figures?

8. The equation describing the sales trend of the Miami Company is

$$S = 13.7 + 1.1t,$$

where S is the trend value of sales (in millions of dollars per month) of the firm, and t is time measured in months from January 1990. The firm's seasonal index of sales is

January	103	May	101	September	121
February	80	June	104	October	101
March	75	July	120	November	75
April	106	August	136	December	78

Construct a monthly sales forecast for the firm for 1992.

Answers

Completion
1. long-term 2. quadratic, exponential 3. Exponential 4. seasonal
5. trough 6. extrapolation 7. Leading indicators 8. exponential smoothing 9. little 10. trend

True or False
1. True 2. True 3. False 4. True 5. False 6. True

Multiple Choice
1. d 2. b 3. d 4. c 5. e 6. d

CHAPTER FIVE

Problems

1. From seasonal variation alone we would expect December's sales to be 110 + 95 = 1.158 times November's sales. Thus, allowing for seasonal variation, sales increased less than expected from November to December.

2. a. Yes.
   b. Sales tend to be high in the summer and low in the winter.
   c. Between April and May we would expect an increase of $\left(\frac{123.0}{106.3} - 1\right)100$, or 15.7 percent. Thus, this increase of 14.3 percent in 1990 is somewhat less than would be expected. Allowing for seasonal variation, sales did not increase between April and May in 1990.

3. a. If January 1984 is $t = 0$, then February 1992 is $t = 97$. Thus, the forecasted value of sales is
   $$5 + 0.1(97) = 5 + 9.7 = 14.7.$$
   That is, the forecast is $14.7 million.
   b. Using this information, we can try to include seasonal factors as well as trend in the forecast. If we are willing to assume that the seasonal variation in the future will be like that in the past, the forecast is
   $$(1.09)(14.7) = 16.02.$$
   That is, the forecast is $16.02 million.

4. a. The least-squares trend line is
   $$Y_t = -1060.536 + 0.53916t,$$
   where Y_t is the trend value of Xerox's sales in year t.
   b.

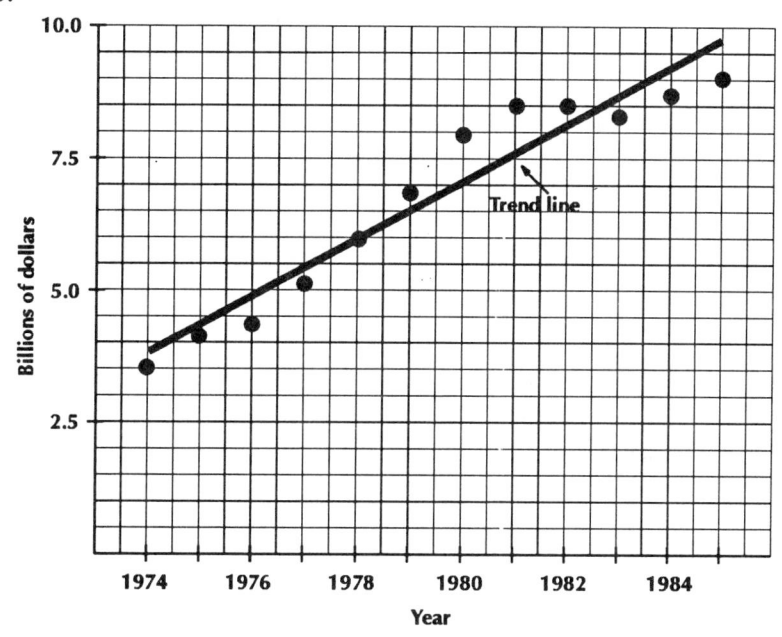

   c. 12.392 billions of dollars.

5. .15(32) + (1 – .15)30 = 4.8 + 25.5 = 30.3 millions of dollars.

6. a. The least-squares trend line is

$$Y_t = -23{,}829 + 12.0804t,$$

where Y_t is the trend value of Rohm and Haas' net income in year t.

b.

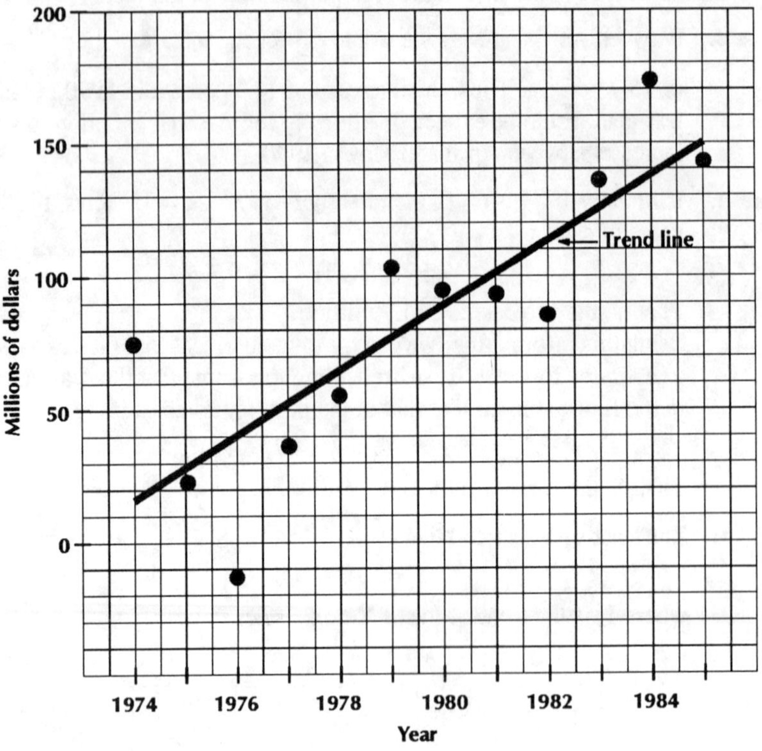

c. 223 millions of dollars.

d. This is a very crude forecasting technique.

7. a.

January	3.30
February	3.54
March	3.71
April	4.08
May	4.75
June	5.00
July	5.54
August	6.02
September	6.80
October	7.48
November	8.33
December	8.91

b. Such figures indicate how sales are changing, when the seasonal factor is removed.

8. For January 1992, $t = 24$. Thus, the trend values of sales are shown below. Multiplying them by the seasonal index, we get the forecasts in the last column.

| | | Millions of dollars | |
Month of 1992	Seasonal index	Trend value	Forecasted Sales
January	103	40.1	41.3
February	80	41.2	33.0
March	75	42.3	31.7
April	106	43.4	46.0
May	101	44.5	44.9
June	104	45.6	47.4
July	120	46.7	56.0
August	136	47.8	65.0
September	121	48.9	59.2
October	101	50.0	50.5
November	75	51.1	38.3
December	78	52.2	40.7

CHAPTER 6

Production Theory

Chapter Profile

The production function is the relationship between the quantities of various inputs used per period of time and the maximum quantity of the good that can be produced per period of time. Given the production function for a particular firm, one can calculate the average product of an input (total output divided by the amount of the input) and the marginal product of an input (the addition to total output resulting from the addition of the last unit of input, when the amounts of other inputs used are held constant).

To determine how much of a particular input to utilize, a firm should compare the marginal revenue product of the input (the amount that an additional unit of the input adds to total revenue) with the marginal expenditure on the input (the amount that an additional unit of the input adds to total cost). To maximize profit, the firm should utilize the amount of the input that results in the marginal revenue product being equal to the marginal expenditure.

An isoquant is a curve showing all possible (efficient) combinations of inputs that are capable of producing a particular quantity of output. The marginal rate of technical substitution shows the rate at which one input can be substituted for another input, if output remains constant. No profit-maximizing firm will operate at a point where the isoquant is positively sloped.

To minimize the cost of producing a particular output, a firm should allocate the expenditures among various inputs in such a way that the ratio of the marginal product to the price is the same for all inputs used. Graphically, this amounts to choosing the input combination where the relevant isoquant is tangent to an isocost curve.

Many firms produce goods in lots. The optimal lot size equals $\sqrt{2SQ/b}$, where S is the cost per setup, Q is the total annual requirement of the relevant good, and b is the annual cost of holding each identical good of this sort in inventory for a year. It is important that firms produce lots of approximately optimal size; otherwise, their costs will be higher than is necessary or desirable.

If the firm increases all inputs by the same proportion and output increases by more (less) than this proportion, there are increasing (decreasing) returns to scale. Increasing returns to scale may occur because of indivisibility of inputs, various geometrical relations, or specialization. Decreasing returns to scale can also occur; the most frequently cited reason is the difficulty of managing a huge enterprise. Whether or not there are constant, increasing, or decreasing returns to scale is an empirical question that must be settled case by case.

CHAPTER SIX

Using techniques of the sort described in Chapter 4, business analysts, engineers, and others have estimated production functions in many firms and industries. Statistical analyses of time series and cross-section data, as well as engineering data, have been carried out. Many studies have fit the so-called Cobb-Douglas production function to the data. Also, competitive benchmarking is frequently used. The results have proved of considerable value to managers, here and abroad.

Questions

Completion

1. At the Manchester Corporation, the average product of labor equals $3L$, where L is the number of units of labor employed per day. The total output produced per day if 4 units of labor are employed per day is _____. The total output produced per day if 5 units of labor are employed per day is _____. The marginal product of the fifth unit of labor employed per day is _____.
2. In the _____, all inputs are variable.
3. The _____ production function can be written $Q = AL^{\alpha_1}K^{\alpha_2}$.
4. A fixed input is _____.
5. A variable input is _____.
6. In both the short run and the long run, a firm's productive processes generally permit substantial _____ in the proportions in which inputs are used.
7. The average product of an input is total product derived by _____.
8. The marginal product of an input is the addition to total output resulting from _____.
9. Underlying the law of diminishing marginal returns is the assumption that technology remains _____.
10. Two isoquants can never _____.

True or False

_____ 1. If the average product of labor equals $10/L$, where L is the number of units of labor employed per day, total output is the same regardless of how much labor is used per day.

_____ 2. The law of diminishing marginal returns is inconsistent with increasing returns to scale.

_____ 3. The marginal rate of technical substitution equals –1 times the slope of the isoquant.

CHAPTER SIX

_____ 4. Isoquants are always straight lines.

_____ 5. All production functions exhibit constant returns to scale.

_____ 6. Increasing returns to scale can occur because of the difficulty of coordinating a large enterprise.

_____ 7. Whether there are increasing, decreasing, or constant returns to scale in a particular case is an empirical question.

_____ 8. Statistical studies of production functions are hampered by the fact that available data do not always represent technically efficient combinations of inputs and outputs.

_____ 9. The production function is not closely related to a firm's or industry's technology.

_____ 10. The law of diminishing marginal returns applies to cases where there is a proportional increase in all inputs.

Multiple Choice

1. At the Martin Company, the average product of labor equals $5 + \sqrt{L}$, where L is the amount of labor employed per day. Thus,

    a. labor always is subject to diminishing marginal returns.
    b. labor is subject to diminishing marginal returns only when L is greater than 5.
    c. labor always is not subject to diminishing marginal returns.
    d. labor always is not subject to diminishing marginal returns when L is greater than 5.
    e. none of the above.

2. Suppose that the production function is as follows:

Quantity of output per year	Quantity of input per year
2	1
5	2
9	3
12	4
14	5
15	6
15	7
14	8

    The average product of the input when 7 units of the input are used is:

    a. 7.
    b. 15.
    c. 15/7.
    d. 7/15.
    e. none of the above.

CHAPTER SIX

3. If the production function is as given in question 2, the marginal product of the input when between 1 and 2 units of the input is used is

   a. 2.
   b. 5.
   c. 3.
   d. 4.
   e. none of the above.

4. If the production function is as given in question 2, the marginal product of the input begins to decline

   a. after 3 units of input are used.
   b. after 2 units of input are used.
   c. after 4 units of input are used.
   d. after 7 units of input are used.
   e. none of the above.

5. If the production function is as given in question 2, the marginal product of the input is negative when more than

   a. 7 units of input are used.
   b. 6 units of input are used.
   c. 5 units of input are used.
   d. 4 units of input are used.
   e. none of the above.

6. The marginal product equals the average product when the latter is

   a. 1/2 of its maximum value.
   b. 1/4 of its maximum value.
   c. equal to its maximum value.
   d. 1 1/2 times its maximum value.
   e. none of the above.

CHAPTER SIX

Problems

1. a. Suppose the production function for a cigarette factory is as given below, there being only one input:

Amount of input (units per year)	Amount of output (units per year)
1	7
2	14.5
3	22
4	29
5	35
6	39
7	39

   Plot the average product curve for the input in the graph below.

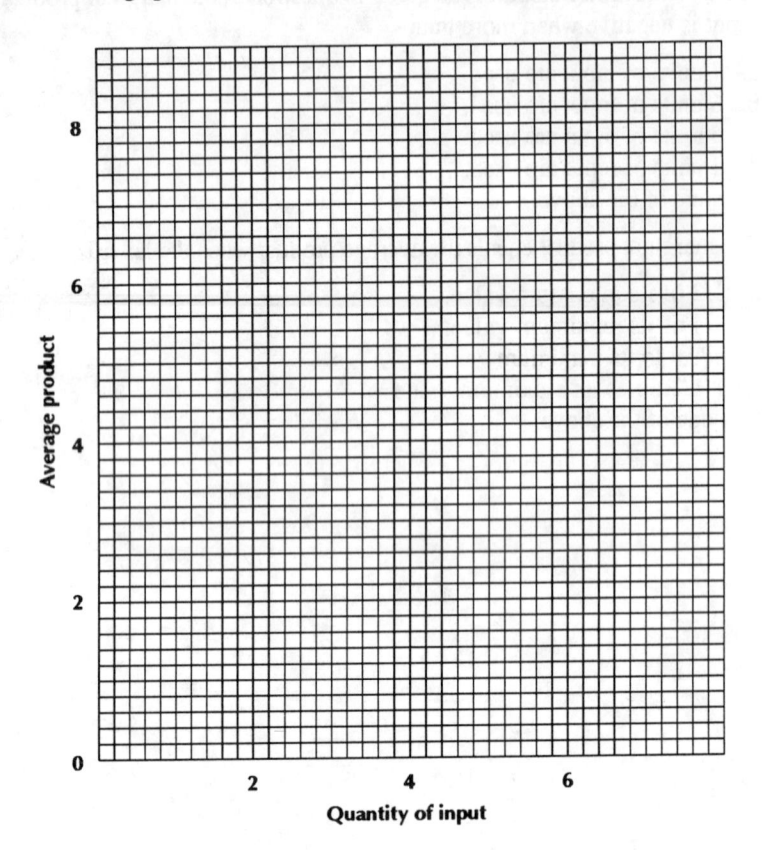

b. On the basis of the production function given in the first part of this question, plot the marginal product curve of the input.

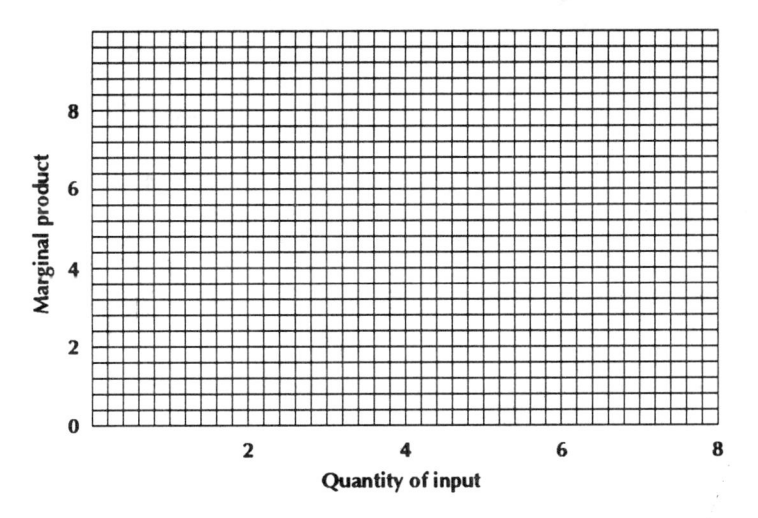

[Graph: Marginal product (y-axis, 0 to 8) vs. Quantity of input (x-axis, 0 to 8)]

2. a. In the Cobb-Douglas production function, is the exponent of labor generally larger or smaller than that of capital?
    b. Suppose that in a chemical plant $Q = AL^{\alpha}K^{\beta}$, where Q is the output rate, L is the rate of labor input, and K is the rate of capital input. Statistical analysis indicates that $\alpha = 0.8$ and $\beta = 0.3$. The owner of the plant claims that there are increasing returns to scale in the plant. Is he right?
    c. What is the value of the output elasticity in the firm in part b?

3. Suppose you are assured by the owner of an aluminum plant that his plant is subject to constant returns to scale, labor and capital being the only inputs. He claims that output per worker in his plant is a function of capital per worker only. Is he right?

4. The Concord Company produces 20,000 parts of a particular type per year. The cost of each setup is $5,000, and the annual cost of holding each identical part of this sort in inventory for a year is $2. What is the optimal lot size?

5. In industries like consumer electronics, steel, and autos, the Japanese have increased their share of the American market. An engineering comparison of a compact-car plant in Japan and the United States is as follows:

	United States	Japan
Parts stamped per hour	325	550
Manpower per press line	7–13	1
Time needed to change dies	4–6 hours	5 minutes
Average production run	10 days	2 days
Time needed per small car	59.9 hours	30.8 hours
Number of quality inspectors	1 per 7 workers	1 per 30 workers

a. One of the concepts at the core of Japanese production management is "just-in-time" production, which calls for goods being produced and delivered just in time to be sold, subassemblies to be produced and delivered just in time to be assembled into finished goods, and fabricated parts to be produced and delivered just in time to go into subassemblies. What are the advantages of this system?
b. What are the disadvantages of this system?
c. Another major Japanese production concept is "total quality control," or "quality at the source," which means that errors should be found and corrected *by the people performing the work*. In the West, inspection is performed by statistical sampling *after* a lot of goods is produced. What are the advantages of the Japanese system?

6. The production function for the Roundtree Laser Company is

$$Q = 10L^{.5}K^{.3}M^{.3},$$

where Q is the number of lasers produced per week, L is the amount of labor used per week, K is the amount of capital used per week, and M is the quantity of raw materials used per week.

a. Does this production function exhibit diminishing marginal returns?
b. Does this production functions exhibit decreasing returns to scale?
c. Does the average product of labor depend on the amount of the other inputs used? Explain.

7. At the Oklahoma Piano Company, the average product of labor equals 5, regardless of how much labor is used.

a. What is the marginal product of the first unit of labor?
b. What is the marginal product of the eightieth unit of labor?
c. By how much will output increase if labor is increased by 100 units?
d. By how much will output fall if labor is reduced by 50 units?
e. Does this case conform to the law of diminishing marginal returns? Why or why not?
f. Does this case seem realistic? Why or why not?

8. The Torch Corporation, a hypothetical producer of paper napkins, claims that in 1990 it has the following production function:

$$Q = 3 + 4L + 2P,$$

where Q is the number of paper napkins it produces per year, L is the number of hours of labor per year, and P is the number of pounds of paper used per year.

a. Does this production function seem to include all of the relevant inputs? Explain.
b. Does this production function seem reasonable, if it is applied to all possible values of L and P? Explain.
c. Does this production function exhibit diminishing marginal returns?

9. Fill in the blanks in the following table:

Number of units of variable input	Total output (number of units)	Marginal product* of variable input	Average product of variable input
3	——	Unknown	30
4	——	20	——
5	130	——	——
6	——	5	——
7	——	——	19½

*These figures pertain to the interval between the indicated amount of the variable input and one unit less than the indicated amount of the variable input.

10. As the quantity of a variable input increases, explain why the point where *marginal* product begins to decline is encountered before the point where *average* product begins to decline. Explain too why the point where *average* product begins to decline is encountered before the point where *total* product begins to decline.

11. The Deering Company's production function is $Q = 20LK$, where Q is the output rate, L is the number of units of labor it uses per period of time, and K is the number of units of capital it uses per period of time. The price of labor is $4 a unit, and the price of capital is $10 per unit. What combination of inputs should the firm use to produce 200 units of output per period of time?

12. The Barton Company is a manufacturer of spectrometers. Barton's vice president for operations has determined that the firm's output (Q) is related in the following way to the number of engineers used (E) and the number of technicians used (T):

$$Q = -5.682 - .316E - .417T + 6.3512\sqrt{E} + 8.5155\sqrt{T} + .3410\sqrt{ET}.$$

Suppose the wage of an engineer is $18,000, the wage of a technician is $12,000, and the total amount that the firm spends on both engineers and technicians is limited to $3 million. Find two equations that must be satisfied simultaneously to obtain the optimal values of E and T.

13. The owner of the Martin Marina believes that the relationship between the number of boats serviced and labor input is

$$Q = -3 + 8.5L - 2L^2,$$

where Q is the number of boats serviced per hour, and L is the number of people employed. Her firm receives $20 for each boat serviced, and the wage rate for each person employed is $10.

a. How many people should she employ to maximize profit?
b. What will be the firm's hourly profit?

CHAPTER SIX

Answers

Completion
1. 48, 75, 27   2. long run   3. Cobb-Douglas   4. fixed in quantity
5. variable in quantity   6. variation   7. the quantity of the input
8. an extra unit of the input   9. constant   10. intersect

True or False
1. True   2. False   3. True   4. False   5. False   6. False   7. True
8. True   9. False   10. False

Multiple Choice
1. a   2. c   3. c   4. a   5. a   6. c

Problems
1. a. The average product curve is as follows:

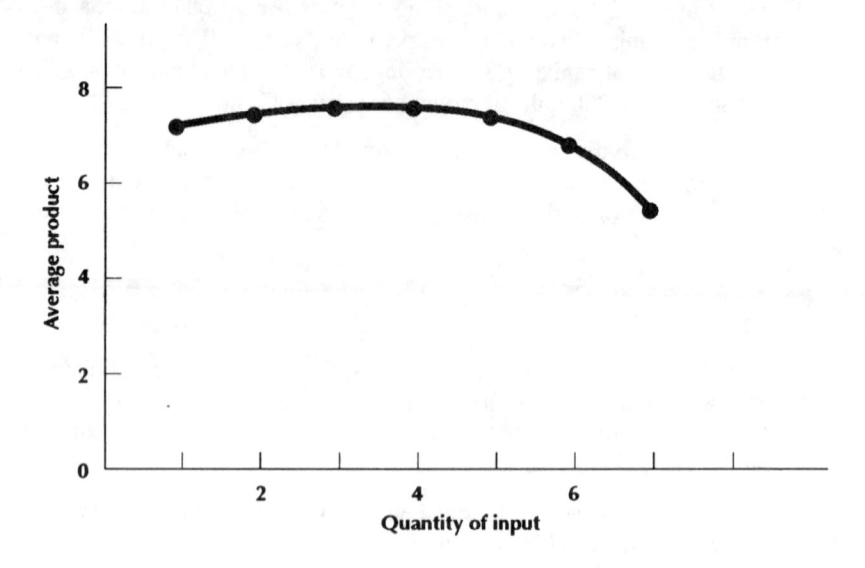

b. The marginal product curve is as follows:

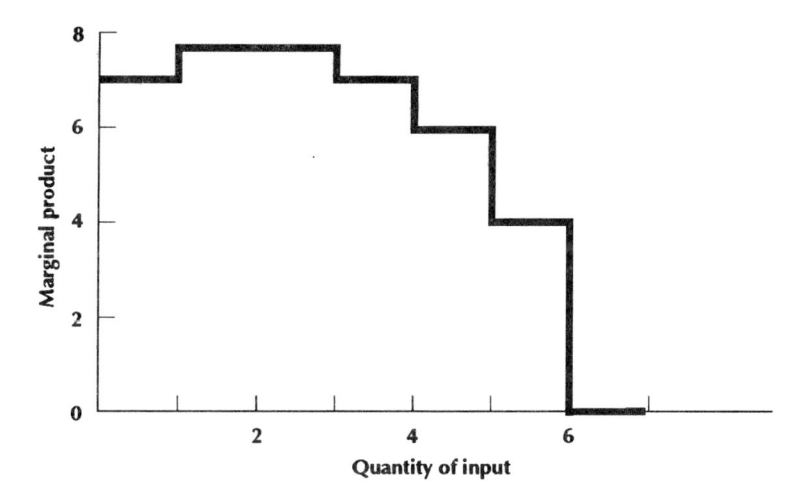

[Figure: Marginal product vs. Quantity of input step curve]

2. a. It is generally larger than the coefficient of capital.
   b. Yes.
   c. 1.1.

3. Yes.

4. The optimal lot size equals $\sqrt{2(5,000)(20,000) \div 2} = 10,000$.

5. a. Because of its hand-to-mouth nature, just-in-time production means that a firm holds fewer inventories of parts, subassemblies, and finished goods. Because it is expensive to hold inventories, this is an advantage. Also, defects tend to be discovered more quickly and their causes may be nipped in the bud.
   b. If goods, subassemblies, and parts are to be produced and delivered just in time for use or sale, they must be produced in small lots, which means that the equipment used to produce them must be set up more often. Each setup is expensive; it often involves moving heavy dies into place, making adjustments, and inspecting the results until the settings are right. To overcome this disadvantage, the Japanese have worked very hard to reduce setup costs. For example, Toyota has reduced the time to set up 800-ton presses used in forming auto hoods and fenders from an hour in 1971 to about 10 minutes or less.
   c. Higher quality of product, less waste of materials, a heightened awareness of the causes of defects on the part of the people doing the work, and fewer inspectors.

6. a. Yes.
   b. No.
   c. Yes.

CHAPTER SIX

7. a. 5.
   b. 5.
   c. 500.
   d. 250.
   e. No.
   f. No.

8. a. No. It seems likely that some capital and land are used.
   b. No. It says that an extra 1/4 hour of labor, or an extra 1/2 pound of paper, will result in an extra paper napkin, regardless of the number of paper napkins produced. Beyond some output level, one would expect the marginal product of labor and of paper to fall. Also, this seems to be a lot of labor to produce one paper napkin!
   c. No.

9. The complete table is:

Number of units of variable input	Total output (number of units)	Marginal product of variable input	Average product of variable input
3	90	Unknown	30
4	110	20	27 1/2
5	130	20	26
6	135	5	22 1/2
7	136 1/2	1 1/2	19 1/2

10. Because of the law of diminishing marginal returns, the marginal product begins to decline at some point. If the marginal product exceeds the average product at that point, the marginal product can fall to some extent without reducing the average product. Only when it falls below zero will the total product begin to decrease.

11. The firm wants to minimize

$$C = 4L + 10K.$$

Since $K = 200 \div (20L) = 10 \div L$, the firm wants to minimize

$$C = 4L + 10\left(\frac{10}{L}\right).$$

Setting $dC/dL = 0$, we find that

$$\frac{dC}{dL} = 4 - \frac{100}{L^2} = 0,$$

so $L = 5$. Thus, $K = 10 \div 5 = 2$. In other words, the firm should use 5 units of labor and 2 units of capital.

CHAPTER SIX

12. If the Barton Company is to maximize output, it must choose a combination of engineers and technicians such that

$$\frac{MP_E}{P_E} = \frac{MP_T}{P_T},$$

where MP_E is the marginal product of an engineer, MP_T is the marginal product of a technician, P_E is the wage of an engineer, and P_T is the wage of a technician. From the production function given in the question,

$$MP_E = \frac{\partial Q}{\partial E} = -.316 + 3.1756\sqrt{\frac{1}{E}} + .1705\sqrt{\frac{T}{E}}$$

$$MP_T = \frac{\partial Q}{\partial T} = -.417 + 4.2578\sqrt{\frac{1}{T}} + .1705\sqrt{\frac{E}{T}}.$$

Substituting for MP_E and MP_T, and noting that $P_E = 18$ and $P_T = 12$ (since wages are measured in thousands of dollars), it follows that

$$\frac{1}{18}\left\{-.316 + 3.1756\sqrt{\frac{1}{E}} + .1705\sqrt{\frac{T}{E}}\right\}$$

$$= \frac{1}{12}\left\{-.417 + 4.2578\sqrt{\frac{1}{T}} + .1705\sqrt{\frac{E}{T}}\right\}.$$

Also, since the firm wants to spend only $3 million on engineers and technicians,

$$18E + 12T = 3{,}000.$$

These last two equations must be solved simultaneously. (It turns out that the Barton Company should hire about 91 engineers and about 114 technicians.)

13. a. The marginal revenue product of a worker equals

$$20\left(\frac{dQ}{dL}\right) = 20(8.5 - 4L) = 170 - 80L.$$

Setting the marginal revenue product equal to the marginal expenditure on labor (which equals the wage), we find that

$$170 - 80L = 10,$$

which means that $L = 2$. She should employ 2 people.

b. Hourly profit equals

$$20[-3 + 8.5(2) - 2(2)^2] - 2(10)$$
$$= 20(17 - 11) - 20 = 100.$$

Thus, hourly profit equals $100.

CHAPTER 7

Technological Change and Industrial Innovation

Chapter Profile

Technological change is the advance of technology, such advance often resulting in a change in the production function for an existing product or in a new product. The rate of technological change is often measured by the change in the total productivity index. Such indexes are often used by firms as rough measures of changes in efficiency.

Research and development can be regarded as a process of uncertainty reduction, or learning. Chance plays a large role in research and development, and many projects use parallel efforts to help cope with uncertainty. Techniques are presented in this chapter to indicate when parallel efforts should be used.

An R and D project's likelihood of economic success is the product of three separate factors: (1) the probability of technical success, (2) the probability of commercialization (given technical success), and (3) the probability of economic success (given commercialization). All three seem to be directly related to how quickly an R and D project is evaluated for its economic, as opposed to only technical potential.

To promote successful R and D, there must be a strong linkage between R and D marketing personnel, the firm's R and D portfolio must be properly balanced between short-term and long-term projects, and project selection techniques must be effective. However, this does not mean that the more complicated quantitative selection techniques need be used.

For a particular innovation, there is likely to be a time-cost trade-off function. If the firm cuts the total time taken to develop and introduce the innovation, it incurs higher costs. Time-cost trade-off functions vary from firm to firm, because some firms are more adept and experienced than others in developing and introducing a particular innovation. The optimal duration of the project is the time interval where the discounted gross profits exceed the discounted cost by the maximum amount.

In many industries, there is a learning curve, which shows the extent to which the average cost of producing an item falls in response to increases in its cumulative total output. This learning curve plays an important role in pricing. For example, Texas Instruments successfully priced its product at less than its then-current average cost to move quickly down the learning curve. Regression techniques can be applied to estimate the learning curve for a particular product.

As the number of firms adopting an innovation increases, the probability of its adoption by a nonuser increases. Also, the probability that a nonuser will adopt the innovation is higher for more profitable innovations than for less profitable innovations, and for innovations requiring small investments than for those requiring large investments. A model based on these propositions can sometimes be of use in forecasting the rate of diffusion of an innovation.

Questions

Completion

1. Technology is _____ regarding the industrial arts.
2. Technological change results in a _____ in the production function.
3. The total productivity index is _____.
4. An invention, when applied for the first time, is called an _____.
5. The rate of diffusion of an innovation depends heavily on the innovation's _____.
6. The proportion of firms using a new process often increases over time in rough accord with the _____ curve.
7. Research and development can be regarded as a process of _____ reduction.
8. As the number of firms adopting a new process increases, the probability of its adoptions by a nonuser (increases, decreases) _____.
9. The closer the link between _____ and R and D, the greater the probability that R and D will be commercialized, given technical completion.

True or False

_____ 1. A firm almost never is wise to wait more than a few weeks in introducing an innovation.

_____ 2. Learning takes place among the users of an innovation but not among the producers of an innovation.

_____ 3. There is no real difference between invention and innovation.

_____ 4. The percentage of total innovation cost devoted to marketing start-up is higher in the United States than in Japan.

_____ 5. The learning curve is often represented as $\log C = \log a + b \log Q$.

_____ 6. The results of the Delphi method can be no better than the foresight of the participating experts.

_____ 7. Technological forecasters sometimes try to forecast the changes in input-output coefficients.

CHAPTER SEVEN

_____ 8. Japanese firms in many high-technology industries have time-cost trade-off functions that are to the left of their American rivals for innovations based on external technology.

_____ 9. IBM does not use parallel efforts in its research and development.

_____ 10. The percentage of total innovation cost devoted in Japan to tooling and manufacturing equipment and facilities is almost double that in the United States.

Multiple Choice

1. The rate of growth of output per hour of labor is
   a. an adequate measure of the rate of technological change.
   b. influenced by the rate of technological change.
   c. independent of the rate of technological change.
   d. constant in the United States.
   e. none of the above.

2. An R and D project's probability of economic success depends on
   a. the probability of technical success.
   b. the probability of commercialization (given technical success).
   c. the probability of economic success (given commercialization).
   d. all of the above.
   e. none of the above.

3. If $R(t)$ is the present value of gross profit when the duration of an R and D project is t years, and if the time-cost trade-off function is $C(t)$,
   a. profit equals $R(t) - C(t)$.
   b. the first order condition for profit maximization is $\frac{dC}{dt} = \frac{dR}{dt}$.
   c. the firm should choose t to minimize $C(t)$.
   d. all of the above.
   e. both (a) and (b).

4. The equation for the logistic curve is
   a. $e^{-(A + Bt)}$.
   b. $1 + e^{-(A + Bt)}$.
   c. $\frac{1}{1 + e^{-(A + Bt)}}$.
   d. all of the above.
   e. none of the above.

5. One simple way to estimate the parameters (A and B) of the logistic curve is to
   a. regress $\ln P(t)$ on t.
   b. regress $\ln[1 - P(t)]$ on t.
   c. regress $\ln \{P(t)/[1 - P(t)]\}$ on t.
   d. all of the above.
   e. none of the above.

CHAPTER SEVEN

Problems

1. Ever since the Arab oil embargo of late 1973, both the private and public sectors have been engaged in a great many projects to develop new ways to power our economy. Shale, found in large amounts in Colorado, Utah, and Wyoming, is a potentially important source of synthetic oil. However, one problem with shale is that it involves a waste-disposal program. The spent shale could fill an enormous volume, and the danger of environmental damage must be considered.

   Another potentially important source of synthetic oil is the tar sands located in Alberta, Canada. Great Canadian Oil Sands, Ltd. (GCOS), 96 percent owned by Sun Oil Company, has invested about $750 million in learning how to obtain oil from these tar sands, which are estimated to be a potential source of as much as 30 billion barrels of synthetic crude oil. GCOS has been the innovator, and the risks have been high. (J. Howard Pew, chairman of Sun Oil, even went against the advice of his own engineers when he set the innovation in motion.) Based on its 45,000-barrel-a-day plant, opened in 1967, it has reported some success in reducing the cost of synthetic crude oil. One factor influencing the rate of adoption of this technique is the Canadian government's policies concerning the exploitation of this natural resource.

   Coal gasification is another potentially important source of energy. The United States is endowed with huge deposits of coal (about 20 percent of the world's supply), but there is no commercially successful way of burning much of it cleanly. One way to get around the environmental problems involved in using coal as a fuel is to convert coal to a clean gas. At present, much of this work is still in the stage of research and development. A substantial portion of this R and D has been funded by the government. Since there is so much uncertainty concerning the relative merits of various processes, the government has helped to finance a number of parallel approaches to the problem. It will be some time before anyone can tell which of these processes, if any, is economically viable.

   a. If any of these technologies were to be successfully commercialized, would this result in an increase in productivity? If so, how quickly would such an increase occur?
   b. Explain how you might use input-output analysis to estimate the effects of these new technologies on the output of energy in the United States.
   c. Why has the government financed a number of parallel approaches to the problem? Why hasn't it focused on a single approach?

2. For a particular machine tool, a doubling of cumulative output results in a 25 percent reduction in average cost. The cost of producing the 100th of these machine tools is $10,000.

   a. What is the cost of producing the 200th of these machine tools?
   b. What is the cost of producing the 400th of these machine tools?

CHAPTER SEVEN

3. An automobile manufacturer is trying to develop an improved engine that will emit fewer pollutants. There are two possible approaches to this technical problem. If either one is adopted, there is a 50–50 chance that it will cost $2 million to develop the engine and a 50–50 chance that it will cost $1 million to do so. The expected cost of development is the sum of the total costs of development if each possible outcome occurs times the probability of the occurrence of this outcome.

   a. If the firm chooses one of the outcomes and carries it to completion, what is the expected cost of developing the engine?
   b. If the two approaches are run in parallel and if the true cost of development using each approach can be determined after $150,000 has been spent on each approach, what is the expected cost of developing the engine?

4. Technological change is called labor saving if it results in a decrease in the marginal rate of technical substitution of labor for capital. Under these circumstances, does technological change result in a greater increase in the marginal product of capital than in the marginal product of labor (at a given capital-labor ratio)? Does it result in the firm's using more capital relative to labor?

5. a. Is the growth of output per hour of labor a complete measure of the rate of technological change? If not, why not? Is it commonly used for this purpose?
   b. What advantages does the total productivity index have over output per hour of labor?

6. a. According to John Kendrick, output per unit of labor input increased by 5.1 percent per year in the tobacco industry during 1899–1953 and by 3.5 percent per year in the chemical industry during 1899–1953. The chemical industry has spent much more on research and development than has the tobacco industry. Does this mean that R and D has relatively little impact on an industry's rate of technological change?
   b. The annual rate of increase of the total productivity index during 1899–1953 was 3.5 percent in the transportation equipment industry and 1.6 percent in the beverage industry. What sorts of factors may be able to explain this difference?

7. Figures provided by the Bureau of Labor Statistics show that output per hour of labor in blast furnaces using the most up-to-date techniques was about twice as large as the industry average. How can such large differences exist at a given point in time? Why don't all firms adopt the most up-to-date techniques at every point in time? Do differences of this sort persist today?

8. The Chester Company produces a numerically controlled machine tool. A member of the firm's engineering staff regresses the logarithm of the input cost (in dollars) of the Qth machine tool produced on the logarithm of Q, the result being

$$\log C = 3 - 0.3 \log Q.$$

   a. What is the estimated input cost of the 10th machine tool produced?
   b. What is the estimated input cost of the 100th machine tool produced?
   c. What is the estimated input cost of the 400th machine tool produced?

9. The Elwyn Corporation wants to estimate the proportion of paper companies that will be using a particular new process in the year 2000. The firm's executive vice president regresses $\ln\{m(t)/[n - m(t)]\}$ on t, where $m(t)$ is the number of paper firms using this process in year t, and n is the total number of paper firms that can use this process. Measuring t in years from 1970, this regression is

$$\ln\left[\frac{m(t)}{n - m(t)}\right] = -3.0 + .15t.$$

Forecast the proportion of paper firms using this new process in the year 2000.

10. The Wilmington Company is developing and introducing a new biotechnology product. The firm's president decides to develop and introduce this product as quickly as possible. Under what conditions is this the optimal strategy? Under what conditions is it a poor strategy?

11. The Cornell Corporation uses three inputs: labor, energy, and materials. In 1991, it uses 10,000 hours of labor, 20,000 kilowatt-hours of energy, and 8,000 pounds of materials to produce 100,000 pounds of output. In 1992, it uses 20,000 hours of labor, 90,000 kilowatt-hours of energy, and 12,000 pounds of materials to produce 300,000 pounds of output. In 1991, the price of labor is $10 per hour, the price of a kilowatt-hour of energy is 2 cents, and the price of a pound of materials is $5.

   a. What was total factor productivity in 1991?
   b. What was total factor productivity in 1992?

12. The manager of a commercial laboratory estimates that the cost (in millions of dollars) of developing and introducing a new product equals

$$C = 50 - 10t + t^2, \text{ for } 1 \leq t \leq 5,$$

where t is the number of years taken to develop and introduce the new drug. The discounted profit (gross of innovation cost) from a new drug of this type (in millions of dollars) is estimated to equal

$$R = 100 - 6t, \text{ for } 1 \leq t \leq 5.$$

   a. The managers of the laboratory are committed to develop and introduce this new drug within 5 years, and it is impossible to develop and introduce it in less than 1 year. What project duration would minimize cost?
   b. What is the optimal project duration? Why?

CHAPTER SEVEN

13. The Japanese emphasis on low-cost manufacturing (and high quality of product) has paid off well. Faced with intense competition from the Japanese and others, many American firms have begun to redesign their products in order to make them cheaper to produce. Consider the Sunbeam Appliance Company, which launched a program in 1982 aimed at getting 30 percent of the world market for steam irons. Sunbeam's existing product used 97 parts with 18 fasteners in 10 configurations. After intensive analysis, Sunbeam's managers decided that the key to cost reduction was to reduce the number of parts. Eventually, a design was developed that used 51 parts and 3 fasteners in 2 configurations. The new design, implemented in 1986, is substantially cheaper to produce than either of Sunbeam's existing designs.[1] Did this new design result in a shift in Sunbeam's production function?

Answers

Completion
1. society's pool of knowledge 2. change 3. $Q + (a_1I_1 + a_2I_2 + \ldots + a_nI_n)$, where Q is output, I_i is the amount of the ith input used, and a_i is the price of the ith input in the base period. 4. innovation 5. profitability 6. logistic 7. uncertainty 8. increases 9. marketing

True or False
1. False 2. False 3. False 4. True 5. True 6. True 7. True 8. True 9. False 10. True

Multiple Choice
1. b 2. d 3. e 4. c 5. c

Problems
1. a. To the extent that these technologies use less input per unit of output than the technologies they replace, productivity will increase. But, in general, productivity will not increase merely because new technologies are introduced (because they are new). The first commercial introduction of a new technology may have little effect. How quickly productivity increases in response to a new technology depends on the rate of diffusion, which depends on the profitability of using the technology, among other things.
   b. One might estimate the changes in the input-output coefficients, and their effects, as indicated in the text.
   c. Because of the uncertainties concerning which approach is best.
2. a. $7,500.
   b. $5,625.

---

[1] A. Lehnard, "Revitalizing the Manufacture and Design of Mature Global Products," in B. Guile and H. Brooks, eds., *Technology and Global Industry* (Washington, D.C.: National Academy Press, 1987).

CHAPTER SEVEN

3. a. If a single approach is used, the expected costs of development are 0.5 × $2 million + 0.5 × $1 million, or $1.5 million, since there is a 0.5 probability that total costs with any single approach will be $2 million and a 0.5 probability that they will be $1 million.
   b. The expected total costs of development are 0.25 × $2 million + 0.75 × $1 million + $150,000, or $1.4 million, if each approach is carried to the point at which $150,000 have been spent on it, and if the cheaper approach is chosen at that point (and the other approach is dropped). Why? Because there is a 0.25 probability that total costs with the better of the two approaches will be $2 million and a 0.75 probability that they will be $1 million. In addition, there is the certainty that a cost of $150,000 will be incurred for the approach that is dropped. The reason why there is a 0.25 chance that total costs with the better of the two approaches is $2 million is that this will occur only when the total cost of both approaches turns out to be $2 million—and the probability that this will occur is 0.5 × 0.5, or 0.25.

4. Yes. Yes.

5. a. No. It is influenced by many factors other than the rate of technological change—for example, changes in capital per worker. Yes.
   b. The total productivity index takes explicit account of capital input as well as labor input.

6. a. No. Many factors other than technological change also influence output per hour of labor.
   b. Differences in R and D expenditures and economies of scale, among others.

7. A profit-maximizing firm generally will not scrap existing equipment merely because somewhat better equipment is available. The new equipment must be sufficiently better to offset the fact that the old equipment is already paid for, whereas this is not the case for the new. Yes.

8. a. $501.
   b. $251.
   c. $166.

9. $\ln \left[\dfrac{m(t)}{n - m(t)} \right] = -3.0 + .15(30) = 1.5.$

   Thus,

   $$\dfrac{m(t)}{n - m(t)} = 4.48,$$

   and

   $$m(t)/n = 4.48 \left[1 - \dfrac{m(t)}{n} \right]$$

   $$m(t)/n = \dfrac{4.48}{5.48} = .82.$$

   The forecasted proportion is .82.

CHAPTER SEVEN

10. It is the optimal strategy if the discounted revenues from the new product fall greatly if the product's introduction is delayed even slightly. Often, however, the discounted revenues do not fall so greatly. Because the discounted costs of developing and introducing the new product often drop if it is delayed, it may be worthwhile to develop and introduce it more slowly.

11. a. $\dfrac{100{,}000}{10{,}000(10) + 20{,}000(.02) + 8{,}000(5)} = \dfrac{100{,}000}{140{,}400} = 0.712.$

    b. $\dfrac{300{,}000}{20{,}000(10) + 90{,}000(.02) + 12{,}000(5)} = \dfrac{300{,}000}{261{,}800} = 1.146.$

12. a. To minimize C, we set $\dfrac{dC}{dt}$ equal to zero, the result being

    $$\dfrac{dC}{dt} = -10 + 2t = 0,$$

    which means that $t = 5$. Thus, to minimize cost, the drug should be developed and introduced in 5 years.

    b. The discounted profit equals

    $$\pi = R - C = 100 - 6t - (50 - 10t + t^2)$$
    $$= 50 + 4t - t^2, \text{ for } 1 \le t \le 5.$$

    Setting $\dfrac{d\pi}{dt} = 0$, we find that

    $$\dfrac{d\pi}{dt} = 4 - 2t = 0,$$

    which means that $t = 2$. Thus, to maximize profit, the drug should be developed and introduced in 2 years.

13. Yes. Note too that the product may have changed somewhat.

CHAPTER 8

The Analysis of Costs

Chapter Profile

Managerial economists define the cost of producing a particular product as the value of the other products that the resources used in its production could have produced instead. This is the product's opportunity cost, and it may differ from historical cost, which is generally the basis of accounting statements.

In the short run, it is important to distinguish between a firm's fixed and variable costs. The firm's total and average costs, total and average fixed costs, and total and average variable costs can all be plotted against output. So can the firm's marginal cost. The resulting cost functions, or cost curves (as they are often called), show how changes in output will affect the firm's costs, a major concern of any firm.

The long-run average cost function shows the minimum cost per unit of producing each output level when any desired scale of plant can be built. The long-run average cost function is tangent to each of the short-run average cost functions at the output where the plant corresponding to the short-run average cost function is optimal. The long-run average cost curve is important for practical decision making because it shows the extent to which larger plants have cost advantages over smaller ones.

Many studies based on the statistical analysis of cross-section and time-series data, as well as engineering studies, have been carried out to estimate the cost functions of particular firms. The regression techniques described in Chapter 4 have played an important role here.

In choosing among plants, a major consideration is flexibility if the output of the plant is highly uncertain. Some plants, while they have higher costs than others at the most likely output, have lower costs than the others over a wide range of output. If one cannot predict output reasonably well, flexible plants of this sort may be best.

Break-even analysis compares total revenue and total cost, graphically or algebraically. A break-even chart combines the total cost function and the total revenue curve, both of which are generally assumed to be linear, and shows the profit or loss resulting from each sales level. The break-even point is the sales level that must be achieved if the firm is to avoid losses. Firms often find it useful to carry out various types of profit contribution analysis. The profit contribution is the difference between total revenue and total variable cost; on a per-unit basis, it is equal to price minus average variable cost.

CHAPTER EIGHT

Questions

Completion

1. If the average fixed cost of producing 10 units of output at the Hollywood Manufacturing Company is $10, the average fixed cost of producing 20 units is _____. If the marginal cost of each of the first 20 units of output is $5, the average variable cost of producing 20 units is _____; and the average total cost of producing 20 units is _____.
2. Total cost equals _____ plus variable cost.
3. Average cost must equal marginal cost at the point where average cost is a _____.
4. The long-run total cost equals output times _____.
5. _____ include opportunity costs of resources owned and used by the firm's owner.
6. An important criticism of cross-section studies of cost functions is that they sometimes are subject to the _____.
7. Some determinants of the shape of the long-run average cost curve are _____.
8. The average variable cost curve turns up beyond some output level because of the _____.
9. The marginal cost curve turns up beyond some output level because of the _____.
10. Average variable cost equals the price of the variable input divided by _____, if the price of the variable input is constant.
11. Marginal cost equals the price of the variable input divided by _____, if the price of the variable input is constant.
12. Statistical estimates of cost functions based on cross-section data sometimes run into problems because firms' _____ methods are different.

True or False

_____ 1. If average variable cost always equals $20 when output is less than 100 units, marginal cost is less than $20 when output is in this range.

_____ 2. Long-run marginal cost can never differ from short-run marginal cost.

_____ 3. Costs that have already been incurred are important factors in making production decisions.

_____ 4. The opportunity cost doctrine says that the production of one good may reduce the cost of another good.

_____ 5. When the firm has constructed the scale of plant that is optimal for producing a given level of output, long-run marginal cost will equal short-run marginal cost at that output.

_____ 6. The shape of the long-run average cost function is due primarily to the law of diminishing marginal returns.

_____ 7. Average cost must exceed marginal cost at the point where average cost is a minimum.

_____ 8. The break-even point lies well above the output level that must be reached if the firm is to avoid losses.

_____ 9. Empirical studies often indicate that the short-run average cost curve is S-shaped.

_____ 10. The survivor technique is a way of estimating a firm's short-run cost function.

Multiple Choice

1. The Moulton Corporation's average total cost per month equals $\$5 \times Q$, where Q is the number of units of output produced per month. The marginal cost of the third unit of output produced per month is
   a. $15.
   b. $20.
   c. $25.
   d. $30.
   e. none of the above.

CHAPTER EIGHT

2. The curve in the graph below has the shape of
   a. a marginal cost curve.
   b. an average variable cost curve.
   c. an average fixed cost curve.
   d. all of the above.
   e. none of the above.

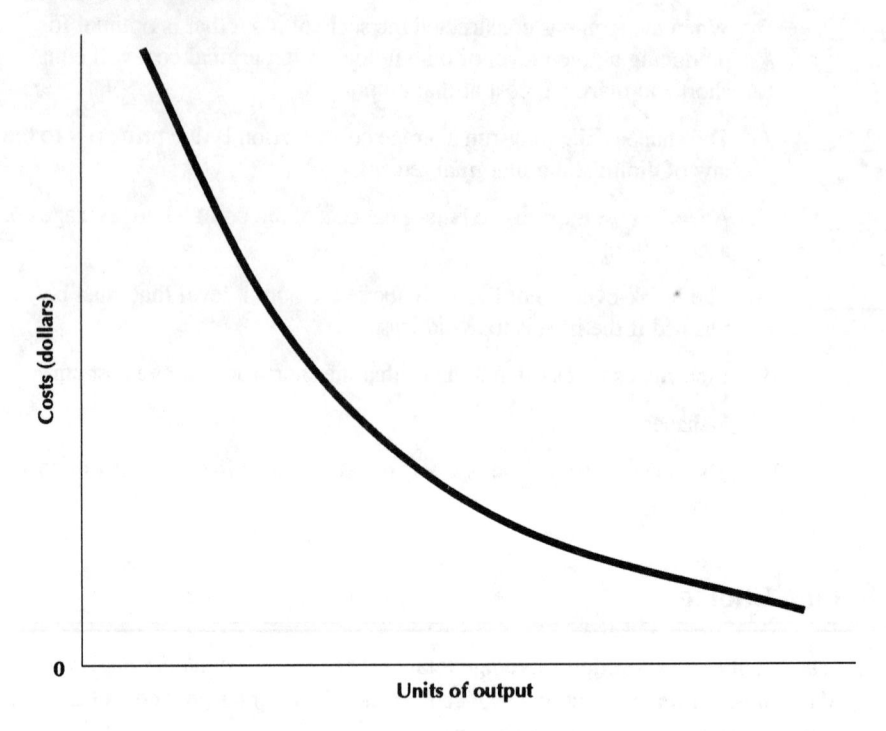

3. The firm's cost functions are determined by
   a. the price of its product.
   b. its assets.
   c. its production function.
   d. the age of the firm.
   e. none of the above.

CHAPTER EIGHT

Problems

1. Suppose that a machine shop's daily costs are as shown below.

Units of output	Total fixed cost (dollars)	Total variable cost (dollars)
0	$500	0
1	500	50
2	500	90
3	500	140
4	500	200
5	500	270
6	500	350
7	500	450
8	500	600

   a. Draw the firm's average fixed cost function below.

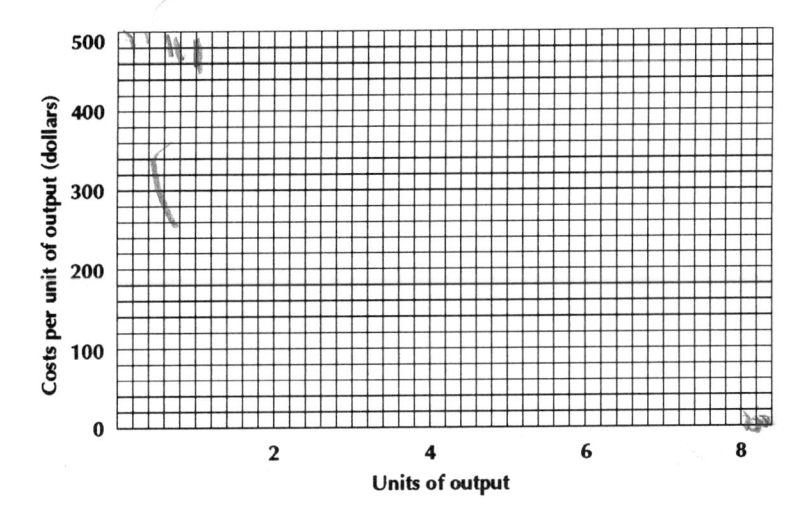

75

CHAPTER EIGHT

b. Draw the firm's average variable cost function below.

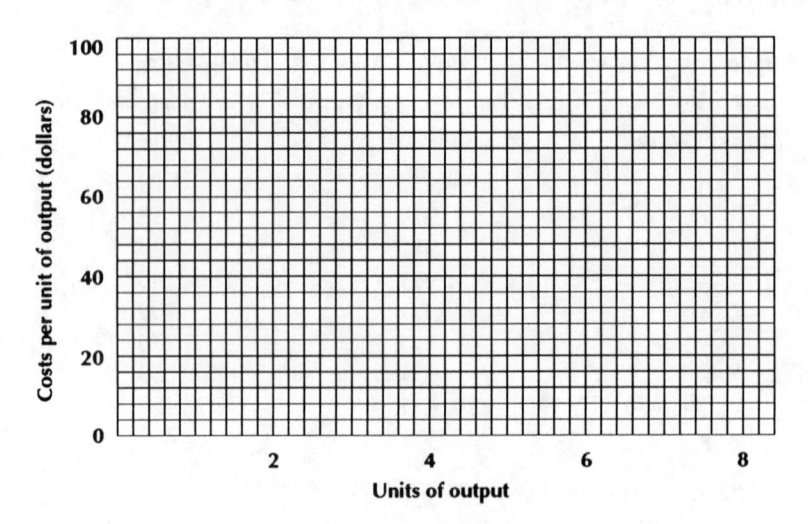

c. Draw the firm's average total cost function below.

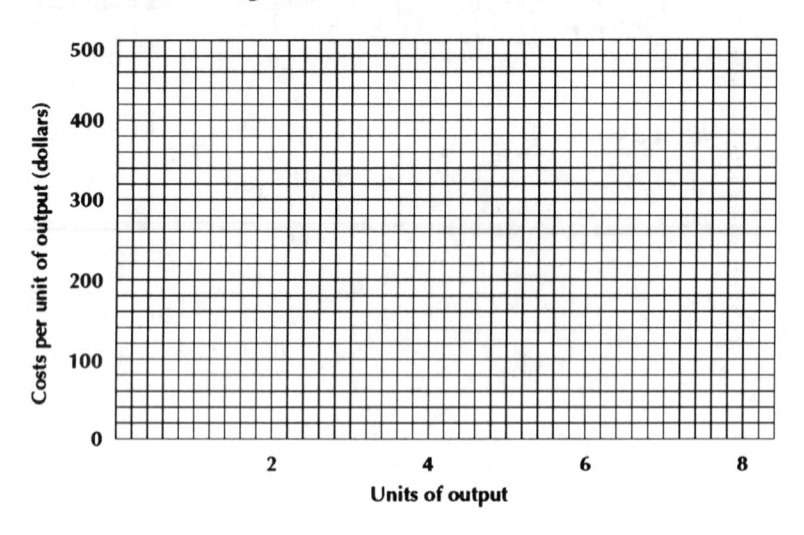

d. Draw the firm's marginal cost function below.

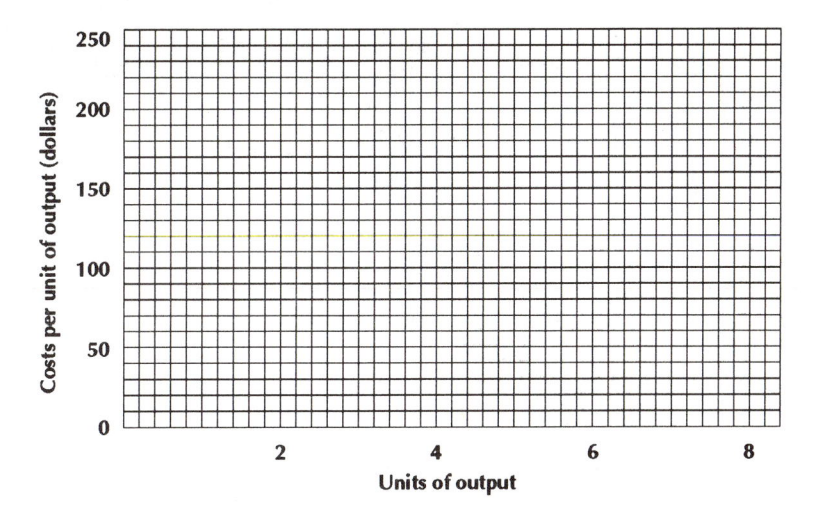

[Graph: y-axis "Costs per unit of output (dollars)" from 0 to 250; x-axis "Units of output" from 0 to 8]

2. a. Suppose you are a consultant to Harper & Row, the book publisher. Suppose the firm is about to publish a book that will sell for $10 a copy. The fixed costs of publishing the books are $5,000; the variable cost is $5 a copy. What is the break-even point for this book?
    b. If the price were $8 rather than $10, what would be the break-even point?

3. a. Suppose two firms have exactly the same marginal cost curve, but their average fixed cost curve is not the same. Will their average variable cost curve be the same? Why or why not?
    b. A firm's marginal product of capital is twice its marginal product of labor; the price of labor is $6, and the price of capital is $3. Is the firm minimizing cost? If not, how can it reduce its costs? Explain.

4. Brady Farms is a profit-maximizing, perfectly competitive producer of tomatoes. It produces tomatoes using one acre of land (price of the land equals $2,000) and varying numbers of workers (wage per worker equals $500 per week). The production function is as follows:

Number of workers (per week)	Output of tomatoes per week (in truckloads)
0	0
1	1
3	2
7	3
12	4
18	5
25	6

    Show that this farm is subject to increasing marginal cost as output increases.

CHAPTER EIGHT

5. The Miracle Manufacturing Company's short-run average cost function in 1990 is

$$AC = 3 + 4Q,$$

where AC is the firm's average cost (in dollars per pound of the product), and Q is its output rate.

a. Obtain an equation for the firm's short-run total cost function.
b. Does the firm have any fixed costs? Explain.
c. If the price of the Miracle Manufacturing Company's product (per pound) is $2, is the firm making profits or losses? Explain.

6. Show that a firm will maximize output—for a given outlay—by distributing its expenditures among various inputs in such a way that the marginal product of a dollar's worth of any input is equal to the marginal product of a dollar's worth of any other input that is used. At any point on a firm's cost function, is the firm maximizing output for a given outlay?

7. a. Suppose that capital and labor are the only inputs used by the Golden Printing Company and that capital costs $1 a unit and labor costs $2 a unit. Draw the isocost curves corresponding to an outlay of $200 and $300.

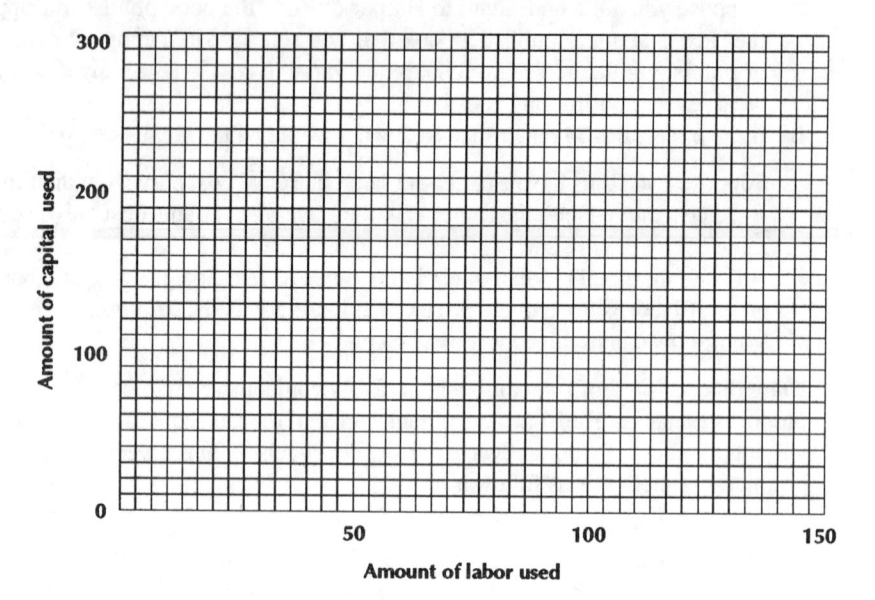

b. To produce each unit of output, the Golden Printing Company must use 1 unit of labor and 1 unit of capital. What is the firm's cost of producing 200 units of output? Of producing 300 units of output?

8. The Barbizon Corporation is considering two types of plants to make an electric motor. For each type of plant, average variable cost is constant so long as output is less than capacity, which is the maximum output of the plant. The cost structure for each type of plant is as follows:

	Plant X	Plant Y
Average variable costs		
Labor	$24.40	$12.10
Materials	14.10	14.05
Other	11.20	10.80
Total	$49.70	$36.95
Total fixed cost	$150,000	$400,000
Annual capacity	80,000	160,000

a. Derive the average cost of producing 40,000, 80,000, and 160,000 motors per year with plant X. (For outputs exceeding the capacity of a single plant, assume that more than one plant of this type is built.)
b. Derive the average cost of producing 40,000, 80,000, and 160,000 motors per year with plant Y.
c. If these are the only plants to produce these motors, plot the points on the long-run average cost curve for the production of these motors for outputs of 40,000, 80,000, and 160,000 per year.

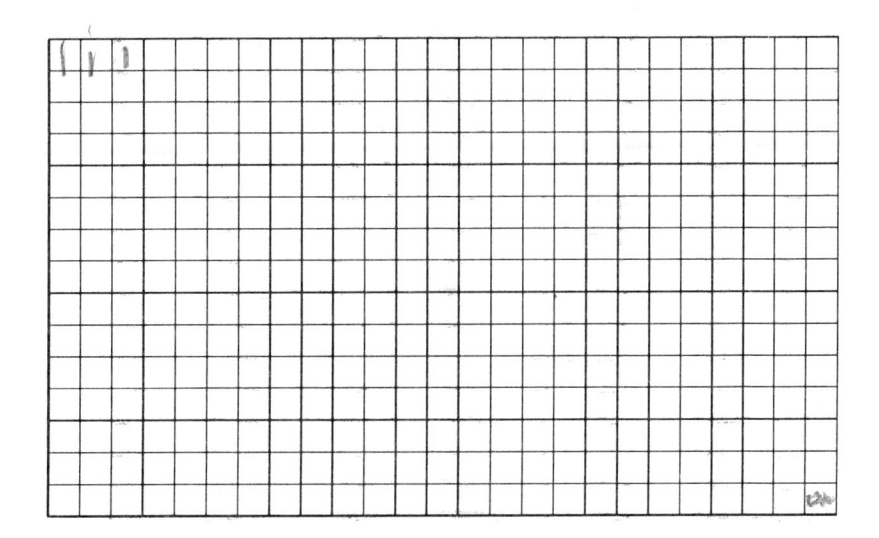

9. The Suffern Company's total cost function is

$$C = 100 + 3Q - 2Q^2 + 3Q^3,$$

where C equals total cost, and Q equals output per day.

a. What is the equation for the firm's average cost curve?
b. What is the equation for the firm's marginal cost curve?
c. At what output is marginal cost a minimum?

CHAPTER EIGHT

10. The Swarthmore Company is considering three types of plants to make a particular product. Plant I is much more highly automated than plant II, which in turn is more highly automated than plant III. For each type of plant, average variable cost is constant so long as output is less than capacity, which is the maximum output of the plant. The cost structure for each type of plant is as follows:

	Plant I	Plant II	Plant III
Average variable costs			
Labor	$1.60	$4.60	$5.80
Materials	1.10	1.50	1.90
Other	.60	.90	1.50
Total	$3.30	$7.00	$9.20
Total fixed costs	$600,000	$200,000	$100,000
Annual capacity (units)	200,000	100,000	50,000

a. Derive the average cost of producing 200,000 units per year with plant I.
b. Derive the average cost of producing 200,000 units per year with plant II. (For outputs exceeding the capacity of a single plant, assume that more than one plant of this type is built.)
c. Derive the average cost of producing 200,000 units per year with plant III. (For outputs exceeding the capacity of a single plant, assume that more than one plant of this type is built.)

11. The Allentown Corporation, a retail seller of sofas, wants to determine how many sofas it must sell in order to earn a profit of $15,000 per month. The price of each sofa is $400, and the average variable cost is $150.
a. What is the required sales volume if the Allentown Corporation's monthly fixed costs are $4,000 per month?
b. If the firm sold each sofa at a price of $500, rather than $400, what would be the required sales volume?
c. If the price is $500 and if average variable cost is $100, rather than $150, what would be the required sales volume?

12. According to a statistical study, the following relationship exists between a firm's total cost (TC) and its output (Q):

$$TC = 40 + 3Q + 2Q^2.$$

At what output is average total cost a minimum?

13. Martin-Brower, a leading food distributor, pared its customer list to only eight fast-food chains. Its strategy was to satisfy the specialized needs of these customers at very low cost. To do so, it stocked only their narrow product lines, located its warehouses near their locations, and geared its order-taking procedures to their purchasing cycles. While Martin-Brower was not the lowest-cost distributor in serving the market as a whole, it was the lowest-cost in serving its particular part of the market, the result being that it has been fast-growing and relatively profitable.[1] Is it always a good strategy for a firm to serve a highly specialized market?

Answers

Completion
1. $5, $5, $10   2. fixed cost   3. minimum   4. long-run average cost
5. Implicit costs   6. regression fallacy   7. economies and diseconomies of scale   8. law of diminishing marginal returns   9. law of diminishing marginal returns   10. average variable product   11. marginal product   12. accounting

True or False
1. False   2. False   3. False   4. False   5. True   6. False   7. False
8. False   9. False   10. False

Multiple Choice
1. c   2. c   3. c

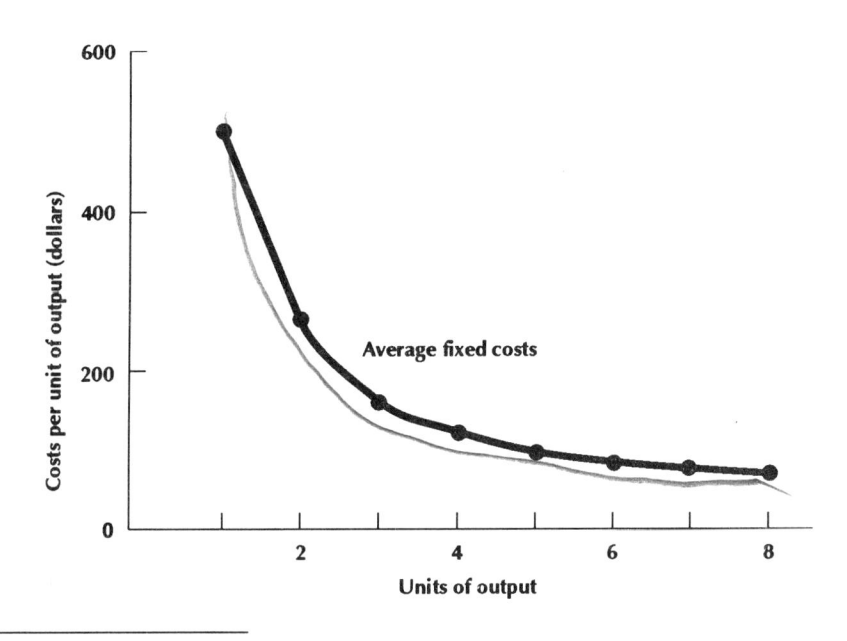

Problems

1. a.

[1] M. Porter, *Competitive Strategy* (New York: Free Press, 1980).

b.

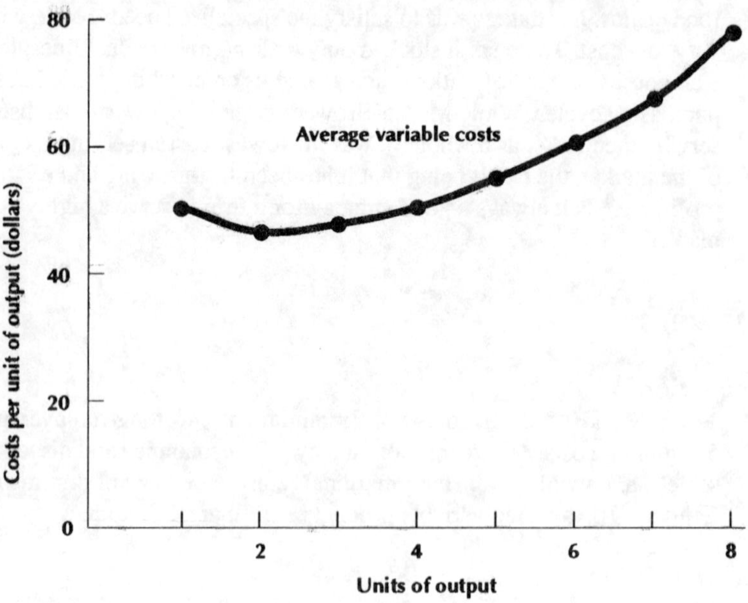
80
60
40
20
0
Costs per unit of output (dollars)
Average variable costs
2
4
6
8
Units of output

c.

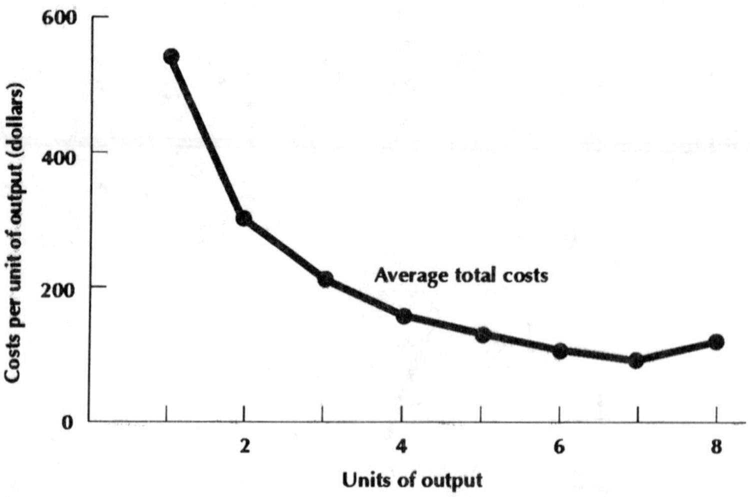
600
400
200
0
Costs per unit of output (dollars)
Average total costs
2
4
6
8
Units of output

d.

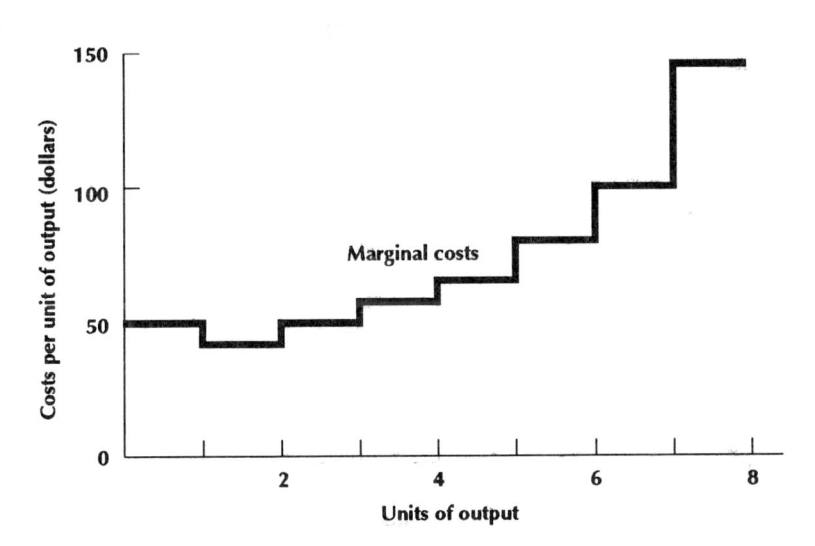

[Graph: Marginal costs step function, x-axis "Units of output" from 0 to 8, y-axis "Costs per unit of output (dollars)" from 0 to 150]

2. a. 1,000 copies sold.
   b. 1,667 copies sold.

3. a. Yes.
   b. No. Since the ratio of the marginal product of capital to the price of capital exceeds the ratio of the marginal product of labor to the price of labor, the firm can lower its costs by substituting capital for labor.

4. The *extra* labor needed to produce the first, second, third, fourth, fifth, and sixth truckloads of tomatoes are 1, 2, 4, 5, 6, and 7 workers. Thus, the marginal costs of the first, second, third, fourth, fifth, and sixth truckloads are $500, $1,000, $2,000, $2,500, $3,000, and $3,500.

5. a. Since total cost equals average cost times output, the firm's total cost function is

$$C = AC \times Q = 3Q + 4Q^2.$$

   b. No, since total cost equals zero when $Q = 0$.
   c. If the price is $2, total revenue ($R$) equals $2Q$. Thus, the firm's profit equals

$$\pi = R - C = 2Q - (3Q + 4Q^2) = -Q - 4Q^2.$$

   If Q is greater than zero, π must be negative, and the firm is incurring losses. If the firm is producing nothing, it is incurring neither profits nor losses. Thus, the firm is better off to produce nothing.

CHAPTER EIGHT

6. Draw the firm's isoquants, as shown below. Also draw the isocost curve corresponding to a given outlay. Clearly, point P is the input combination that maximizes output for this outlay. Since the firm's isoquant is tangent to the isocost curve at point P, the slope of the isocost curve (which equals −1 times the price of input 1 ÷ price of input 2) must equal the slope of the isoquant (which equals −1 times the marginal product of input 1 ÷ marginal product of input 2). Thus, at point P, the ratio of the marginal product to the price of each input must be the same. Yes.

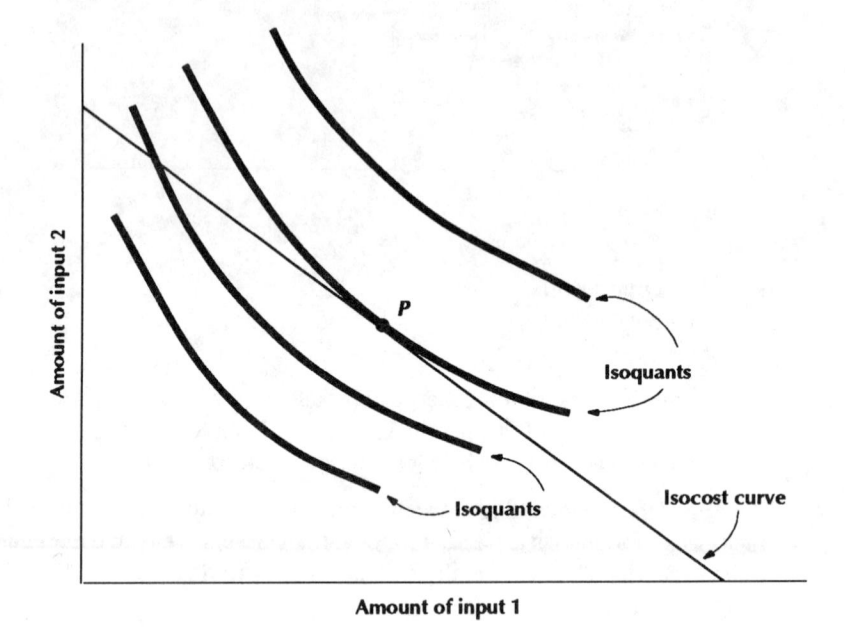

7. a. The isocost curves are as follows:

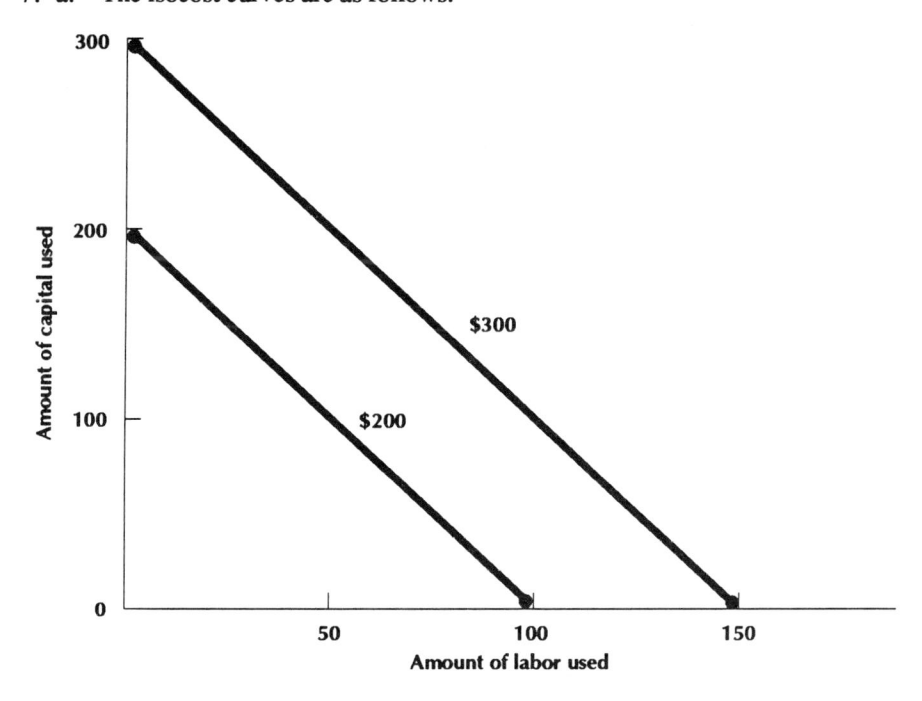

b. $600, $900.

8. a. The average cost of producing 40,000 motors per year is $49.70 + $\frac{\$150,000}{40,000}$ = $49.70 + $3.75 = $53.45. For 80,000 and 160,000 motors, it is $49.70 + 1.88 = $51.58.

b. For 40,000 motors, it is $36.95 + $\frac{\$400,000}{40,000}$ = $46.95. For 80,000 motors, it is $36.95 + $\frac{\$400,000}{80,000}$ = $41.95. For 160,000 motors, it is $36.95 + $\frac{\$400,000}{160,000}$ = $39.45.

c.

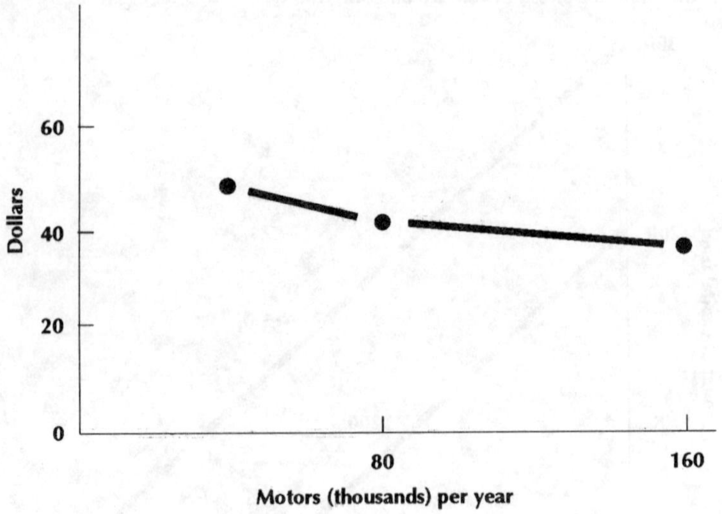
60
40
20
0
Dollars
80
160
Motors (thousands) per year

9. a. $AC = \frac{100}{Q} + 3 - 2Q + 3Q^2.$

b. $MC = 3 - 4Q + 9Q^2.$

c. $\frac{dMC}{dQ} = -4 + 18Q.$

Setting $\frac{dMC}{dQ}$ equal to zero, $Q = 4/18 = 0.22$.

10. a. $\$3.30 + \frac{\$600{,}000}{200{,}000} = \$6.30.$

b. $\$7.00 + \frac{\$200{,}000}{100{,}000} = \$9.00.$

c. $\$9.20 + \frac{\$100{,}000}{50{,}000} = \$11.20.$

11. a. Profit equals $250Q - 4{,}000$, where Q is the number sold. If $250Q - 4{,}000 = 15{,}000$, $Q = 19{,}000 \div 250 = 76$.

b. $Q = 19{,}000 \div 350 = 54.3.$

c. $Q = 19{,}000 \div 400 = 47.5.$

CHAPTER EIGHT

12. Average total cost equals

$$ATC = \frac{40}{Q} + 3 + 2Q,$$

and

$$\frac{dATC}{dQ} = \frac{-40}{Q^2} + 2.$$

Setting $\frac{dATC}{dQ} = 0$, $Q = \sqrt{20} = 4.47$.

13. No. A firm frequently can make more money by serving a broader market.

CHAPTER 9

Linear Programming

Chapter Profile

Linear programming is a technique that allows decision makers to solve maximization and minimization problems where there are certain constraints that limit what can be done. It is useful to look at production decisions from the programming point of view because, unlike conventional theory, linear programming does not take the production function as being given to the analyst or manager before he or she attacks the problem. Also, the programming analysis is easier to apply in many respects, and powerful computational techniques are available to obtain solutions.

A firm often has to choose which one (or which combination) of a number of alternative processes to use to produce a particular product, given that it has only a limited amount of certain inputs. We solved this problem by graphical techniques. Isoprofit curves were constructed and superimposed on a diagram showing the feasible input combinations, and the point was chosen that, among those that were feasible, was on the highest isoprofit curve. In addition, we considered a variant of this problem in which the firm is no longer constrained by limitations on inputs.

Frequently, a firm produces more than one product, and has various fixed facilities that set limits on the amount of each product that can be produced. The firm's managers must determine the optimal combination of outputs of the products. This problem was also solved by graphical means, with isoprofit lines superimposed on a diagram showing feasible output combinations. In addition, in the context of this example, we discussed the fact that the optimal solution of a linear-programming problem will lie at one of the extreme points or corners of the feasible area.

Every linear-programming problem has a corresponding problem called its **dual**; the original problem is called the **primal problem**. If the primal is a maximization problem, the dual is a minimization problem; if the primal is a minimization problem, the dual is a maximization problem. In the example concerning the optimal combination of outputs of two products, whereas the primal looked for optimal output rates for the two products, the dual seeks to impute values to the fixed facilities. These imputed values, or shadow prices, are very useful, since they show what would happen to the firm's profits if the company somehow were able to increase each type of capacity.

A slack variable represents the amount of an input that is unused. When slack variables are introduced, the constraints can be converted from inequalities into equations.

Once such a conversion is made, one can use algebraic techniques to solve a linear-programming problem. The procedure is to evaluate the objective function, which is what we are trying to maximize or minimize, at each corner of the feasible area. The corner where the objective function is highest or lowest is the optimal solution.

*Most linear-programming problems faced by firms are too complex to be solved by graphical methods. Instead, computer programs are used. For example, LINDO (Linear Interactive Discrete Optimizer) is one easy-to-use software package.

Questions

Completion

1. When linear programming is applied, there is some _____ function to be maximized or minimized.
2. In linear-programming problems, the objective function is a _____ function of the variables to be determined.
3. In linear-programming problems, the values of the variables must satisfy certain _____, which are in the form of _____.
4. Every linear-programming problem has a corresponding problem called its _____.
5. If the primal problem is a minimization problem, its dual is a _____ problem.
6. If a resource is not fully utilized, its shadow price will be _____.
7. If a resource is fully utilized and its opportunity cost is positive, its shadow price will be _____.
8. A _____ variable is used to represent the amount of an input that is unused.
9. If the slack variable for an input turns out to be positive in the solution to a firm's problem, some of this input is _____.
10. If the primal problem is to find the outputs of two products that maximize profit, subject to constraints on labor and equipment time, the dual problem is to _____ the total value of _____ and _____ available.

True or False

_____ 1. Linear programming involves constraints that are inequalities.
_____ 2. Linear programming is a purely mathematical technique.

---
*This paragraph refers to the appendix.

CHAPTER NINE

_____ 3. Linear programming seems to conform more closely than conventional analysis to the way managers tend to view production.

_____ 4. Linear programming works only when there are fewer than 10 constraints.

_____ 5. Isoquants are horizontal in the case of linear programming.

_____ 6. The optimal solution of a linear programming problem will occur at an extreme point.

_____ 7. The simplex method is a technique designed to determine how many processes the firm should utilize.

_____ 8. To every linear-programming problem there corresponds a dual problem.

_____ 9. The solutions to the dual problem are the shadow prices.

_____ 10. If the slack variable for an input turns out to be positive, some of this input is redundant.

Multiple Choice

1. In linear programming, isoquants are

   a. positively sloped.
   b. smooth.
   c. a series of connected line segments.
   d. all of the above.
   e. none of the above.

2. In linear programming, the objective function is

   a. a summary of the constraints.
   b. what you want to maximize or minimize.
   c. always nonnegative.
   d. all of the above.
   e. none of the above.

3. If the slack variable for an input turns out to be zero,

   a. this input is fully utilized when the firm is maximizing profit.
   b. this means that some of this input is redundant.
   c. none of this input should be used.
   d. all of the above.
   e. both a and b.

4. The shadow price of a resource is

   a. the opportunity cost of using this resource.
   b. zero if an extra unit of the resource would not increase profit.
   c. positive if the resource is fully utilized and more of it would increase profit.
   d. all of the above.
   e. only a and b.

Problems

1. The Hogan Company can use three processes, A, B, and C, to produce motors. To make one motor, process A requires 1 hour of labor and 4 hours of machine time, process B requires 2 hours of labor and 2 hours of machine time, and process C requires 5 hours of labor and 1 hour of machine time.

   a. In the graph below, draw the rays corresponding to the three processes.
   b. In the graph below, draw the isoquant corresponding to an output of 200 motors.

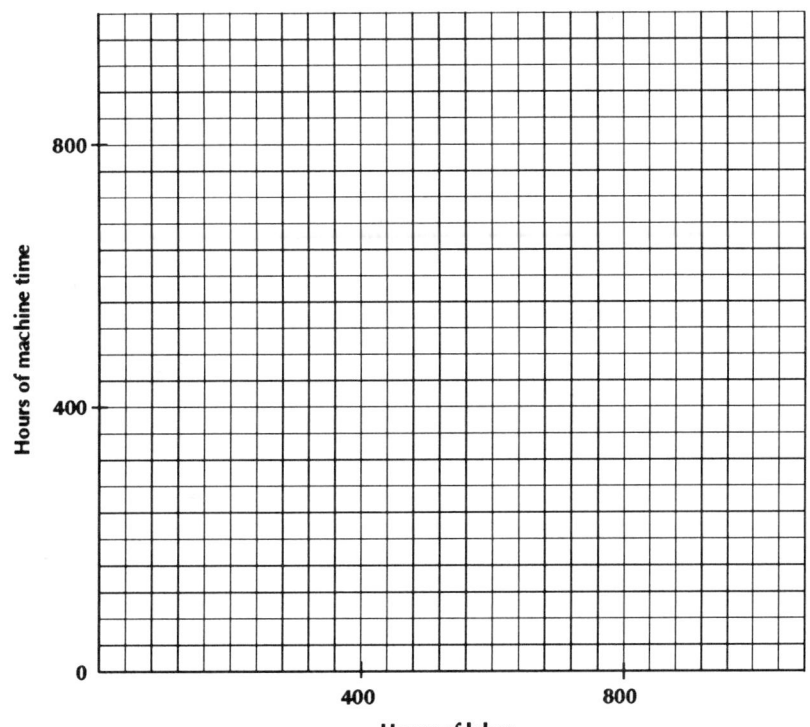

CHAPTER NINE

2. The Hogan Company must pay $10 an hour for labor and $15 an hour for machine time.

   a. If the firm can hire as much labor and machine time as it wants, draw two isocost curves for this firm in the graph below.
   b. Which of the three processes described in question 1 should Hogan's managers choose?

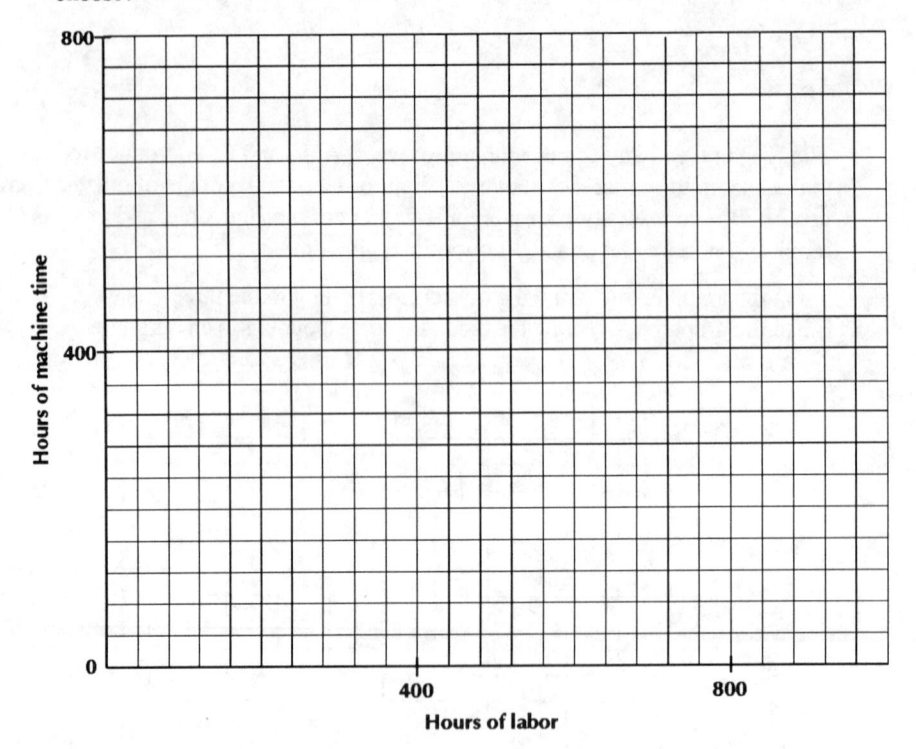

3. Suppose that the Hogan Company can use no more than 1,000 hours of labor time and 2,000 hours of machine time, and that, regardless of which process the firm uses, it receives a price of $100 per motor.

   a. How much profit does the firm receive for each motor made by process A?
   b. How much profit does the firm receive for each motor made by process B?
   c. How much profit does the firm receive for each motor made by process C?

CHAPTER NINE

4. Under the circumstances set forth in question 3, the Hogan Company wants to know how it should allocate its available labor time and machine time among the three processes.

   a. What is the objective function?
   b. What are the constraints?
   c. In the graph below, plot the feasible input combinations.
   d. In the graph below, plot several isoprofit curves.
   e. Solve the firm's problem.

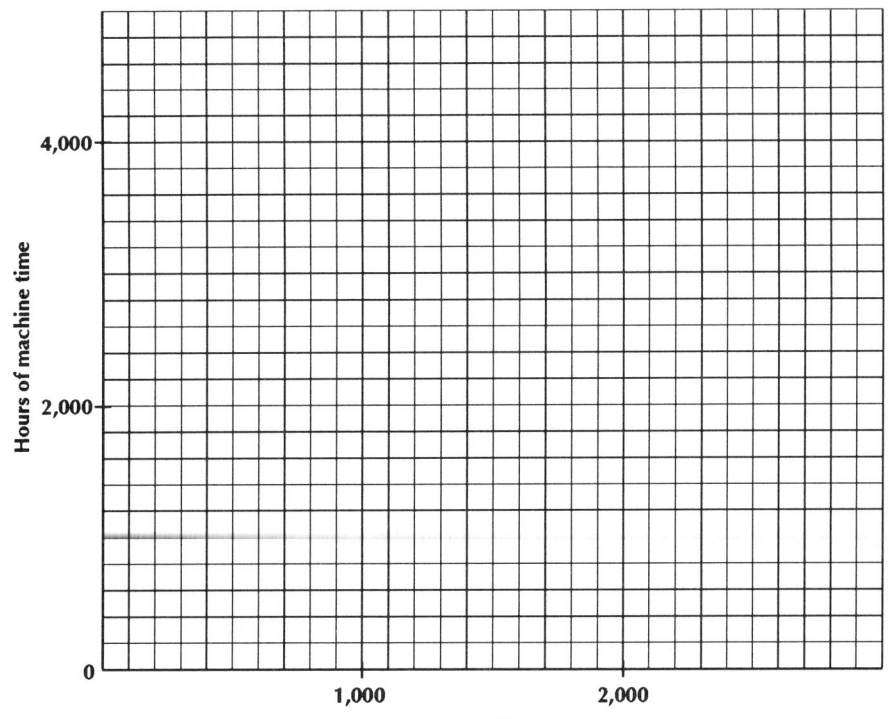

93

CHAPTER NINE

5. The Cook Company produces large and small chairs. The profit contribution per chair is $100 for a large chair and $40 for a small chair. To produce each large chair, the firm requires 20 hours of labor and 10 hours of machine time. To produce each small chair, the firm requires 10 hours of labor and 3 hours of machine time. The firm has available only 1,000 hours of labor and 400 hours of machine time per day.

   a. If the Cook Company wants to maximize the total profit contribution from the two types of chairs, what is the objective function?
   b. What are the constraints?
   c. In the graph below, plot the feasible combinations of output of large and small chairs.
   d. In the graph below, plot three isoprofit lines, and solve the firm's problem.

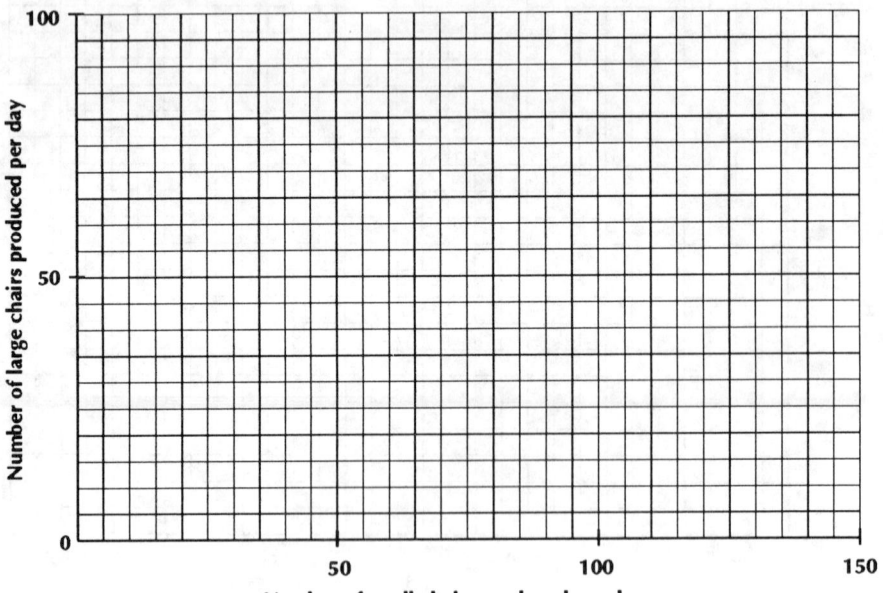

6. a. In question 5, what is the dual problem?
   b. In the dual problem, what is being maximized or minimized?
   c. In the dual problem, what are the constraints?
   d. In the dual problem, what is the solution?
   e. What are the shadow prices of labor time and machine time, and why are they of importance to the managers of the Cook Company?

7. a. In question 5, show how slack variables can be used to convert the constraints from inequalities into equalities.
   b. If one of these slack variables turns out to be zero in the solution of the problem, what does this mean?

8. The Livermore Company has two factories and three warehouses. The factories are in New Jersey and Wisconsin. The warehouses are in Georgia, Tennessee, and Oregon. The cost of shipping a ton of the firm's product from each factory to each warehouse is as follows:

	--------- Warehouse ---------		
Factory	*Georgia*	*Tennessee*	*Oregon*
New Jersey	$ 8	6	14
Wisconsin	10	9	11

The capacity of the New Jersey factory is 1,000 tons per week; for the Wisconsin factory, it is 2,000 tons per week. The weekly requirements of the three warehouses are: Georgia 800 tons; Tennessee, 1,200 tons; and Oregon, 1,000 tons.

   a. If the Livermore Company wants to minimize shipping cost, what is the objective function?
   b. What are the constraints?
 * c. What is the solution?
 * d. What is the minimum value of the firm's weekly shipping cost?

Answers

Completion
1. objective 2. linear 3. constraints, inequalities 4. dual
5. maximization 6. zero 7. positive 8. slack 9. unutilized
10. minimize, labor, equipment

True or False
1. True 2. True 3. True 4. False 5. False 6. True 7. False
8. True 9. True 10. True

Multiple Choice
1. c 2. b 3. a 4. d

---

* This question is for students having access to a computer package like LINDO. See the appendix to Chapter 9.

CHAPTER NINE

Problems

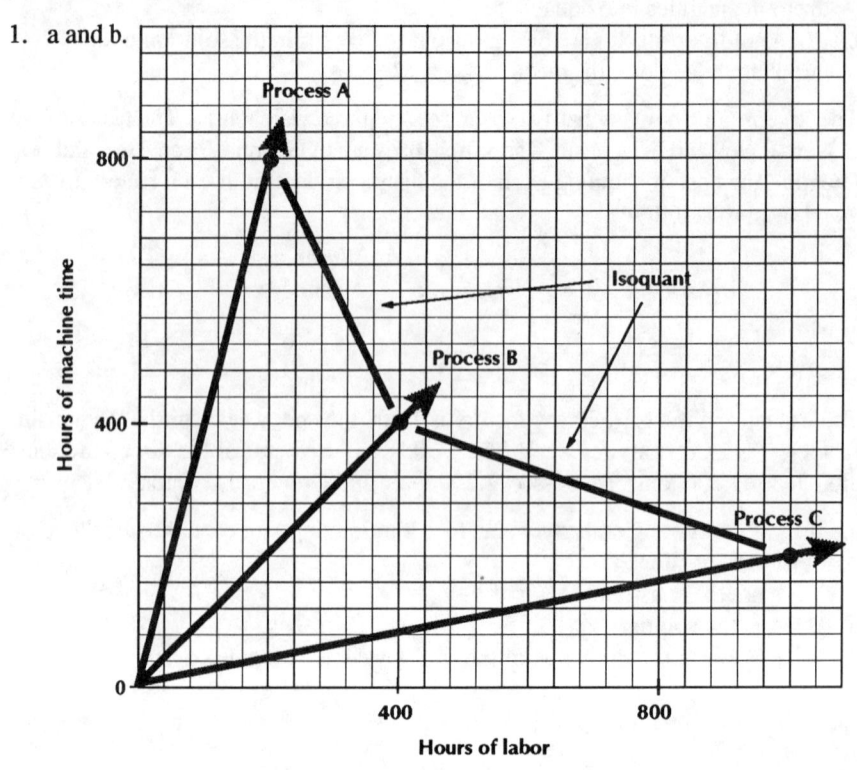

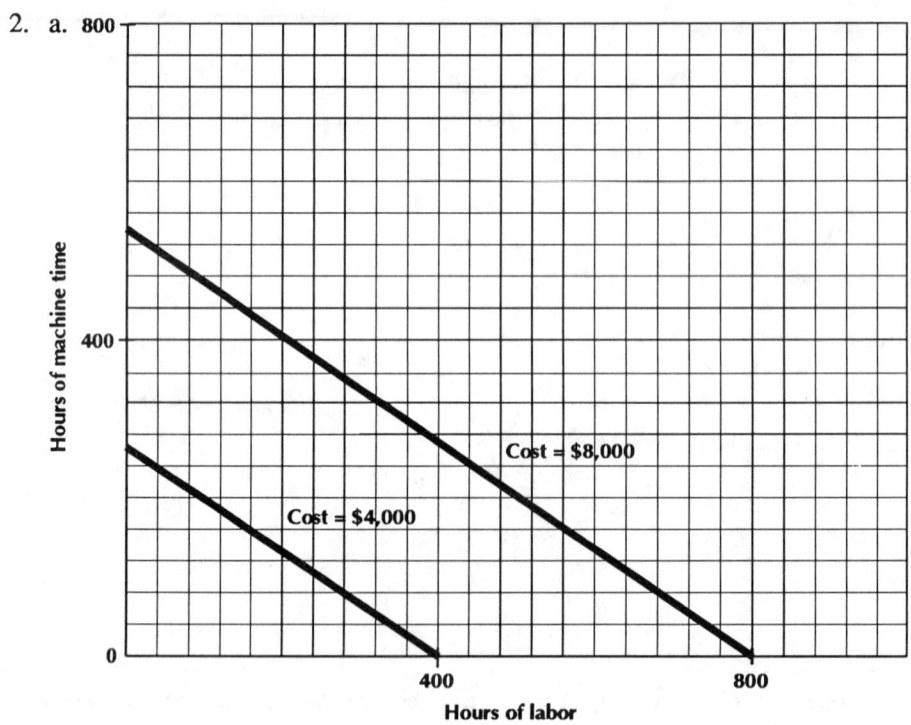

1. a and b.

2. a.

96

CHAPTER NINE

    b. Process B.
3. a. $100 – $70 = $30.
   b. $100 – $50 = $50.
   c. $100 – $65 = $35.
4. a. Maximize $30A + 50B + 35C$.
   b. $A + 2B + 5C \leq 1,000$.
   $4A + 2B + C \leq 2,000$.
   $A \geq 0, B \geq 0, C \geq 0$.
   c. The feasible input combinations are in the rectangle $OXYZ$.

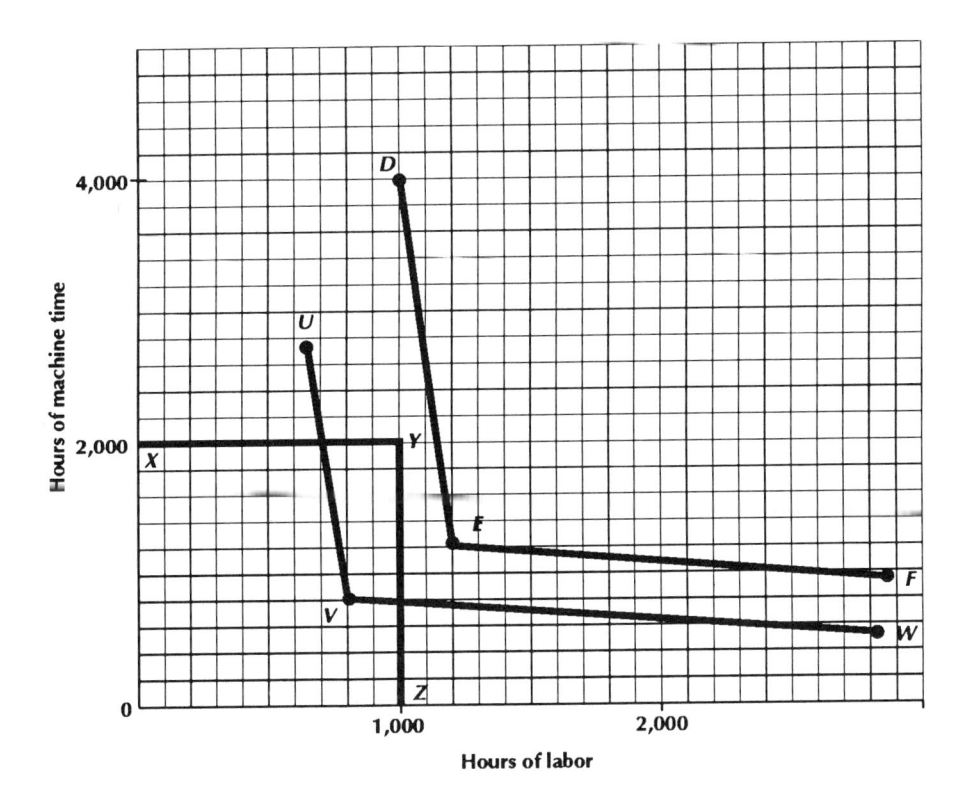

[Graph: Hours of machine time (y-axis) vs Hours of labor (x-axis). Points labeled D (near 4,000 machine time), U (around 2,666), X (at 2,000), Y, E, F, V, W, Z (at 1,000 labor).]

d. Let's construct the isoprofit curve for a profit level of $20,000. To obtain this much profit from process A, $20,000 ÷ $30 = 666 2/3 motors must be produced, which requires 666 2/3 hours of labor and 2,666 2/3 hours of machine time. To obtain this much profit from process B, $20,000 ÷ $50 = 400 motors must be produced, which requires 800 hours of labor and 800 hours of machine time. To obtain this much profit from process C, $20,000 ÷ $35 = 571 motors must be produced, which requires 2,855 hours of labor and 571 hours of machine time. Thus, the isoprofit curve is UVW in the graph in the answer to part c. Using the same technique, we can derive the isoprofit curve for a profit level of $30,000, which is DEF in this graph.

97

CHAPTER NINE

e. Based on the diagram in the answer to part c, it is evident that the point in the feasible area 0XYZ that is on the highest isoprofit curve is point Y. Since points U and D pertain to process A and points V and E pertain to process B, only processes A and B are used. Thus,

$$A + 2B = 1{,}000$$

$$4A + 2B = 2{,}000,$$

where A is the number of motors produced with process A, and B is the number of motors produced with process B. Solving these two equations simultaneously, $A = 333\ 1/3$ and $B = 333\ 1/3$. Thus, the optimal solution is for the firm to produce 333 1/3 motors with process A and 333 1/3 motors with process B.

5. a. The Cook Company should maximize $100L + 40S$, where L is the number of large chairs produced, and S is the number of small chairs produced per day.

b. $20L + 10S \leq 1{,}000$
$10L + 3S \leq 400$
$L \geq 0, S \geq 0.$

c. If the constraint on labor time is satisfied,

$$20L + 10S \leq 1{,}000,$$

which implies that

$$L \leq \frac{1{,}000}{20} - \frac{10S}{20} = 50 - 0.5S.$$

If the constraint on machine time is satisfied,

$$10L + 3S \leq 400,$$

which implies that

$$L \leq \frac{400}{10} - \frac{3S}{10} = 40 - 0.3S.$$

Thus, the feasible combinations of output are points within $0ABC$ in the graph below:

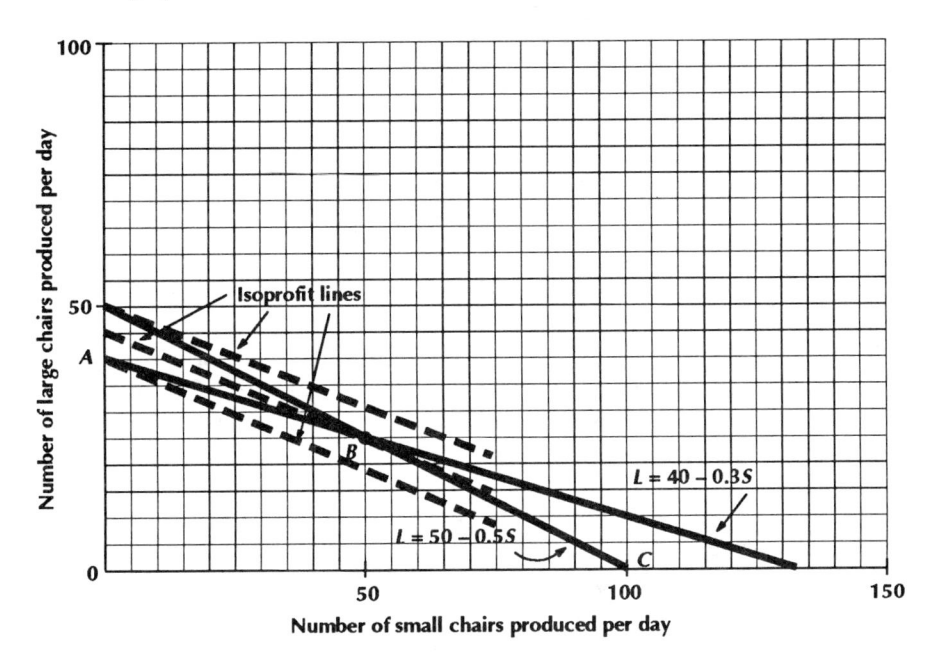

d. The total profit contribution is $100L + 40S$. Thus, if the total profit contribution per day equals π,

$$L = \frac{\pi}{100} - \frac{40}{100} S.$$

To obtain the isoprofit lines in the graph above, we set $\pi = 5{,}000$, $4{,}500$, and $4{,}000$.

Clearly, the point in the feasible area ($0ABC$) on the highest isoprofit line is point B. This is the point of intersection between the following two lines:

$$L = 40 - 0.3S$$
$$L = 50 - 0.5S.$$

Solving these two equations simultaneously, we get $L = 25$ and $S = 50$, which are the coordinates of point B. Thus, the Cook Company should produce 25 large chairs and 50 small chairs per day.

6. a. Minimize $1{,}000G + 400H$ subject to
$$20G + 10H \geq 100$$
$$10G + 3H \geq 40$$
$$G \geq 0, H \geq 0.$$

b. $1{,}000G + 400H.$

c. $20G + 10H \geq 100$
$10G + 3H \geq 40$
$G \geq 0, H \geq 0.$

CHAPTER NINE

d. If the first constraint is satisfied,

$$G \geq \frac{100}{20} - \frac{10H}{20} = 5 - 0.5H.$$

If the second constraint is satisfied,

$$G \geq \frac{40}{10} - \frac{3H}{10} = 4 - 0.3H.$$

Thus, if both constraints are satisfied, only points on or above XYZ in the graph below can be considered. Letting $1{,}000G + 400H = M$,

$$G = \frac{M}{1{,}000} - \frac{400}{1{,}000}H = \frac{M}{1{,}000} - 0.4H.$$

Each dashed line in the graph below shows the values of G and H resulting in a given value of M (5,000 or 4,500). To minimize M, we must find the point on or above XYZ that is on the lowest dashed line. Clearly, this point is Y, where $G = 2.5$ and $H = 5$.

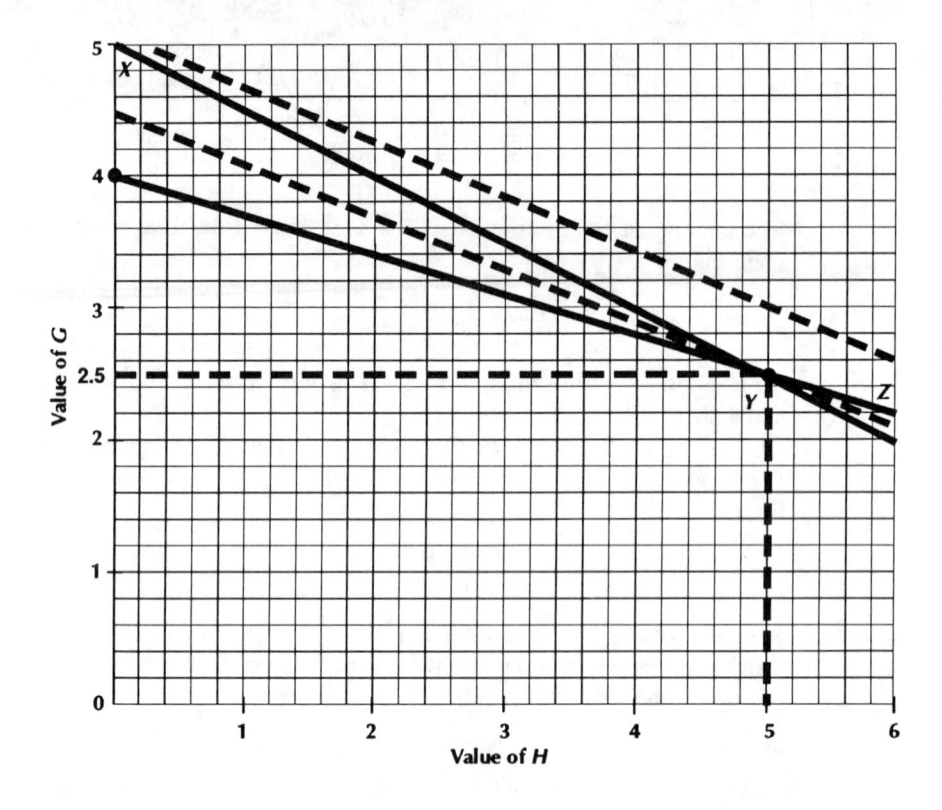

e. The solutions to the dual problem—that is, the values of G and H found in part d—are the shadow prices of labor time and of machine time. Thus, the shadow price of labor time is $2.50 per hour, and the shadow price of machine time is $5 per hour. These shadow prices are important because they indicate what an extra hour of labor time or machine time would be worth to the Cook Company.

7. a. Let U be the number of hours of available labor time that is unutilized. Let V be the number of available machine time that is unutilized. Then the constraints on labor time and machine time are

$$20L + 10S + U = 1{,}000$$
$$10L + 3S + V = 400.$$

Because of the utilization of the slack variables (U and V), these constraints are now equalities, not inequalities.

b. It means that all of the relevant resource is used. Thus, if U equals zero, all of the available labor time is used. If V equals zero, all of the available machine time is used.

8. a. Livermore wants to minimize

$$8I + 6J + 14K + 10N + 9P + 11R,$$

where I is the number of tons per week shipped from the New Jersey factory to the Georgia warehouse, J is the number of tons per week shipped from the New Jersey factory to the Tennessee warehouse, K is the number of tons per week shipped from the New Jersey factory to the Oregon warehouse, N is the number of tons shipped per week from the Wisconsin factory to the Georgia warehouse, P is the number of tons shipped per week from the Wisconsin factory to the Tennessee warehouse, and R is the number of tons shipped per week from the Wisconsin factory to the Oregon warehouse.

b. $I + J + K \le 1{,}000$
$N + P + R \le 2{,}000$
$I + N \ge 800$
$J + P \ge 1{,}200$
$K + R \ge 1{,}000$
$I \ge 0, J \ge 0, K \ge 0, N \ge 0, P \ge 0, R \ge 0.$

CHAPTER NINE

c. The solution is that the New Jersey factory should ship 1,000 tons per week to the Tennessee warehouse, and the Wisconsin factory should ship 800 tons per week to the Georgia warehouse, 200 tons per week to the Tennessee warehouse, and 1,000 tons per week to the Oregon warehouse. The computer printout is shown below:

```
  min 8I + 6J + 14K + 10N + 9P + 11R
? s.t.
? I + J + K < 1000
? N + P + R < 2000
? I + N > 800
? J + P > 1200
? K + R > 1000
? I > 0
? J > 0
? K > 0
? N > 0
? P > 0
? R > 0
? end
: look all

MIN        8 I + 6 J + 14 K + 10 N + 9 P + 11 R
SUBJECT TO
           2)    I + J + K <=    1000
           3)    N + P + R <=    2000
           4)    I + N >=    800
           5)    J + P >=    1200
           6)    K + R >=    1000
           7)    I >=    0
           8)    J >=    0
           9)    K >=    0
          10)    N >=    0
          11)    P >=    0
          12)    R >=    0
END
```

```
: go
LP OPTIMUM FOUND    AT STEP      4
          OBJECTIVE FUNCTION VALUE
   1)           26800.0000

   VARIABLE        VALUE             REDUCED COST
          I         .000000             1.000000
          J      1000.000000             .000000
          K         .000000             6.000000
          N       800.000000             .000000
          P       200.000000             .000000
          R      1000.000000             .000000

      ROW     SLACK OR SURPUS        DUAL PRICES
       2)         .000000             3.000000
       3)         .000000              .000000
       4)         .000000           -10.000000
       5)         .000000            -9.000000
       6)         .000000           -11.000000
       7)         .000000              .000000
       8)      1000.000000              .000000
       9)         .000000              .000000
      10)       800.000000              .000000
      11)       200.000000              .000000
 - -More- -
      12)      1000.000000              .000000

   NO. ITERATIONS=    4
```

d. As the above printout shows, the minimum cost is $26,800 per week.

CHAPTER 10

Perfect Competition, Monopoly, and Monopolistic Competition

Chapter Profile

A perfectly competitive firm will set its output so that price equals marginal cost. If there exists an output rate where price exceeds average variable costs, it will pay the firm to produce, even though price does not cover average total costs. But if there does not exist an output rate where price exceeds average variable costs, the firm is better off to produce nothing at all. In the long run, the firm will produce at the minimum point on its long-run average total cost curve. Price tends to be at the level where the market demand curve intersects the market supply curve.

Under monopoly, a firm will maximize profit if it sets its output rate at the point where marginal revenue equals marginal cost. It does not follow that a firm that holds a monopoly over the production of a particular product must make a profit. If the monopolist cannot cover its variable costs, it, like a perfectly competitive firm, will shut down, even in the short run.

Many monopolists, as well as other firms, own and operate more than a single plant. To maximize profit, such firms must determine how to allocate output among their plants. To minimize cost, a firm should allocate output so that marginal cost is the same for all plants that produce at all. To maximize profit, price and total output should be set so that this common value of marginal cost equals marginal revenue.

In contrast to perfect competition, where all firms sell an identical product, firms under monopolistic competition sell somewhat different products. Producers differentiate their product from that of other producers. Thus, the demand curve facing each firm slopes downward to the right—and is not horizontal, as it would be under perfect competition. Each firm will set marginal revenue equal to marginal cost. In the long run, each firm will produce to the left of the minimum point on its long-run average total cost curve.

Monopolistically competitive firms spend very large amounts on advertising. To maximize its profits, a firm should set its advertising so that the marginal revenue from an extra dollar of advertising equals the price elasticity of demand. A graph showing how both the price elasticity and the marginal revenue from an extra dollar of advertising vary with the amount spent by the firm on advertising can shed useful light on this topic.

Advertising of price changes may increase the price elasticity of demand for the product whose price is changed. This is because the advertising makes more consumers aware of the price changes. Measures of brand loyalty are useful in guiding decisions concerning promotional activities to increase sales of particular brands.

CHAPTER TEN

Questions

Completion

1. In the long run, a perfectly competitive firm's equilibrium position is at the place where its long-run average cost equals _____.
2. For a firm in a perfectly competitive market, if price is more than marginal cost, increases in output will _____ profit.
3. A monopolist can sell 12 units of output when it charges $8 a unit, 11 units of output when it charges $9 a unit, and 10 units of output when it charges $10 a unit. The marginal revenue from the eleventh unit of output equals _____. The marginal revenue from the twelfth unit of output equals _____.
4. A monopolist's demand curve is the same as the industry _____.
5. For a monopolist, marginal revenue is _____ than price.
6. Price will be _____ under monopoly than under perfect competition.
7. Output will be _____ under monopoly than under perfect competition.
8. A monopolistically competitive firm is in long-run equilibrium. Its marginal revenue equals $10. If its marginal revenue plus its economic profit equals one-half of its price, its price equals _____, and its marginal cost equals _____.
9. A measure of brand loyalty is the percentage of customers buying a particular brand today that will buy this brand _____.
10. In the case of coffee, coupon users tend to have a relatively (low, high) _____ brand loyalty.

True or False

_____ 1. In the long run, equilibrium price under perfect competition may be above or below average total cost.

_____ 2. Under perfect competition, one producer can produce a somewhat different good from other producers in the industry.

_____ 3. Under perfect competition, each firm must be careful not to produce too much and spoil the market.

_____ 4. At the equilibrium price, price will equal marginal cost (for all firms that choose to produce) under perfect competition.

_____ 5. A profit-maximizing monopolist will always choose an output in the short run where average total cost is less than average revenue.

_____ 6. A monopolist always produces an output such that the price elasticity of demand is 1.

CHAPTER TEN

_____ 7. A monopolistically competitive firm's short-run demand and cost curves are as follows:

Price (dollars)	Quantity demanded	Output	Total cost (dollars)
8	1	1	5
7	2	2	7
6	3	3	9
4	4	4	11
3	5	5	20

This firm, if it maximizes profit, will choose an output rate of 5.

_____ 8. One effect of advertising price changes is likely to be an increase in the price elasticity of demand for the product whose price is changed.

_____ 9. To maximize profit, a firm should set the marginal revenue from an extra dollar of advertising equal to the income elasticity of demand.

_____ 10. To maximize profit, a firm with two plants, A and B, will allocate output between them so that the average cost at plant A equals the average cost at plant B.

Multiple Choice

1. The market demand curve for a particular kind of table is as follows:

Price (dollars)	Quantity demanded
30	200
20	300
10	400
5	600
3	800

The industry producing this kind of table has a horizontal long-run supply curve, and each firm has the following long-run total cost curve:

Output	Total cost (dollars)
1	10
2	12
3	15
4	30

(Each firm can produce only integer numbers of units of output.)
In the long run, the total number of firms in this industry will be about

a. 100.
b. 200.
c. 300.
d. 400.
e. 500.

2. The long-run average cost curve of the Longacre Company, a perfectly competitive firm, is given below. Given that this curve does not shift, the long-run equilibrium output of this firm will be

   a. 4 units.
   b. 5 units.
   c. 6 units.
   d. 7 units.
   e. 8 units.

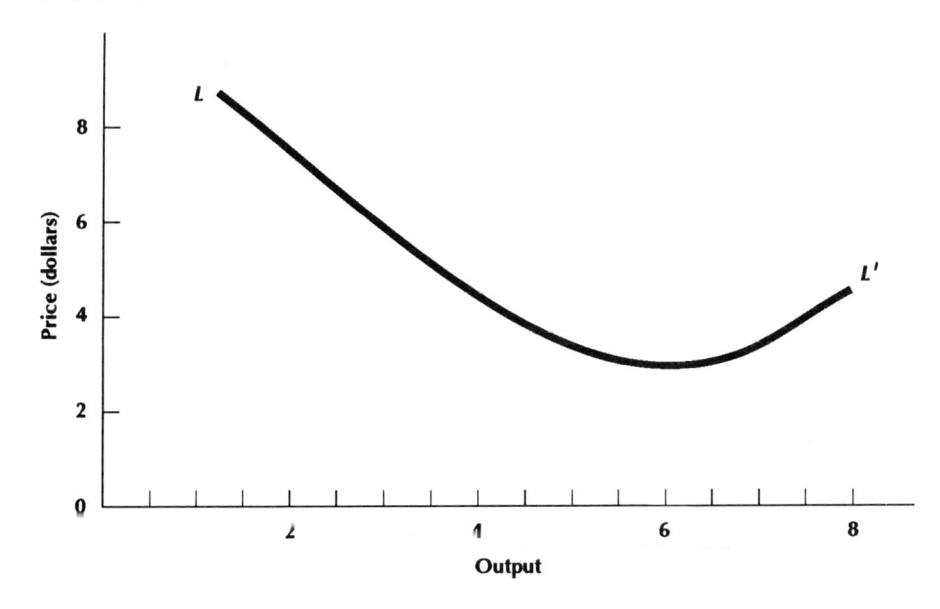

CHAPTER TEN

3. The total cost and total revenue of the Connors Company, a perfectly competitive firm, are shown below:

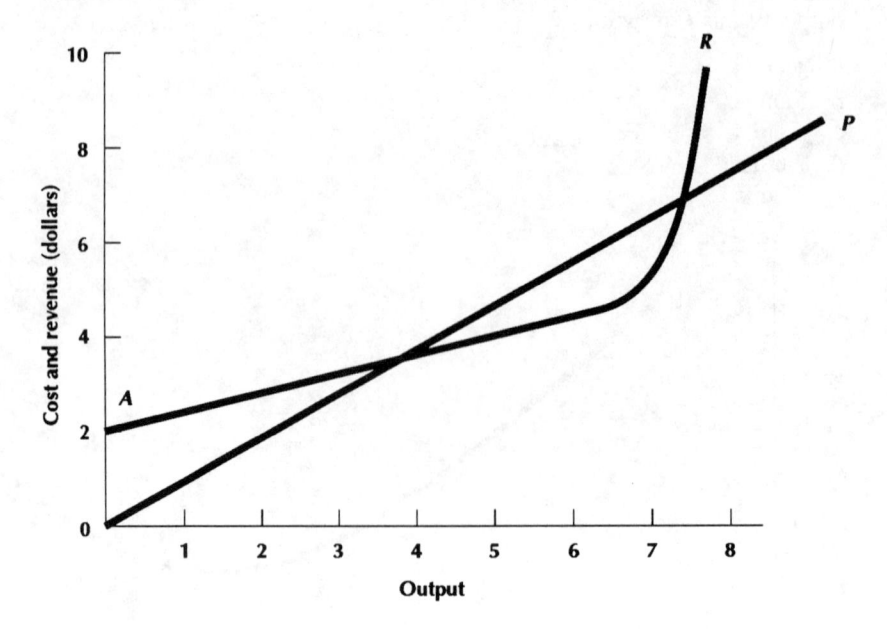

The line *OP* is

a. the total cost curve.
b. the total revenue curve.
c. the relationship between price and output.
d. all of the above.
e. none of the above.

4. A monopolist's total cost equals $100 + 3Q$, where Q is the number of units of output it produces per month. Its demand curve is $P = 200 - Q$, where P is the price of the product. The marginal revenue from the twentieth unit of output per month equals

a. $3,600.
b. $3,439.
c. $180.
d. $140.
e. none of the above.

5. A monopolistic firm will expand its output when

a. marginal revenue exceeds marginal cost.
b. marginal cost exceeds marginal revenue.
c. marginal cost equals marginal revenue.
d. marginal revenue is negative.
e. none of the above.

CHAPTER TEN

6. A profit-maximizing monopoly, if it owns a number of plants, will always
   a. produce some of its output at each plant.
   b. transfer output from plants with high marginal cost to those with low marginal cost.
   c. transfer output from plants with low marginal cost to those with high marginal cost.
   d. produce all of its output at a single plant and shut down the rest.
   e. none of the above.

Problems

1. In the cotton textile industry, each firm's marginal cost curve is

   $$MC = 5 + 3Q,$$

   where MC is its marginal cost (in dollars per ton), and Q is its output per day (in tons).

   a. If there are 1,000 firms in the cotton textile industry, derive the industry's short-run supply curve.
   b. If the price is $8, how much will the cotton textile industry produce per day?
   c. Can you derive each firm's total cost function? Why or why not?

2. Each firm in a perfectly competitive industry has the short-run total cost function shown below.

Output	Total cost (dollars)
0	10
1	12
2	16
3	22
4	30
5	40

   There are 1,000 firms in this industry, and the market demand curve is as follows:

Price (dollars)	Quantity demanded
3	3,000
5	2,000
7	1,500
9	1,000

   a. What is the equilibrium price of the product? (Assume that the price must be $3, $5, $7, or $9.)
   b. What will be the output of each firm?
   c. If you were considering investing in this industry, would you forecast that in the long run firms would tend to enter or leave this industry?

CHAPTER TEN

3. The Jackson Company, a perfectly competitive firm, has the following total cost function:

Total Output	Total cost (dollars)
0	20
1	30
2	42
3	55
4	69
5	84
6	100
7	117

   How much will the Jackson Company produce, if the price is

   a. $13?
   b. $14?
   c. $15?
   d. $16?
   e. $17?

4. The Murphy Corporation's marginal cost curve is

   $$MC = 4 + 3Q,$$

   where MC is the cost (in dollars) of producing the Qth unit of its product, and Q is the number of units of its product produced per day. The price of a unit of its product is $3. A consultant hired by the Murphy Corporation argues that based on this evidence, the firm would make more money by shutting down than by continuing to operate. Do you agree? Explain.

5. The Landau Company's average cost curve is

   $$AC = \frac{400}{Q} + 3Q,$$

   where AC is its average cost (in dollars), and Q is the number of units of its product that is produced per day. The price of a unit of its product is $3.

   a. If the firm produces more than one unit per day, is it making profits or losses? Explain.
   b. Is the firm better off to shut down or operate? Explain.

6. In the early 1950s, it was proposed that New York subway fares should be increased. William Vickrey of Columbia University was asked by the Mayor's Committee on Management Survey of the City of New York to make a study to help evaluate the proposal. Vickrey estimated the demand curve; part of his results are shown below. How would these data be useful in deciding whether or not to raise the subway fare from the then-prevailing level of 10 cents? What additional data would you need in order to come to a conclusion on this score? Do you think that data of this sort would be as useful now as in the early 1950s?

Fare (cents)	Passengers	Total revenue (dollars)
5	1,945	$ 97.2
10	1,683	168.3
15	1,421	213.2
20	1,159	231.8
25	897	224.2
30	635	190.5

Source: W. S. Vickrey. Passengers and revenues are in millions per year.

7. The Ardmore Company's marginal cost of production is zero if its output is less than (or equal to) 40 units per day.

   a. If its output rate is 20 units per day, does its average total cost exceed its average fixed cost?
   b. If the Ardmore Company is a perfectly competitive firm, will it produce less than 40 units per day? Why or why not?
   c. If the Ardmore Company is a monopolist, under what conditions (if ever), will it produce less than 40 units per day? Explain.

8. The Towne Food Corporation has bought exclusive rights to sell chocolate bars in a local sports arena. The fee it paid for this concession was $1,000 per game. The cost (excluding this fee) of obtaining and marketing each candy bar is 10 cents. The demand schedule for candy bars in this arena is as follows:

Price per candy bar (cents)	Thousands of candy bars sold per game
20	10
25	9
30	8
35	7
40	6
45	5
50	4

It is assumed that prices must be multiples of a nickel.

   a. What price should the Towne Food Corporation charge for a candy bar?
   b. What is the maximum amount that the Towne Food Corporation should pay for this concession for a single game?

CHAPTER TEN

9. Beer manufacturers try to differentiate their products by advertising and by other means. In recent decades, there has been a reduction in the number of beer producers: in 1947, there were 404; in 1963; 150; and in 1974, 58. The rate of return, after taxes, on owner's equity in this industry was usually below 8 percent in the post–World War II period, but it increased to 9.1 percent in 1967, 10.1 percent in 1969, and 8.8 percent in 1971. For all manufacturing, the comparable rate of return in 1967, 1969, and 1971 was 11.7, 11.5, and 9.7 percent, respectively.

   a. Would you characterize the beer industry in the United States as monopolistically competitive? Why or why not?
   b. With regard to production differentiation, does it have the characteristics of a monopolistically competitive industry?
   c. Is its profit performance similar to what would be expected in a monopolistically competitive industry?
   d. Do you think that it is becoming closer to monopolistic competition than it used to be? Why or why not?

10. The Haas Company believes that the price elasticity of demand for its product equals 2. It also believes that an extra $1 million in advertising would increase its sales by $1.5 million.

    a. Is the Haas Company spending the optimal amount on advertising? Why or why not?
    b. If not, should it spend more or less on advertising? Explain.

11. For the Schmidt Company, the marginal revenue from an extra dollar of advertising is as shown below.

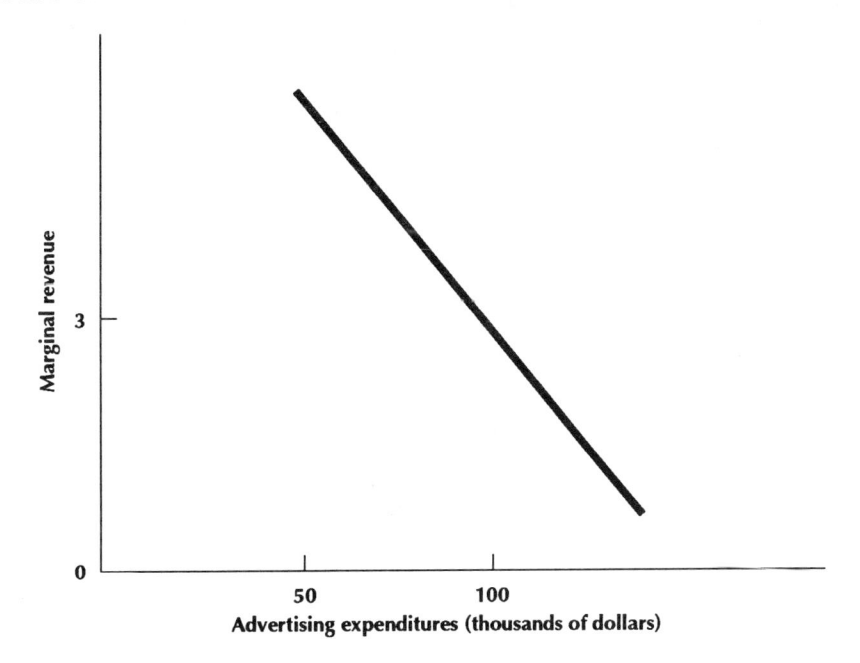

If the price elasticity of demand for the Schmidt Company's product is 3, regardless of how much is spent on advertising, how much should the firm spend on advertising?

12. The Rosemont Company is a member of a perfectly competitive industry. Like all members of the industry, its total cost function is

$$TC = 160{,}000 + 100Q + 4Q^2,$$

where TC is the firm's monthly total cost (in dollars), and Q is the firm's monthly output.

   a. If the industry is in long-run equilibrium, what is the price of the Rosemont Company's product?
   b. What is the firm's monthly output?

13. The London Corporation's total cost function (where TC is total cost in dollars, and Q is quantity) is

$$TC = 400 + 6Q + 3Q^2.$$

   a. If the firm is perfectly competitive and if the price of its product is $36, what is its optimal output rate?
   b. At this output rate, what are its profits?

CHAPTER TEN

14. The supply and demand curves for a product are as follows:

$$Q_S = 10{,}000P$$
$$Q_D = 25{,}000 - 15{,}000P,$$

where Q_S is the quantity (tons) supplied, Q_D is the quantity (tons) demanded, and P is the price per ton (in hundreds of dollars per ton).

a. What is the equilibrium price?
b. What is the equilibrium quantity?

15. The Nibelungen Company, an unregulated monopoly, finds that its marginal cost curve is $MC = 80 + 4Q$, where MC is marginal cost (in dollars), and Q is output. The demand curve for its product is $P = 200 - 2Q$, where P is the product price (in dollars), and Q is output.

a. If this firm wants to maximize profit, what output should it choose?
b. What price should it charge?

16. The Garfield Company's marketing manager believes that the price elasticity of demand for its product equals 1.8, and that the relationship between the amount spent by the firm on advertising and its sales is as follows:

Advertising expenditure	Sales
$200,000	$0.6 million
300,000	0.9 million
400,000	1.1 million
500,000	1.2 million

a. If the Garfield Company is spending $300,000 on advertising, what is the marginal revenue from an extra dollar of advertising?
b. Is $300,000 the optimal amount for the firm to spend on advertising?
c. If $300,000 is not the optimal amount, would you recommend that the firm spend more or less on advertising?

Answers

Completion
1. price   2. increase   3. −$1, −$3   4. demand curve   5. less
6. higher   7. lower   8. $20, $10   9. again when next they buy the product
10. low

True or False
1. False   2. False   3. False   4. True   5. False   6. False   7. False
8. True   9. False   10. False

Multiple Choice
1. b   2. c   3. b   4. e   5. a   6. b

CHAPTER TEN

Problems

1. a. If Q is the quantity supplied by the industry (in tons per day) and P is the price (in dollars per ton),
$$Q = \frac{-5{,}000}{3} + \frac{1{,}000P}{3}.$$
   b. 1,000 tons.
   c. No.

2. a. $5.
   b. 2 units.
   c. They will tend to leave this industry.

3. The Jackson Company's marginal cost curve is

Output	Marginal cost (dollars)
0 to 1	10
1 to 2	12
2 to 3	13
3 to 4	14
4 to 5	15
5 to 6	16
6 to 7	17

   a. If the price is $13, the Jackson Company will produce 2 or 3 units.
   b. 3 or 4 units.
   c. 4 or 5 units.
   d. 5 or 6 units.
   e. 6 or 7 units.

4. According to this evidence, the marginal cost of the first unit of output is $4 + (3)(1) = \$7$. Clearly, if the price of a unit of the product is $3, the firm loses money on each unit it sells. Indeed, it does not even cover its variable costs. Thus, the consultant is right; the firm should produce nothing.

5. a. The firm's total cost function is
$$C = AC \times Q = \left(\frac{400}{Q} + 3Q\right)Q = 400 + 3Q^2.$$
The firm's total revenue equals $R = 3Q$. Thus, its profit equals
$$\pi = R - C = 3Q - 400 - 3Q^2 = -400 - 3(Q^2 - Q) = -400 - 3Q(Q - 1).$$
If $Q > 1$, the firm incurs losses because $\pi = -400 - 3Q(Q - 1)$ is negative.
   b. Since $\pi = -400 - 3Q(Q - 1)$, the maximum value of π is not achieved at $Q = 0$. For example, if $Q = 1/2$, $\pi = -400 - 3(1/2)(-1/2) = -399\ 1/4$. This is a higher value of π than -400, which is the value of π when $Q = 0$. Thus, assuming that the firm can produce fractional units of output per day, it is better off to operate than to shut down.

CHAPTER TEN

6. The demand for subway travel is shown by the table to be price inelastic at the then-prevailing fare of 10 cents. This means that increases in the fare would increase total revenues. Also, they would reduce the subway deficit because fewer passengers would mean lower costs (or at least no higher costs). But this is not the only consideration. You would probably want to investigate how such a fare increase would affect various parts of the population—the poor, the rich, rush-hour traffic, non-rush-hour traffic, and so on. Data of this sort would be just as relevant now as in the early 1950s.

7. a. No. They are equal.
   b. No, since marginal cost (which is zero) must be less than price (unless it too is zero).
   c. It will produce less than 40 units per day if marginal revenue equals zero (and thus is equal to marginal cost) at an output less than 40 units per day.

8. a. Since total cost (excluding the fee) is 10 cents times the number of candy bars sold, the Towne Food Corporation's total profit per game (before paying the fee) is shown below, under various assumptions concerning the price.

Thousands of candy bars	Price (cents)	Total revenue (dollars)	Total cost (dollars) (excluding fee)	Total profit (dollars)
10	20	2,000	1,000	1,000
9	25	2,250	900	1,350
8	30	2,400	800	1,600
7	35	2,450	700	1,750
6	40	2,400	600	1,800
5	45	2,250	500	1,750
4	50	2,000	400	1,600

Thus, the Towne Food Corporation will maximize profit if it sets a price of 40 cents.
   b. $1,800, since this is the maximum amount it could make per game.

9. a. The beer industry has some characteristics of monopolistic competition, but it departs from it in other respects. In a particular geographical market, there may be a limited number of beers that are distributed. In contrast, monopolistic competition occurs where there are a great many sellers. Also, the barriers to entry in the beer industry are not inconsiderable, whereas monopolistic competition assumes free entry.
   b. Yes, the beer industry is characterized by product differentiation.
   c. Its profits have not been above-average. In this respect, at least, its profit performance is similar to a monopolistically competitive industry.
   d. No, because the number of breweries has declined, and it seems to be increasingly oligopolistic.

10. a. No. It should set the marginal revenue from an extra dollar of its advertising equal to its price elasticity of demand.
    b. Less.

CHAPTER TEN

11. $100,000.

12. a. Average cost equals
$$AC = \frac{160,000}{Q} + 100 + 4Q.$$
Thus, the minimum value of average cost occurs when
$$\frac{dAC}{dQ} = \frac{-160,000}{Q^2} + 4 = 0$$
$$Q = 200.$$
Substituting 200 for Q in the equation for average cost, the minimum value of average cost equals
$$\frac{160,000}{200} + 100 + 4(200) = 1,700.$$
Thus, in the long run, price equals $1,700.
   b. 200.

13. a. Since marginal cost equals
$$MC = \frac{dTC}{dQ} = 6 + 6Q,$$
marginal cost equals price when
$$6 + 6Q = 36$$
$$Q = 5.$$
Thus, the optimal output rate is 5 units.
   b. $5(36) - (400 + 6(5) + 3(25)) = 180 - 505 = -325.$

14. a. Since Q_D must equal Q_S,
$$10,000P = 25,000 - 15,000P$$
$$P = 1.$$
   b. 10,000 tons.

15. a. Setting marginal cost equal to marginal revenue,
$$80 + 4Q = 200 - 4Q$$
$$Q = 15.$$
   b. $P = 200 - 2(15) = 170.$

16. a. 2.
    b. No.
    c. More.

117

CHAPTER 11

Oligopoly and Strategic Behavior

Chapter Profile

Oligopoly is characterized by a small number of firms and a great deal of interdependence, actual and perceived, among them. A good example of an oligopoly is the American oil industry, where a small number of firms account for the bulk of the industry's capacity.

Oligopolistic industries, like others, tend to pass through a number of phases—introduction, growth, maturity, and decline. As an industry goes through these phases, the nature of firm behavior often shifts. During the early stages, there often is considerable uncertainty regarding the industry's technology and concerning which markets will open up soonest. During the maturity phase, there frequently is a tendency for firms to attack the market shares of their rivals. In decline, there may be a tendency to get cash out of the firm as quickly as possible, but this may not be the best policy.

There is no single model of oligopoly. Instead, there are many models, depending on the circumstances. In some cases, the demand curve facing an oligopolist is kinked, demand being more price elastic for price increases than for price decreases. Under these circumstances, price would be expected to be quite rigid.

Conditions in oligopolistic industries tend to promote collusion, since the number of firms is small and firms recognize their interdependence. The advantages to be derived by the firms from collusion seem obvious: increased profits, decreased uncertainty, and a better opportunity to control the entry of new firms. However, collusive arrangements are often hard to maintain, since once a collusive agreement is made, any of the firms can increase its profits by "cheating" on the agreement. An interesting example is the United Arab Emirates, which openly refused to abide by the production quotas set by the OPEC cartel.

In considering whether to make a move that threatens its rivals, an oligopolist should consider how likely it is that retaliation will occur, how soon it is likely to come, and how effective (and painful) it will be. It frequently is important that you convince your firm's rivals that your firm is committed to a strategic move it is making, that, if they make particular moves, your firm is committed to retaliate swiftly and effectively, and that your firm is committed not to make particular threatening moves against them.

The prisoners' dilemma is a type of game that is useful in analyzing oligopolistic situations, such as whether or not cartel members should cheat. If the game is played once, there are strong incentives to cheat, but if it is repeated, other strategies such as

CHAPTER ELEVEN

"tit for tat" may be better. Most-favored-customer clauses can be devices to discourage price cutting.

Another model of oligopolistic behavior is based on the supposition that one of the firms in the industry is a price leader, because it is a dominant firm. We have shown how under these circumstances this firm should set its price to maximize its profits. Also, game theory was used to analyze entry deterrence by oligopolists, as well as preemptive strategies.

Statistical studies based on data pertaining to hundreds of firms indicate (a) that the single most important factor influencing a business unit's profitability is the quality of its products and services, relative to those of rivals, and (b) that market share and profitability are strongly related.

Questions

Completion

1. All firms in an industry have marginal costs equal to $10 per unit of output. If they combine to form a cartel, the cartel's marginal cost (will, will not) _____ be $10 per unit of output. If the cartel maximizes profit, its marginal revenue will be (greater than, smaller than, equal to) _____ $10 per unit. Its price will be (greater than, smaller than, equal to) _____ $10 per unit.
2. Under oligopoly, each firm is aware that its actions are likely to elicit _____ in the policies of its competitors.
3. A good example of oligopoly in the United States is the _____ industry.
4. According to the kinked oligopoly demand curve, firms think that if they raise their price, their rivals will _____.
5. According to the kinked oligopoly demand curve, firms think that if they lower their price, their rivals will _____.
6. A most-favored-customer clause means that if a firm reduces its price subsequently, earlier customers will get a _____ so they will pay _____ more than those buying _____ the price reduction.
7. Most-favored-customer clauses can be devices to discourage _____.
8. Excess _____ can be used to forestall and resist entry.
9. According to PIMS data, the most important single factor influencing a business unit's profitability is the _____ of its products and services relative to those of rivals.

CHAPTER ELEVEN

True or False

_____ 1. Collusion is often difficult to achieve and maintain because an oligopoly contains an unwieldy number of firms, or because the product is quite heterogeneous.

_____ 2. If a perfectly competitive industry is operating along the elastic portion of its demand curve, there is no point in trying to cartelize the industry.

_____ 3. Because a cartel maximizes profit, there is no incentive for a member to violate the rules of the cartel.

_____ 4. Cartels have been common and legally acceptable in Europe.

_____ 5. Cartels tend to be unstable because the demand curve facing a "cheater" is highly inelastic.

_____ 6. According to the dominant-firm model, the dominant firm allows the smaller firms to sell all they want at the price it sets.

_____ 7. Whether or not an industry remains oligopolistic in the face of relatively easy entry depends on the size of the market for the product relative to the optimal size of the firm.

_____ 8. A limit price is a price that is the maximum price the oligopolists can charge without courting the possibility of government antitrust action.

_____ 9. A Nash equilibrium exists for any and every game.

_____ 10. According to a tit-for-tat strategy, if one firm cheats on an agreement, the other firm should do the same.

Multiple Choice

1. The Oakland Corporation's demand curve, given below, is kinked.

Price (dollars)	Quantity demanded
3	64
4	62
5	60
6	55
7	50

If the price must be an integer number of dollars, at what price is the kink?

a. $3.
b. $4.
c. $5.
d. $6.
e. $7.

2. If *D* is the industry demand curve and marginal cost equals $2, the price that maximizes a cartel's profits is

   a. $12.
   b. $14.
   c. $16.
   d. $2.
   e. none of the above.

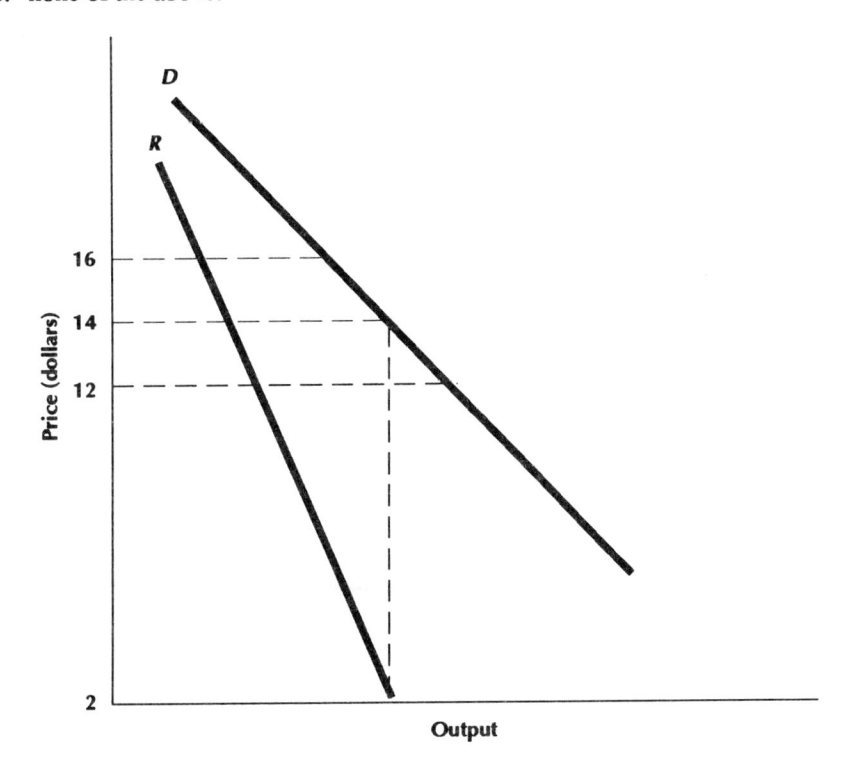

3. In the previous question, the *R* curve is

   a. the marginal revenue curve.
   b. the marginal cost curve.
   c. the reaction curve.
   d. all of the above.
   e. none of the above.

4. A dominant strategy is a strategy where

   a. the player loses.
   b. a seond-best approach is used.
   c. pure strategies are mixed with impure strategies.
   d. all of the above.
   e. none of the above.

CHAPTER ELEVEN

5. In the following graph, which of the curves is a kinked oligopoly curve?

   a. A.
   b. B.
   c. C.
   d. all of the above.
   e. none of the above.

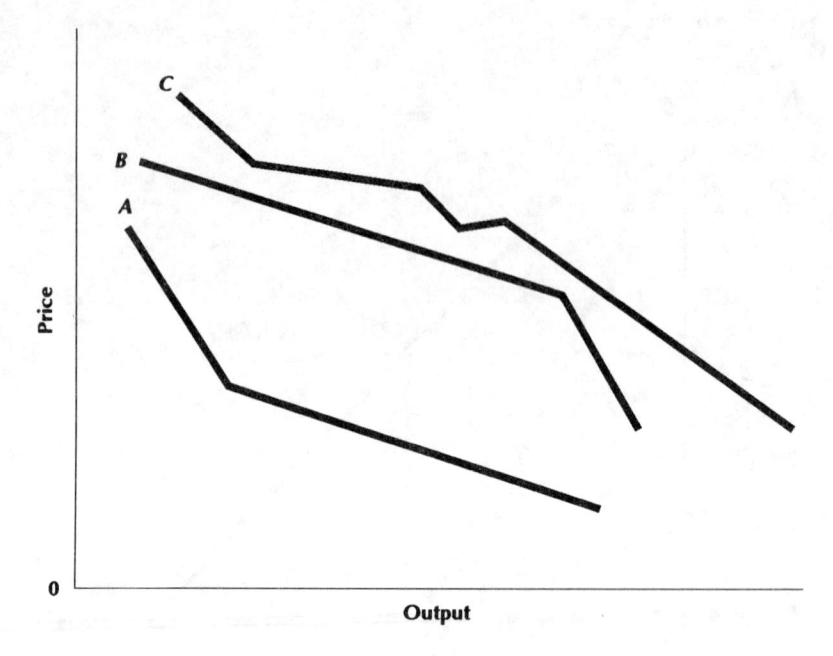

6. In the dominant-firm model, the dominant firm finds the demand curve for its output by

   a. using the unadjusted industry demand curve.
   b. adding up the small firms' demand curves.
   c. subtracting the small firms' supply from the industry demand curve.
   d. all of the above.
   e. none of the above.

Problems

1. During the 1960s and 1970s, the major U.S. automobile manufacturers were not very enthusiastic about producing small cars, owing in part to the fact that they made a larger profit on a larger car than a small one. But the explosion of gasoline prices and the press of foreign competition during the 1970s led the American producers to introduce new lines of smaller, fuel-efficient cars in the fall of 1980. The prices at which they and their Japanese competitors were offered were as follows:

Chevrolet Citation	$6,337	Subaru wagon	$5,612
GM "J" cars	6,300	Datsun 310	5,439
Ford Escort	6,009	Subaru hatchback	5,212
Dodge Omni	5,713	Mazda GLC	4,755

   a. According to some observers, "Detroit . . . priced these cars relatively high to replenish its depleted coffers as soon as possible." Is this necessarily the effect of charging relatively high prices?
   b. Some auto executives stated that the U.S. demand for smaller cars would be so great in the early 1980s that Detroit would be able to sell all such cars that it could produce. What implicit assumptions were they making?

2. Firms C and D are the only two producers and sellers of a particular type of electrical equipment. They each have two possible strategies for product development. The payoff matrix is as follows:

Possible strategies for firm C	Possible strategies for firm D A	B
1	Firm C's profit: $5 million Firm D's profit: $6 million	Firm C's profit: $4 million Firm D's profit: $5 million
2	Firm C's profit: $6 million Firm D's profit: $5 million	Firm C's profit: $5 million Firm D's profit: $4 million

   a. What is firm C's optimal strategy?
   b. What is firm D's optimal strategy?
   c. Is this an example of the prisoner's dilemma?
   d. Is there a dominant strategy for firm C? Explain.
   e. Is there a dominant strategy for firm D? Explain.

CHAPTER ELEVEN

3. If two firms are engaged in a game with the characteristics of the prisoner's dilemma, can the equilibrium depend on whether the game is played repeatedly or just once? Explain.

4. Two firms that are the only producers of a particular scientific instrument agree to maintain their prices at the monopoly level. In the event that either cheats on this agreement, both firms will adopt a strategy of tit for tat. Describe how each firm may attempt to determine whether the other firm is cheating.

5. There are ten identical producers of spring water. Each of these firms has zero costs of production, so long as it produces less than (or equal to) 10 gallons of water per hour. It is impossible for each firm to produce more than 10 gallons per hour. Suppose the market demand curve for this water is as follows:

Price (dollars per gallon)	Number of gallons demanded per hour	Price (dollars per gallon)	Number of gallons demanded per hour
11	0	5	60
10	10	4	70
9	20	3	80
8	30	2	90
7	40	1	100
6	50	1/2	105

   a. If the firms take the price of water as given (as in the case of perfect competition), what will be the price and output of each firm?
   b. If the firms form a completely effective cartel, what will be the price and output of each firm?
   c. How much money will each firm be willing to pay to achieve and enforce the collusive agreement described in part b?
   d. Suppose that one of the firms secretly breaks the terms of the agreement and shades price. What effect will this have on its profits?

6. John Milton and Alexander Pope are arrested for holding up a bank. The district attorney talks *separately* to each one, saying, "We've got lots of evidence indicating you robbed the bank, so you'd better confess. If you do, I'll give you a break. If you *alone* confess, I'll see to it you get only 6 months in jail. If you *both* confess, I'll see to it you get 10 years. But if you don't confess, and your partner *does*, I'll see to it you get 20 years." Both Milton and Pope are sure that if neither confesses, they will get 2 years.

   a. In this situation, what is the payoff matrix?
   b. What strategy will each choose, given that each tries to save his own skin?

7. The Aloha Company and the Crowe Corporation are producers of a product whose marginal cost equals $2. The marginal revenue curve for their combined output is

$$MR = 10 - 2Q,$$

where MR is marginal revenue (in dollars), and Q is the number of units of output sold by both together per hour. If the two producers decide to collude and share the monopoly profits, how much will be their combined output? Why?

8. A cartel is formed by three firms. Their total cost functions are as follows:

Units of output	Firm A	Firm B	Firm C
0	20	25	15
1	25	35	22
2	35	50	32
3	50	80	47
4	80	120	77
5	120	160	117

Total cost (dollars)

If the cartel decides to produce 11 units of output, how should the output be distributed among the three firms, if they want to minimize cost?

9. In its annual report, Aluminum, Ltd., of Canada once noted, "World stocks of aluminum are not excessively large. They are in firm hands and do not weigh unduly upon the world market." What did it mean by "firm hands"? Do you think this phenomenon was at all related to the firmness of world aluminum prices during the relevant period? Under perfect competition, do you think aluminum prices would remain fairly constant in the face of sharp reductions in sales?

10. U.S. Steel (now USX) often was regarded as the price leader in steel, as was Alcoa in virgin aluminum, American Viscose in rayon, and Du Pont in nylon and polyester fibers. What characteristics tend to distinguish price leaders from other firms? If you had to predict which of a number of firms in an industry was the price leader, what variables would you use to make the forecast?

11. If the payoff matrix is as given below, what strategy will firm A choose? What strategy will firm B choose?

Possible strategies for firm A	Possible strategies for firm B		
	1	2	3
	Profits for firm A, or losses for firm B (dollars)		
I	$10	$9.0	$11
II	8	8.5	10

12. According to the Federal Trade Commission, there was collusion among the leading bakers and food outlets in the state of Washington in the late 1950s and early 1960s. Prior to the conspiracy, bread prices in Seattle were about equal to the U.S. average. During the period of the conspiracy, bread prices in Seattle were 15 to 20 percent above the U.S. average. Is this consistent with the theory of collusive behavior? Why do you think bread prices in Seattle were not double or triple the U.S. average during the conspiracy?

CHAPTER ELEVEN

Answers

Completion
1. will, equal to, greater than   2. changes   3. steel (among many others)
4. maintain their present price   5. lower their price too   6. rebate, no, after
7. price cutting   8. capacity   9. quality

True or False
1. True   2. False   3. False   4. True   5. False   6. True   7. True
8. False   9. False   10. True

Multiple Choice
1. c   2. b   3. a   4. e   5. b   6. c

Problems
1. a. No. If a firm charges relatively high prices, it may sell relatively few units of its product, the result being that its profits may be lower than they would be if its price were somewhat lower.
   b. They were assuming that U.S. consumers would not buy imported smaller cars (instead of U.S. smaller cars) in such numbers that Detroit would be unable to sell all it could produce.

2. a. Strategy 2.
   b. Strategy A.
   c. No.
   d. Yes. Strategy 2.
   e. Yes. Strategy A.

3. Yes. See the text.

4. In some cases, trade associations have been authorized to collect detailed information concerning each firm's transactions.

5. a. The industry supply curve would be as shown below. This is the horizontal sum of the firm's marginal cost curves. Since this supply curve intersects the demand curve at a price of $1, this is the equilibrium price. Since the supply and demand curves intersect at an output of 100 gallons, this is the industry output. Each firm produces one-tenth of this output, or 10 gallons.

The industry supply curve is

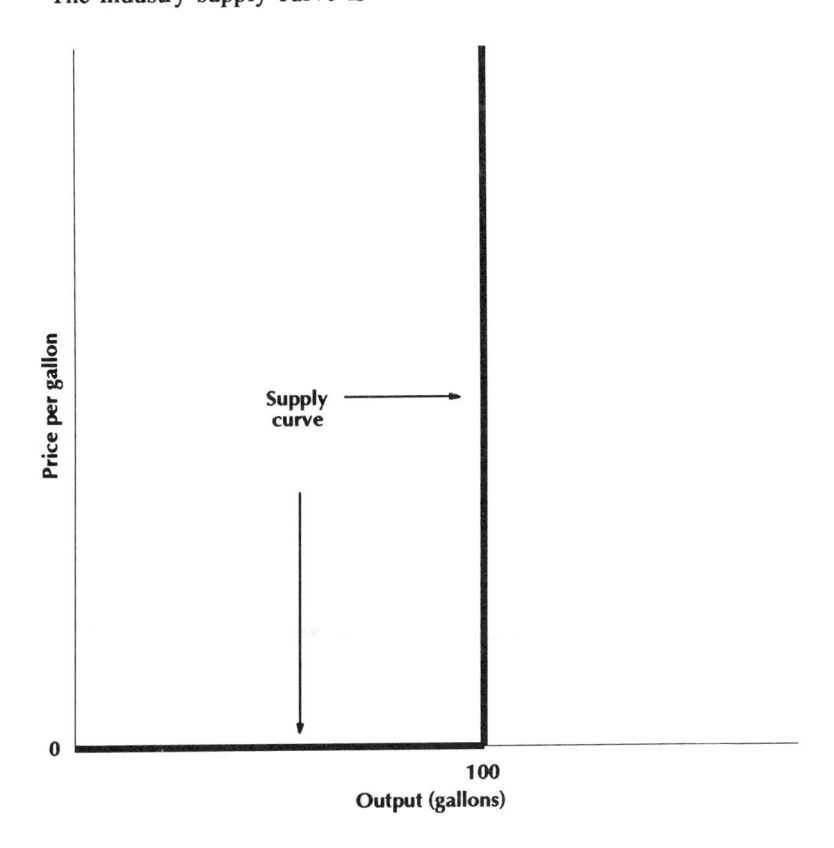

b. The cartel would expand output only so long as marginal revenue exceeds marginal cost. Since marginal cost is zero, this means that the cartel would expand output only so long as marginal revenue is positive. Marginal revenue is shown below.

Output	Total revenue (dollars)	Marginal revenue (dollars)
0	0	
10	100	10
20	180	8
30	240	6
40	280	4
50	300	2
60	300	0
70	280	-2
80	240	-4
90	180	-6
100	100	-8

Clearly, the cartel would restrict output to 50 gallons and charge $6 per gallon. (Alternatively, it could set output at 60 gallons, and charge $5 per gallon. The profit would be the same.)

c. If the alternative to the cartel is the arrangement described in part a, each firm would be willing to pay up to $20 per hour to achieve and enforce the cartel. With the cartel, each firm makes $30 per hour, since each produces 5 gallons per hour, and charges $6 per gallon. Under the arrangement in part a, each firm makes $10 per hour, since each produces 10 gallons per hour and charges $1 per gallon. Thus, each firm's profit per hour is $20 higher under the cartel.

d. If the cartel sets a price of $6 per gallon, this firm can increase its profits by selling an additional 5 gallons per hour at a price per gallon of $5. But if a substantial number of firms begin to act in this way, the cartel will break apart.

6. a. The payoff matrix is as follows:

Possible strategies for Pope	Milton's payoff — Possible strategies for Milton — Confess	Milton's payoff — Not confess (Years of imprisonment for Milton)	Pope's payoff — Possible strategies for Milton — Confess	Pope's payoff — Not confess (Years of imprisonment for Pope)
Confess	10	20	10	1/2
Not confess	1/2	2	20	2

CHAPTER ELEVEN

b. Milton's payoff matrix shows that if Pope confesses, he is better off to confess than not to confess. If Pope does not confess, he is also better off to confess than not to confess. Thus, Milton's optimal strategy is to confess. Similarly, Pope's payoff matrix shows that he is better off to confess if Milton confesses and that he is also better off to confess if Milton does not confess. Thus, his optimal strategy too is to confess.

7. The two producers will choose the monopoly output, where marginal revenue equals marginal cost. Since marginal cost equals $2, this means that

$$MR = 10 - 2Q = 2,$$

so

$$Q = \frac{8}{2} = 4.$$

Thus, their combined output will be 4 units per hour.

8. They should set the marginal cost at one firm equal to the marginal cost at each other firm. If firm A produces 4 units, firm B produces 3 units, and firm C produces 4 units, the marginal cost at each firm equals $30. Thus, this seems to be the optimal distribution of output.

9. It meant that the holders of these inventories were unlikely to sell them (and depress the price). Yes, by holding output off the market, producers could maintain prices. No.

10. The price leaders tend to be the largest firms. Also, historical factors play a role, and there is sometimes a tendency for low-cost (or medium-cost) firms to be leaders.

11. Firm A will choose strategy I.

    Firm B will choose strategy 2.

12. Yes. Because of possible entry, for one thing.

CHAPTER 12

Pricing Techniques

Chapter Profile

Empirical studies indicate that cost-plus pricing is used frequently by firms. In this approach, the firm estimates the cost per unit of output of the product (based on some assumed output level) and adds a markup to include costs that cannot be allocated to any specific product and to provide a return on the firm's investment. On the surface, it is questionable whether this approach can maximize profit, but if marginal cost (not average cost) is really what is being marked up, and if the markup is determined (in the appropriate way) by the price elasticity of demand of the product, cost-plus pricing can result in profit maximization.

Firms generally produce and sell more than one product. It is important for them to recognize the demand interrelationships among the products they sell. Also, a firm's products are often interrelated in production. If two products are produced jointly in fixed proportions, the profit-maximizing output is where the total marginal revenue curve—the vertical summation of the marginal revenue curves for the individual products—intersects the marginal cost curve for the bundle of products (assuming that the marginal revenue of each product is nonnegative).

If two products are produced jointly in variable proportions, one can construct isocost curves, each of which shows the combinations of outputs that can be produced at the same total cost. Also, isorevenue lines can be constructed, each of which shows the combinations of outputs that yield the same total revenue. For an output combination to be optimal, it must be at a point where an isorevenue line is tangent to an isocost curve. To determine which output combination is optimal, one compares the profit levels at the tangency points. The tangency point where profit is highest is the optimal output combination.

Price discrimination occurs when the same commodity is sold at more than one price, or when similar products are sold at prices that are in different ratios to marginal cost. A firm will be able and willing to practice price discrimination if various classes of buyers with different price elasticities of demand can be identified and segregated, and if the commodity cannot be transferred easily from one class to another. If the total market is divided into such classes, a firm that discriminates will maximize its profits by choosing prices and outputs so that the marginal revenue in each class is equal to marginal cost.

Many large firms are decentralized, and one division of the firm sells its product to another division of the firm. To maximize the firm's overall profit, it is important that

CHAPTER TWELVE

the price at which this transfer takes place—the so-called transfer price—is set properly. If there is no market outside the firm for the transferred product, the transfer price should equal the marginal production cost at the optimal output. If there is a perfectly competitive market for the transferred product outside the firm, the transfer price should equal the price of this product in that market.

Questions

Completion

1. If a firm is maximizing profit, the percentage markup on a product is (directly, inversely) _____ related to the product's price elasticity of demand.
2. The price at which one division of a firm sells to another division is the _____ price.
3. If there is a perfectly competitive market for the transferred product, the transfer price should equal the _____ .
4. If two products are produced jointly in fixed proportions, the profit-maximizing output is where the _____ of the marginal revenue curves of the individual products intersects the _____ for the bundle of products.
5. The statement in the previous question assumes that the marginal revenue of each product is _____ .
6. If the Johnstown Company produces 1 unit of good X, it automatically produces 2 units of good Y. Goods X and Y are _____ products produced in _____ proportions.
7. From a production point of view, goods X and Y (in the previous question) are not separate products but should be view as a _____ .
8. A markup is meant to include costs that (can, cannot) _____ be allocated to any specific product and to provide a _____ on the firm's investment.

True or False

_____ 1. General Electric at times has established a target rate of return of 20 percent.

_____ 2. Surveys of business-pricing practices show that few firms use cost-plus pricing.

_____ 3. If marginal cost is what is being marked up, and if the markup (in absolute terms) equals $MC\left(1 - \dfrac{1}{\eta}\right)$, the firm can maximize profit.

131

CHAPTER TWELVE

_____ 4. If two goods are joint products, they must be produced in variable proportions.

_____ 5. If there is no external market for the transferred good, the optimal transfer price is the average cost of the product.

_____ 6. Price discrimination is unlikely to occur unless consumers can be segregated into classes and the commodity cannot be transferred from one class to another.

_____ 7. Price discrimination always occurs when differences in price exist among roughly similar products, even when their costs are not the same.

_____ 8. Price discrimination is profitable even when the price elasticity of demand is the same among each class of consumer in the total market.

_____ 9. If a monopoly practices price discrimination, it does not set marginal revenue equal to marginal cost.

_____ 10. First-degree price discrimination occurs frequently, particularly in the auto industry.

Multiple Choice

1. If the price elasticity of demand for a product equals 2, and if its producer wants to maximize profit, its marginal cost should be marked up by

   a. 50 percent.
   b. 100 percent.
   c. 150 percent.
   d. 200 percent.
   e. none of the above.

2. If the price elasticity of demand for a product equals 3, and if its producer wants to maximize profit, its price should be

   a. double its average cost.
   b. 150 percent of its average cost.
   c. double its marginal cost.
   d. 150 percent of its marginal cost.
   e. none of the above.

3. The Montana Company produces and sells two products, A and B. If they are complements, an increase in the quantity sold of product A will

   a. reduce the total revenue from product B.
   b. increase the total revenue from product B.
   c. have no effect on the total revenue from product B.
   d. be impossible to attain.
   e. none of the above.

CHAPTER TWELVE

4. The Milwaukee Corporation produces and sells two products, D and E. If they are substitutes, an increase in the quantity sold of product D will

   a. reduce the total revenue from product E.
   b. increase the total revenue from product E.
   c. have no effect on the total revenue from product E.
   d. be impossible to attain.
   e. none of the above.

5. For first-degree price discrimination to occur, a firm must have

   a. an infinite number of buyers.
   b. knowledge of the maximum prices buyers are willing to accept.
   c. a small number of buyers.
   d. both a and b.
   e. both b and c.

6. Second-degree price discrimination is

   a. more common than first-degree price discrimination.
   b. often practiced by electric and gas companies.
   c. a way for sellers to increase their profits.
   d. all of the above.
   e. none of the above.

7. To determine how a discriminating monopolist will allocate output between two classes of consumers, one must

   a. compare the marginal revenues in the classes.
   b. compare the prices in the classes.
   c. compare the slopes of the demand curves in the classes.
   d. compare the heights of the demand curves in the classes.
   e. none of the above.

Problems

1. a. Under what conditions will a firm be able and willing to engage in price discrimination?
   b. Under price discrimination, will price tend to be relatively high in markets where the price elasticity of demand is relatively high? Why or why not?

2. The Logan Company sells in two distinct markets, which are sealed off from each other. The demand curve for the firm's output in the one market is

$$P_1 = 200 - 10Q_1,$$

where P_1 is the price of the product, and Q_1 is the amount sold in the first market. In the second market, the demand curve for the firm's product is

$$P_2 = 100 - 5Q_2,$$

where P_2 is the price of the product, and Q_2 is the amount sold in the second market. The firm's marginal cost curve is

$$MC = 10Q,$$

where Q is the firm's entire output.

a. How many units should the firm sell in the first market?
b. What price should it charge in the first market?
c. How many units should the firm sell in the second market?
d. What price should it charge in the second market?

3. The makers of methyl methacrylate used to sell it at 85 cents per pound for commercial purposes, but for denture purposes, it was sold to the dental profession for $45 per pound. Assuming that there was no difference in quality, why would the producers of methyl methacrylate, Du Pont and Rohm and Haas, find it profitable to charge different prices? In which of these markets (the commercial market or the dental market) do you think the price elasticity of demand was lower?

4. The Montana Company estimates its average total cost to be $22 per unit of output when it produces 15,000 units, which it regards as 75 percent of capacity. It wants to earn 20 percent on its total investment, which is $175,000.

   a. If it uses cost-plus pricing, what price should it set?
   b. What percentage markup will it use?

5. The Dakota Company's total annual indirect costs (for all products) are estimated to be $3 million, and its total annual variable costs (for all products) are estimated to be $1.5 million. Indirect costs are allocated among the firm's products on the basis of their average variable costs.

   a. If the average variable cost of product X is $14, how much would the firm add on for indirect cost?
   b. What would the estimated fully allocated cost per unit be for product X?
   c. If the markup for product X is 50 percent, what will its price be?

6. The Ohio Company sells a product with marginal cost equal to $9. If the Ohio Company maximizes profit, what must be the price elasticity of demand for this product if

   a. the product's price is $18?
   b. the product's price is $27?
   c. the product's price is $13.50?

7. The California Corporation is composed of a marketing division and a production division. The marginal cost of producing a unit of the firm's product is $8 per unit, and the marginal cost of marketing it is $6 per unit. The demand curve for the firm's product is

$$P = 200 - .015Q,$$

where P is the price per unit (in dollars), and Q is output (in units). There is no external market for the good made by the production division.

   a. What is the California Corporation's optimal output?

b. What price should it charge?
c. How much should the production division charge the marketing division for each unit of the product?

8. The Beiswanger Company sells a plastic toy in the United States and Europe. According to the firm's marketing department, marginal revenue is $8 per unit in both these markets. The firm's president says that it should sell more in Europe and less in the United States. The vice president of marketing disagrees.

   a. Who is right? (Assume that marginal cost is the same in the United States as in Europe.)
   b. Can you determine whether the price elasticity of demand is the same in both markets? Why or why not?
   c. Can you determine whether the price of a toy is the same in both markets? Why or why not?

9. The Hayes Company is composed of a marketing division and a production division. The production division produces a raw material that it transfers to the marketing division. There is an external market for this raw material, the price in this market (which is perfectly competitive) being $18 per pound. The production division's average cost of production is $22 per pound.

   a. The vice president of production argues that the transfer price for this raw material should be $22. Otherwise his division cannot cover its costs. Is he correct? Why or why not?
   b. The vice president of marketing argues that the transfer price should be $18. Otherwise his division is paying more than it needs to. Is he correct? Why or why not?

Answers

Completion
1. inversely   2. transfer   3. price in the perfectly competitive market
4. vertical summation, marginal cost curve   5. nonnegative   6. joint, fixed
7. bundle   8. cannot, return

True or False
1. True   2. False   3. False   4. False   5. False   6. True   7. False
8. False   9. False   10. False

Multiple Choice
1. b   2. d   3. b   4. a   5. e   6. d   7. a

Problems
1. a. The firm must be able to identify and segregate buyers into classes with different price elasticities of demand for the product, and the buyers must be unable to transfer the product easily from one class to another.
   b. No.

135

CHAPTER TWELVE

2. a. Since marginal revenue in the first market equals $200 - 20Q_1$, and marginal revenue in the second market equals $100 - 10Q_2$, it follows that

$$200 - 20Q_1 = 100 - 10Q_2 = 10(Q_1 + Q_2).$$

Thus, $Q_1 = 10 - 2Q_2$, and $200 - 20(10 - 2Q_2) = 100 - 10Q_2$, which means that $Q_2 = 2$. Consequently, $Q_1 = 10 - 2(2)$, or 6.
   b. $200 - 10(6) = 140$.
   c. 2.
   d. $100 - 5(2) = 90$.

3. Because the price elasticity of demand was different in the two markets. The dental market.

4. a. To earn 20 percent on its investment of $175,000, its profit must be $35,000. Thus, the per-unit markup must be $35,000 ÷ 15,000 = $2.33, and price must equal $22 + $2.33 = $24.33.
   b. $\dfrac{\$2.33}{\$22} = 10.6\%$.

5. a. $28.
   b. $42.
   c. $63.

6. a. 2.
   b. 1.5.
   c. 3.

7. a. Since the firm's marginal cost equals $8 + $6 = $14, and the firm's marginal revenue equals $200 - .03Q$, the profit-maximizing level of output is the one where

$$200 - .03Q = 14,$$

   $Q = 6,200$.
   b. Price should equal $200 - .015(6,200) = 107$ dollars.
   c. $8.

8. a. The vice president of marketing.
   b. No, because marginal revenue depends both on the price elasticity of demand and price.
   c. No. See the answer to part b.

9. a. No, the transfer price should be $18.
   b. Yes.

CHAPTER 13

Risk Analysis

Chapter Profile

The probability of a particular outcome is the proportion of times that this outcome occurs over the long run if this situation exists over and over again. Expected profit is the sum of the amount of money gained (or lost) if each outcome occurs times the probability of occurrence of the outcome.

A decision tree represents a decision problem as a series of choices, each of which is depicted by a decision fork or a chance fork. A decision tree can be used to determine the course of action with the highest expected monetary value. As an example, we took up the decision of whether or not to drill an oil well.

The expected value of perfect information is the increase in expected monetary value if the decision maker could obtain completely accurate information concerning the outcome of the relevant situation (but he or she does not yet know what this information will be). This is the maximum amount that the decision maker should pay to obtain such information. Using methods described in this chapter, one can calculate the expected value of perfect information.

Risk is often measured by the standard deviation or coefficient of variation of the probability distribution of profit. Whether a decision maker wants to maximize expected profit depends on his or her attitudes toward risk. The decision maker's attitudes toward risk can be measured by his or her utility function.

To construct such a utility function, we begin by setting the utility attached to two monetary values arbitrarily. Then we present the decision maker with a choice between the certainty of one of the other monetary values and a gamble where the possible outcomes are the two monetary values whose utilities we set arbitrarily. Repeating this procedure over and over, we can construct the decision maker's utility function.

One way to adjust the basic valuation model for risk is to use certainty equivalents in place of the expected profit figures in equation (13.7) in the text. Based on the decision maker's utility function, one may be able to construct indifference curves showing the certainty equivalent corresponding to each uncertain outcome.

Another way to introduce risk into the valuation model is to adjust the discount rate. Based on the decision maker's utility function, one may be able to construct indifference curves between expected rate of return and risk. Using such indifference curves, one can estimate the risk premium (if any) that is appropriate.

CHAPTER THIRTEEN

Uncertainty refers to a situation where the relevant probabilities cannot be estimated. Many rules, including the minimax rule, have been proposed as aids to decision making under conditions of uncertainty. According to the minimax rule, the decision maker should choose the course of action where the worst possible outcome is least damaging. There are important problems in this rule, as well as others proposed to handle the situation of uncertainty.

Questions

Completion

1. If a decision maker's utility function is _____ the decision maker maximizes expected monetary value.
2. The Millrose Company stores spare parts at two warehouses, one in Scranton and one in Cleveland. The number of defective and acceptable spare parts at each warehouse is given below.

	Number of spare parts		
Warehouse	Defective	Acceptable	Total
Scranton	200	800	1,000
Cleveland	50	450	500

    If one of the 1,500 spare parts kept by the firm is chosen at random (i.e., if each spare part has a 1/1,500 chance of being chosen), the probability that it will be defective is _____ .
3. In the previous question, the probability that the chosen spare part will be at the Scranton warehouse is _____ .
4. In question 2, the probability that the chosen spare part will be *both* defective and at the Scranton warehouse is _____ .
5. In calculating the expected value of perfect information, it is important to recognize that the decision maker (does, does not) _____ know what this information will be.
6. When a decision maker applies the minimax rule, he or she assumes that nature (or whatever force determines the outcome of the situation) dictates that if any course of action is taken, the _____ outcome will occur.
7. Whether a decision maker wants to maximize expected profit depends on his or her attitude toward _____ .
8. A _____ fork is a juncture representing a choice where the decision maker is in control of the outcome.
9. A _____ fork is a juncture where "chance" controls the outcome.
10. If the decision maker's utility function is linear, she (will, will not) _____ maximize expected profit.

CHAPTER THIRTEEN

True or False

_____ 1. The maximization of expected utility results in the same decisions as the minimax rule if the utility function is linear.

_____ 2. Under conditions of uncertainty, it is easy to formulate optimal general rules for decision makers; they should maximize expected utility, using the known probabilities of the relevant outcomes.

_____ 3. Risk and uncertainty are indistinguishable.

_____ 4. According to the subjective definition of probability, the probability of a particular outcome is the proportion of times that this outcome occurs over the long run if this situation exists over and over again.

_____ 5. One problem with the minimax rule is that it ignores the maximum amount that the decision makers can lose.

_____ 6. If James Johnson is indifferent between the certainty of a $50,000 gain and a gamble where there is a 0.4 probability of a $40,000 gain and a 0.6 probability of a $60,000 gain, the utility he attaches to a $50,000 gain equals $0.4U(40) + 0.6U(60)$, where $U(40)$ is the utility he attaches to a $40,000 gain, and $U(60)$ is the utility he attaches to a $60,000 gain.

_____ 7. If a firm accepts a particular gamble, there is a 0.3 chance that it will gain $1 million and a 0.6 chance that it will lose $2 million. Based on this information, one cannot calculate the expected monetary value of this gamble to the firm.

_____ 8. If John Jeffries is a risk averter, his utility function is linear.

_____ 9. If Mary Solomon is a risk lover, her utility function is linear.

_____ 10. Martin Bush is willing to accept greater risks only if he obtains a higher expected rate of return. Thus, he is risk averter.

Multiple Choice

1. If a decision maker is indifferent to risk, and if the expected value of perfect information is $40,000, the decision maker should be willing to pay the following for perfect information:

    a. $35,000.
    b. $45,000.
    c. $55,000.
    d. $65,000.
    e. $75,000.

CHAPTER THIRTEEN

2. If a decision maker is a risk averter for values of monetary gain above $10,000, then he or she

   a. must be a risk averter for values of monetary gain below $10,000.
   b. must be indifferent to risk for values of monetary gain below $10,000.
   c. must be a risk lover for values of monetary gain below $10,000.
   d. must be either a or b.
   e. none of the above.

3. William Moran rolls a true die. If the die comes up a 2, he receives $6,000; if it does not come up a 2, he pays $1,000. The expected monetary value of this gamble to him is

   a. $1,167.
   b. $833.
   c. $167.
   d. –$167.
   e. –$833.

4. William Moran's utility function is $U = 10 + 3M$, where U is utility, and M is monetary gain (in dollars). He will prefer the certainty of a gain of $20 over a gamble where there is a 0.3 probability of a $9 gain and a 0.7 probability of

   a. a $31 gain.
   b. a $29 gain.
   c. a $27 gain.
   d. a $25 gain.
   e. none of the above.

5. In the previous question, if William Moran has a 0.4 probability of receiving $100 and a 0.6 probability of losing $200, the expected utility of this gamble is

   a. –70.
   b. –80.
   c. –230.
   d. –250.
   e. none of the above.

6. The difference between the expected rate of return on a specific risky investment and that on a riskless investment is called

   a. the risk-adjusted discount rate.
   b. the risk premium on this investment.
   c. the investment's level of risk.
   d. all of the above.
   e. none of the above.

CHAPTER THIRTEEN

Problems

1. The Deming Company must determine whether or not to add a new product line. If the new product line is a success, the firm will increase its profits by $1 million; if it is not a success, its profits will decrease by $0.5 million. Deming's managers feel that the probability is 0.6 that the new product line will be a success and 0.4 that it will not be a success.

   a. If Deming's managers are indifferent to risk, should they add the new product line?
   b. How would you determine whether they are indifferent to risk?
   c. What is the expected value of perfect information to them?

2. A newspaper publisher in a small town must decide whether or not to publish a Sunday edition. The publisher thinks that the probability is 0.7 that a Sunday edition would be a success and that it is 0.3 that it would be a failure. If it is a success, he will gain $200,000. If it is a failure, he will lose $100,000.

   a. Construct the decision tree for this problem, and use it to solve the problem, assuming that the publisher is indifferent to risk.
   b. What is the expected value of perfect information?
   c. How would you go about trying to determine whether the publisher is in fact indifferent to risk?

3. A Tucson restaurant owner must decide whether or not to expand his restaurant. He thinks that the probability is 0.6 that the expansion will prove successful and that it is 0.4 that it will not be successful. If it is successful, he will gain $100,000. If it is not successful, he will lose $80,000.

   a. Construct the decision tree for this problem, and use it to solve the problem, assuming that the restaurant owner is indifferent to risk.
   b. List all forks in the decision tree you constructed, indicate whether each is a decision fork or a chance fork, and state why.

4. In the previous problem, would the restaurant owner's decision be altered if he felt that

   a. the probability that the expansion will prove successful is 0.5, not 0.6?
   b. the probability that the expansion will prove successful is 0.7, not 0.6?
   c. What value of the probability that the expansion will prove successful will make the restaurant owner indifferent between expanding and not expanding the restaurant?

5. The president of the Hawaii Company says that she is indifferent between the certainty of receiving $100,000 and a gamble where there is a 0.5 chance of receiving $250,000 and a 0.5 chance of receiving nothing. In the graph below, plot three points on her utility function.

141

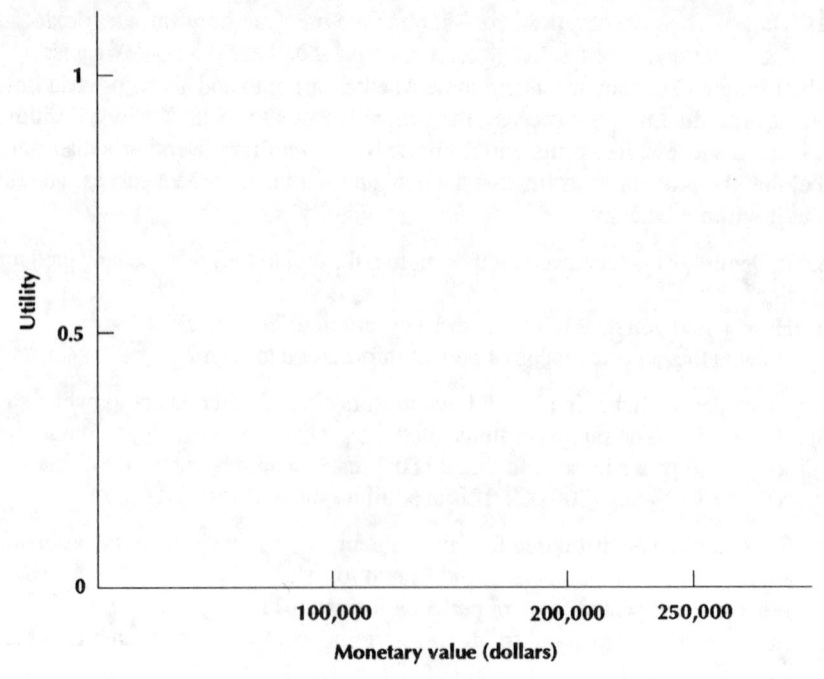

6. The utility function of the president of Manhattan Company is shown below.

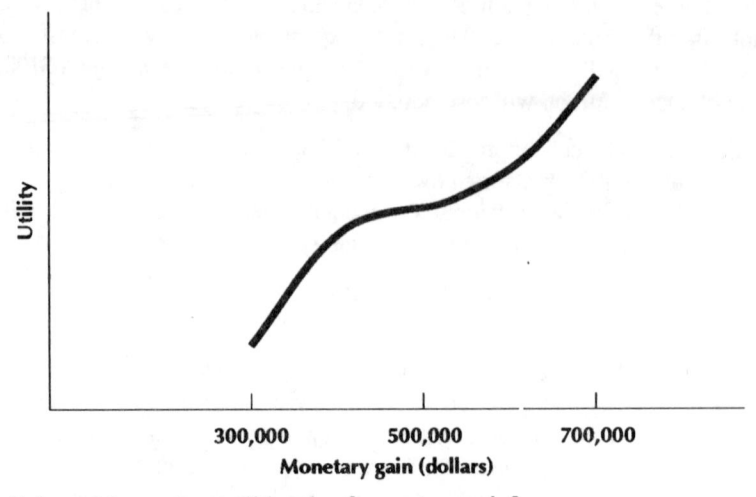

   a. Is he a risk averter at all levels of monetary gain?
   b. Is he a risk lover at all levels of monetary gain?
   c. Does he prefer the certainty of gaining $400,000 over a gamble where there is a 0.5 probability of gaining $300,000 and a 0.5 probability of gaining $500,000?

7. If each card in a standard 52-card deck of playing cards has the same probability of being drawn, what is the probability that a single card that is drawn will be

   a. a red 9?
   b. a black ace?
   c. a black card?
   d. neither a red card nor a queen?
   e. a queen, king, or ace?

CHAPTER THIRTEEN

8. a. The Rosetree Corporation is considering the purchase of a firm that produces tools and dies. Rosetree's management feels that there is a 50–50 chance, if Rosetree buys the firm, that it can make the firm into an effective producer of auto parts. If the firm can be transformed in this way, Rosetree believes that it will make $1 million if it buys the firm; if it cannot be transformed in this way, Rosetree believes that it will lose $2 million. What is the expected monetary value to Rosetree of buying the firm?
   b. In fact, the Rosetree Corporation decides to purchase the firm described in the previous question. Does this mean that Rosetree's management is (i) indifferent to risk, (ii) a risk averter?

9. The utility function of the president of the Howe Company can be represented by the following equation:

$$U = 10 + 2M,$$

   where U is utility, and M is monetary gain (in thousands of dollars). He has the opportunity to invest $25,000 in a small electronics firm. He believes there is a 0.5 probability that he will lose his entire investment and a 0.5 probability that he will gain $32,000.

   a. If he makes the investment, what is his expected utility?
   b. Should he make the investment?

10. An appliance firm must decide whether or not to offer Roland Whelan a job. If Whelan turns out to be a success, the firm will increase its profits by $100,000; if he turns out not to be a success, the firm's profits will decrease by $80,000. The firm feels that the chances are 50–50 that he will be a success.

    a. What is the expected value of perfect information?
    b. What is the expected monetary value to the firm if it does not hire Whelan?
    c. What is the expected monetary value to the firm if it hires Whelan?

11. A firm must decide whether or not to go forward with an R and D project to develop a new process. If the project is successful, it will gain $5 million; if it is not successful, it will lose $1 million. Suppose that the firm has no idea of what the probabilities of success or failure may be. If the minimax rule is applied, should the firm go forward with the R and D project? Why or why not?

12. a. The Contact Engineering Company must decide whether or not to buy a piece of equipment. If it buys this equipment, and if the price of ammonia increases by more than 10 percent in the next year, it will make $3 million; if it buys the equipment and the price of ammonia does not increase by this amount in the next year, it will lose $2 million. If it does not buy the equipment, it gains (and loses) nothing, regardless of what happens to the price of ammonia. Construct a table showing the firm's profits if each possible outcome occurs, given that the firm takes each possible course of action.

CHAPTER THIRTEEN

b. What decision should the Contact Engineering Company make, if it applies the minimax rule? What criticisms can be made of this rule?

13. William McCarthy's indifference curve between expected rate of return and risk is shown below:

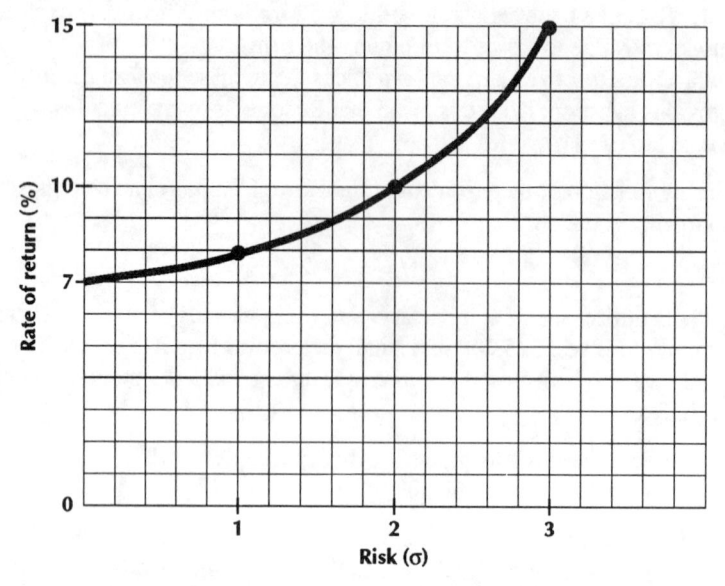

a. For him, what is the risk premium for an investment where $\sigma = 3$?
b. If $\sigma = 2$, what is the risk-adjusted discount rate?
c. What is the riskless discount rate?

Answers

Completion
1. linear   2. 250/1,500 = 1/6   3. 1,000/1,500 = 2/3   4. 200/1,500 = 2/15
5. does not   6. worst   7. risk   8. decision   9. chance   10. will

True or False
1. False   2. False   3. False   4. False   5. False   6. True   7. True
8. False   9. False   10. True

Multiple Choice
1. a   2. e   3. c   4. e   5. c   6. b

Problems
1. a. Yes.
   b. Construct the utility function of the decision maker.
   c. $200,000.

2. a.

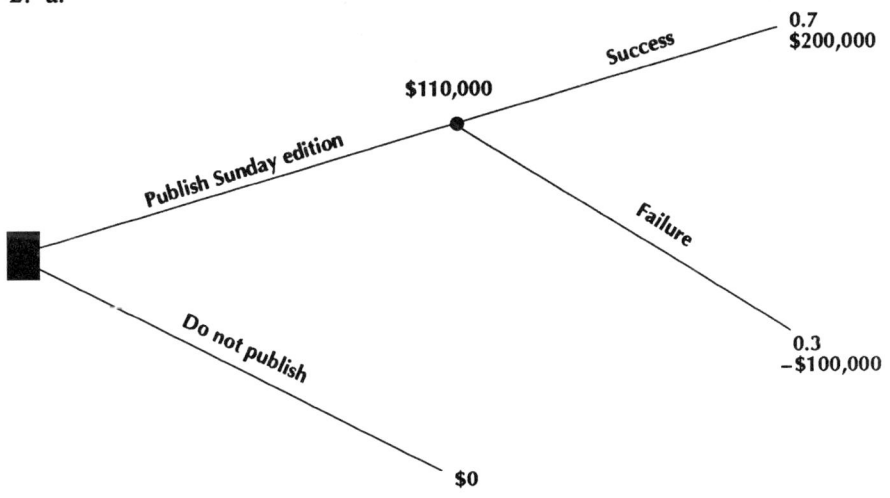

```
                                    Success         0.7
                                   ───────────    $200,000
                       $110,000
         Publish Sunday edition ●
   ■                              Failure
                                  ───────────      0.3
         Do not publish                          -$100,000

                         $0
```

He should publish the Sunday edition.
b. .7($200,000) + .3(0) – $110,000 = $30,000.
c. Construct his utility function.

3. a.

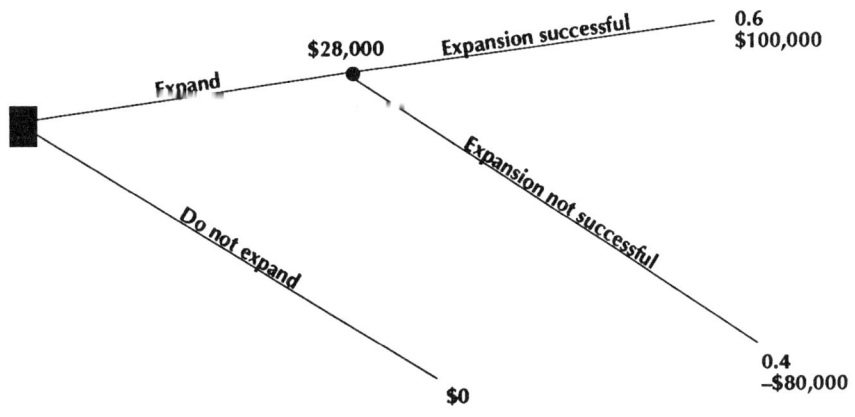

```
                    $28,000   Expansion successful    0.6
                                ───────────────    $100,000
              Expand    ●
   ■                     Expansion not successful
         Do not expand                              0.4
                                                  -$80,000
                    $0
```

Since the expected monetary value if he expands is 0.6 ($100,000) + 0.4 (–$80,000) = $28,000, he should expand the restaurant.

b. The first fork on the left is a decision fork since the restaurant owner decides whether or not to expand. The next fork is a chance fork, since "chance" decides whether or not the expansion is successful.

4. a. No.
   b. No.
   c. 4/9.

5. a. Let zero be the utility of receiving nothing, and 1 be the utility of receiving $250,000. Then, since she is indifferent between the certainty of receiving $100,000 and the gamble described in the problem, the utility of receiving $100,000 must equal

$$0.5(1) + 0.5(0) = 0.5.$$

Thus, three points on her utility function are given below.

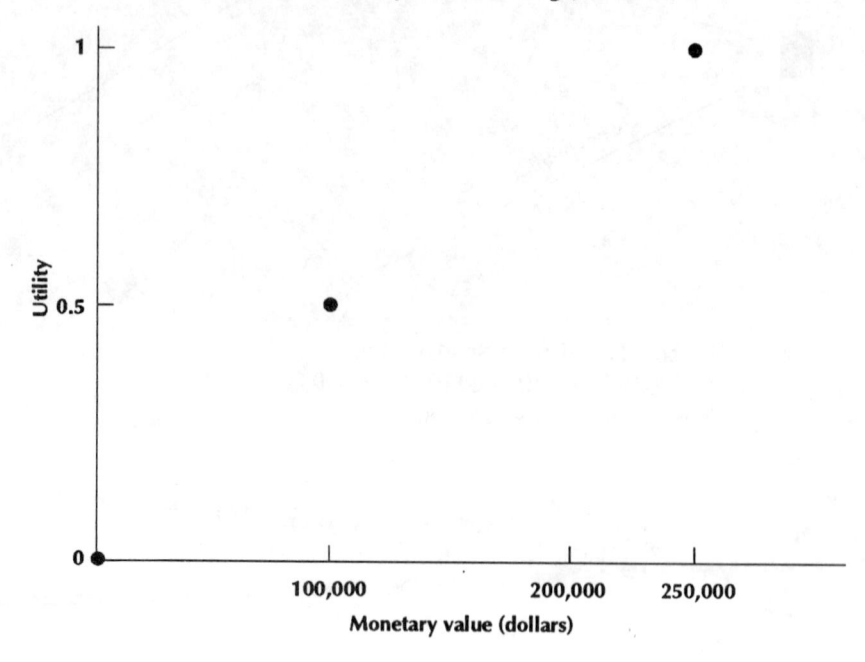

6. a. No.
   b. No.
   c. Yes.

7. a. 1/26.
   b. 1/26.
   c. 1/2.
   d. 6/13.
   e. 3/13.

8. a. 0.5($1 million) + 0.5(–2 million) = –$0.5 million.
   b. (i) No, since it would have chosen not to purchase it if it were indifferent to risk.
   (ii) No. Since it would have chosen not to purchase it if it were risk averse.

9. a. The utility of –$25,000 equals 10 + 2(–25) = –40. The utility of +$32,000 equals 10 + 2(32) = 74. His expected utility equals 0.5(–40) + 0.5(74) = 17.
   b. Since the expected utility if he makes the investment (17) exceeds the expected utility if he does not make it (10), he should make it.

10. a. 0.5($100,000) + 0.5(0) − $10,000 = $40,000.
    b. zero.
    c. 0.5($100,000) + 0.5(−$80,000) = $10,000.

11. No, because the maximum loss if it goes ahead with the project is $1 million, whereas the maximum loss if it does not go ahead with it is zero.

12. a.

	Price of ammonia increases by more than 10%	*Price of ammonia increases by 10% or less*
	(Profits of Contact Engineering Company)	
Contact buys equipment	+$3 million	−$2 million
Contact does not buy equipment	zero	zero

   b. It should not buy the equipment. It assumes that the worse outcome will occur, if each action is taken. This may be far too pessimistic.

13. a. 8 percent.
    b. 10 percent.
    c. 7 percent.

CHAPTER 14

Capital Budgeting

Chapter Profile

The investment selection process is composed of four steps. (a) The firm must generate proposals for alternative investment projects. (b) For each of these proposed projects, it must estimate cash flows for the project. (c) It must evaluate each of the proposed projects, and select those to be implemented. (d) It should review the projects after implementation.

For each proposed project, the difference between the cash flows with and without the project should be estimated each year on an after-tax basis. Indirect effects of the project on parts of the firm's activities seemingly far removed from the investment should be taken into account if the firm's cash flows are impacted.

If the outlays for an investment project all occur in the current year, the net present value of the project equals

$$\sum_{t=1}^{n} F_t/(1+k)^t - I,$$

where F_t equals the cash flow in year t, and I equals the investment outlay. If a project's net present value is greater than zero, it should be accepted; if not, it should be rejected.

Another measure of the profitability of a proposed project is its internal rate of return, which is defined as the interest rate that equates the present value of the net cash flows from the project to its investment outlay. Generally, if a firm accepts projects where the internal rate of return exceeds the firm's cost of capital, the results are the same as if the net present value criterion is used. (However, recall note 4 of Chapter 14 of the textbook.)

The cost to the firm of debt capital is the rate of return that must be paid to the investors. New long-term debt is often issued by firms at (or close to) par. If so, the after-tax cost of debt capital is the coupon interest rate times $(1 - t)$, where t is the firm's marginal tax rate.

The cost of equity capital is the equilibrium rate of return required by the investors in the firm's common stock. Assuming that the firm's dividends per share will increase at a constant compound annual rate of g, the cost of internal equity is $(D_1/W) + g$, where D_1 is the annual dividend paid next year, and W is the price per share of the firm's stock. The capital asset pricing model can also be used to estimate the cost of equity capital.

CHAPTER FOURTEEN

In calculating the net present value of a project, the firm should base the interest rate, k, on the weighted cost of capital, which is the weighted average of the costs of debt and equity capital, the weights being the proportions of debt and equity financing in the firm's desired financial structure.

The interest rate, k, should also be modified to reflect the riskiness of the project, as well as the attitudes of the firm's decision makers with regard to risk. The ways such modifications can be made have already been described in Chapter 13.

Questions

Completion

1. The decision maker should carry out any investment project with a _____ present value.

2. Mr. Smith buys a bond for $1,000. If the bond pays interest of $50 per year indefinitely, the interest rate is _____ percent. If the price of the bond increases to $1,500, the interest rate is _____ percent. If the price of the bond falls to $500, the interest rate is _____ percent.

3. If the interest rate is 10 percent, a dollar received a year from now is currently worth _____, and a dollar received 2 years from now is currently worth _____. Thus, a business venture that will pay you both a dollar a year from now and a dollar 2 years from now is currently worth _____.

4. If the present value of a dollar received 2 years from now is 85.7 cents, the interest rate must be _____ percent. If the interest rate is more than _____ percent, one dollar received 20 years from now is worth less than 15 cents now.

5. A _____ expenditure is a _____ outlay that is expected to result in a flow of future cash benefits (extending beyond one year in the future).

6. The first step of the investment selection process is to generate _____ for investment projects.

7. The cash flows used in evaluating an investment project should be the difference between the cash flows _____ and _____ the project.

8. To calculate the internal rate of return, we find the value of _____ that sets the project's net present value equal to _____.

9. The _____ is the relationship between risk and expected return for all stocks in the market.

10. _____ risk is due to cyclical changes in the economy and other broad movements that affect all stocks.

CHAPTER FOURTEEN

True or False

_____ 1. If an investment yields $100 per year indefinitely into the future, and the interest rate is 10 percent, the present value of this investment is $500.

_____ 2. If the firm maximizes profit, it will accept investments where the interest rate exceeds the rate of return.

_____ 3. If a firm borrows money to buy equipment at an interest cost that is less than the rate of return from the equipment, it will lose money.

_____ 4. Capital budgeting refers to decisions concerning a firm's choice of investment projects.

_____ 5. The stock market as a whole has a beta of zero.

_____ 6. Firms frequently assume that if they do not invest in new equipment, their profits will stay at current levels.

_____ 7. The cost of internal equity is $D + (W + g)$, where D is the annual dividend, W is the price per share of the firm's stock, and g is the annual compound rate at which the firm's dividends per share increase.

_____ 8. Noncash items like depreciation are irrelevant in evaluating investment projects.

_____ 9. Estimates of incremental cash flow depend on what the alternative is, if the investment project is not carried out.

_____ 10. There may be no unique value of the internal rate of return.

Multiple Choice

1. The Mangrum company buys a painting for $1,000 in 1990. If maintenance of the painting is costless, and if the interest rate is 0.10, how much must it sell the painting for in 1993 if the present value of the investment in the painting is to be nonnegative?

   a. At least $(1.10)^3 \times \$1,000$.
   b. At least $(1.30) \times \$1,000$.
   c. At least $1,000.
   d. At least $\$1,000 + (.30)^3 \times \$1,000$.
   e. None of the above.

2. The Mangrum Company can pay $50 now (for the coming year) and $50 a year from now (for the next year) for a service that protects against termites. Alternatively, it can pay $100 now (for the coming two years) for the service. The firm should be indifferent between these two alternatives if the rate of interest is

   a. zero.
   b. 2 percent.
   c. 5 percent.
   d. 10 percent.
   e. none of the above.

CHAPTER FOURTEEN

3. In the previous question, if the rate of interest is 10 percent, the cost of the second alternative exceeds that of the first alternative by

   a. zero.
   b. $4.55.
   c. −$5.00.
   d. $500.
   e. none of the above.

4. In question 2, if the rate of interest is 8 percent, the firm should be indifferent between the first alternative and paying _____ now (for the coming two years) for this service.

   a. $96.00.
   b. $96.30.
   c. $100.00
   d. $104.00.
   e. none of the above.

5. Suppose the rate of return on alternative investments is 6 percent, and that a particular asset will yield $1,500 per year indefinitely. The asset is worth

   a. $9,000.
   b. $25,000.
   c. $90,000.
   d. $250,000.
   e. $100,000.

6. If a firm maximizes profit, the rate of return of the least productive project that is accepted by the firm must be _____ the interest rate at which the firm can borrow.

   a. less than
   b. 1/2
   c. greater than or equal to
   d. twice
   e. less than or equal to

7. The cost of internal equity is $\frac{D_1}{W} + g$, where

   a. D_1 is the annual profit of the firm.
   b. W is the price of the firm's product.
   c. g is the annual rate of increase of the firm's dividends per share.
   d. all of the above.
   e. none of the above.

CHAPTER FOURTEEN

Problems

1. The following excerpt from congressional testimony by executives of the Armstrong Cork Company describes the procedure it used to decide which investment projects to undertake.

   The more important aspects of the Armstrong Cork Company system can be summarized as follows:

   1. The economics of proposed capital appropriation requests are examined by the controller's office in consultation with the interested staffs like central engineering, research, industrial engineering, economic and marketing research, purchasing, and so forth, before presentation to top management.
   2. The basic evaluation is made in return on investment terms.
   3. An evaluation of risk is made, based on the length of time required to recover the cash to be expended.
   4. Management relies on these valuations in making appropriation decisions.
   5. Follow-up reports of the in-process status and actual results of capital appropriations granted are made annually by the controller's office to top management, which, in turn, discuss the results with the accountable persons.

   "Return on investment" or, as we use the phrase, "return on capital employed" (ROCE), is nothing more than the ratio of net profit after tax to total book assets. In the Armstrong Cork Company, ROCE is accepted as the basis for measuring operating management performance; the success or failure of all our individual and collective efforts to improve operations is reflected in our ROCE results. . . .

   All matters related to financing are reserved to a staff vice-president. The determination of what shall be financed is reserved, depending upon the amounts involved, for the executive committee of our board of directors or the board itself. In practice, the board of directors and its executive committee control "what shall be financed" almost entirely through our system of capital appropriation requests. This control of capital expenditures automatically controls the basic level of working capital. The general level of cash, accounts receivable, and inventories required by operations is determined basically by the types of businesses in which we operate. Since we are primarily a manufacturing company, the types of businesses we operate are established by the plant, property, and equipment we buy. Therefore, the board of directors and its executive committee, in controlling such purchases, indirectly but effectively control the types of business we operate and, consequently, the basic levels of cash, accounts receivable, and inventories.

   Our procedures for reviewing capital appropriation requests are designed specifically to fit the needs of our organization. They do this by profit and loss statements expressed in terms of ROCE. We place our emphasis on accuracy of perspective rather than on accuracy of detail. Our aim is to discover the best of the many potential expenditures.

   We don't attempt to provide the figure that makes approval or disapproval of a request automatic. The figures we develop are relative, not absolute. One of the most valuable results of our system will never be measured since it is the elimination of projects of low ROCE potential from consideration before an undue amount of valuable technical and management effort is expended upon them.[1]

---

[1] This description pertains to the situation a number of years ago.

CHAPTER FOURTEEN

   a. Does this procedure attempt to accomplish the same objective as the present-value rule? Explain.
   b. What differences can you detect between this procedure and the present-value rule?

2. A government program involves the training of disadvantaged teenagers. The cost of training each person is $8,000. With this training, he or she makes $500 more each year than he or she otherwise would. If this income differential is an adequate measure of the social benefit, and if the interest rate is 10 percent, is this program worthwhile?

3. The Winston Company is considering a $3 million investment in a new piece of equipment. If this investment is accepted, the company's cash inflow will be reduced by $3 million this year, its production costs are expected to fall by $450,000 per year over the next five years, and its inventory costs are expected to fall by $875,000 over the next five years. The piece of equipment will be depreciated over five years, using straight-line depreciation. The firm's marginal tax rate is 34 percent.

   a. Determine the incremental after-tax cash flow each year from this investment.
   b. If the marginal tax rate were 48 percent, not 34 percent, what would be the incremental after-tax cash flow each year?
   c. If the cost of capital is 10 percent, what is the net present value of this investment, if the firm's marginal tax rate is 34 percent?

4. The Salem Corporation is considering the purchase of a new machine that costs $30,000, and that will reduce labor costs by $17,500 per year for the next four years. Its marginal tax rate is 34 percent.

   a. If the discount rate is 15 percent, should the firm buy this machine?
   b. If the discount rate is 8 percent, should the firm buy this machine?

5. The Trenton Company's common stock sells currently at $80 per share. Its dividend per share is expected to be $8 next year. In the past decade, its dividend per share has been increasing at a 10 percent annual rate, and this growth rate is expected to continue in the future.

   a. What is the Trenton Company's cost of equity capital?
   b. If the firm's common stock were to sell for $100, not $80, what would be its cost of equity capital?
   c. If the dividend per share were to increase at 5 percent, not 10 percent (and if the common stock price were $100), what would be its cost of equity capital?

6. The Hartford Company wants to estimate its cost of equity capital. The beta for its stock is 0.9, the risk-free rate of return is 7 percent, and the rate of return on the average stock is 12 percent.

   a. What is this firm's cost of equity capital?
   b. If its beta were 1.2 rather than 0.9, what would be its cost of equity capital?
   c. If its beta were 1.5 rather than 0.9, what would be its cost of equity capital?

CHAPTER FOURTEEN

7. The Riverside Corporation issues new long-term debt at par—that is, at $1,000 per bond. The coupon interest rate is 10$^{1}\!/_{2}$ percent. The company's marginal income tax rate is 34 percent.

    a. What is the firm's after-tax cost of debt?
    b. If the company's marginal income tax rate were 48 percent rather than 34 percent, what would be the firm's after-tax cost of debt?

8. The Buffalo Company is considering the purchase of a new truck, which would result in a $25,000 incremental after-tax cash outflow this year and a $8,000 incremental after-tax cash inflow for each of the next four years.

    a. What is the internal rate of return from this investment?
    b. If the cash outflow were $30,000 rather than $25,000 this year, what would be the internal rate of return?

9. The Evanston Company's after-tax cost of debt capital is 10 percent, and its cost of equity capital is 15 percent. What is its weighted cost of capital if

    a. the proportion of debt financing in the firm's desired financial structure is 40 percent and the proportion of equity financing in the firm's desired financial structure is 60 percent?
    b. these proportions are 30 and 70 percent, rather than 40 and 60 percent?

10. The Marble Orchard Bank is considering a large investment in new data-processing equipment. The effect on the bank's after-tax cash flow would be as follows:

Year	Effect on cash flow (million of dollars)
1990	−10
1991	3
1992	4
1993	3
1994	2
1995	1

    a. If the bank's cost of capital is 10 percent, what is the present value of the investment?
    b. If the bank's cost of capital is 12 percent, what is the present value of the investment?

CHAPTER FOURTEEN

Answers

Completion
1. positive   2. 5, 3 1/3, 10   3. 90.9 cents, 82.6 cents, 173.5 cents
4. 8, 10   5. capital, cash   6. proposals   7. with, without
8. the interest rate, zero   9. security market line   10. Systematic

True or False
1. False   2. False   3. False   4. True   5. False   6. True   7. False
8. False   9. True   10. True

Multiple Choice
1. a   2. a   3. b   4. b   5. b   6. c   7. c

Problems

1. a. In crude terms, both seem to attempt to promote the wealth (or something like it) of the firm. The firm's executives are supposed "to use the capital they are allocated by the board to obtain the best possible return on it." However, this decision-making procedure does not focus directly on the wealth of the firm, and is not the same as the present-value rule.

   b. Armstrong Cork used the ratio of net profit (after tax) to investment as a measure of the desirability of an investment project, whereas the present-value rule uses the present value of the investment project.

2. If the benefit continued indefinitely, its present value would be $500 ÷ 0.10, or $5,000. This is an overestimate, since the benefit will not continue indefinitely. Since the cost is $8,000, the investment is not worthwhile. (Note that these figures are hypothetical, and that no judgment should be made concerning the effects of actual or proposed government programs.)

3. a.

Year	Incremental after-tax cash flow (million of dollars)
0 (this year)	−3
1	(1 − .34)(.725) + 3/5 = 1.0785
2	1.0785
3	1.0785
4	1.0785
5	1.0785

   b.

Year	Incremental after-tax cash flow (million of dollars)
0	−3
1	(1 − .48)(.725) + 3/5 = 0.977
2	0.977
3	0.977
4	0.977
5	0.977

155

CHAPTER FOURTEEN

c.

t	Net cash flow (millions of dollars)	$\frac{1}{(1+.10)^t}$	$\frac{\text{Net cash flow}}{(1+.10)^t}$
1	1.0785	.9091	.98046
2	1.0785	.8264	.89127
3	1.0785	.7513	.81028
4	1.0785	.6830	.73662
5	1.0785	.6209	.66964
			Sum 4.08827

Thus, $\sum_{t=1}^{5} \frac{F_t}{(1+k)^t} - I = 4.08827 - 3 = 1.08827$ millions of dollars.

4. a. If the firm buys the new machine, the incremental after-tax cash flow in each of the next four years equals ($17,500 − $7,500) (1 − .34) + $30,000/4 = $14,100. Thus, the next present value equals

$$\$14,100 \left(\frac{1}{1.15} + \frac{1}{1.15^2} + \frac{1}{1.15^3} + \frac{1}{1.15^4} \right) - \$30,000 =$$

$$\$14,100 (.8696 + .7561 + .6575 + .5718) - \$30,000 =$$

$$\$14,100 (2.8550) - \$30,000 = \$10,255.$$

Since it exceeds zero, it appears that the firm should buy the machine.

b. The net present value equals

$$\$14,100 \left(\frac{1}{1.08} + \frac{1}{1.08^2} + \frac{1}{1.08^3} + \frac{1}{1.08^4} \right) - \$30,000 =$$

$$\$14,100(3.312) - \$30,000 = \$16,699.$$

Since it exceeds zero, it appears that the firm should buy the machine.

5. a. $\frac{8}{80} + .10 = .20$. Thus, the cost of internal equity seems to be about 20 percent.

b. $\frac{8}{100} + .10 = .18$. Thus, the cost of internal equity would be about 18 percent.

c. $\frac{8}{100} + .05 = .13$. Thus, the cost of internal equity would be about 13 percent.

6. a. .07 + 0.9(.12 − .07) = .115.
   b. .07 + 1.2(.12 − .07) = .13.
   c. .07 + 1.5(.12 − .07) = .145.

7. a. .105(1 − .34) = .0693. The firm's after-tax cost of debt is 6.93 percent.
   b. .105(1 − .48) = .0546. The firm's after-tax cost of debt is 5.46 percent.

8. a. $25{,}000 = \left(\dfrac{1}{1+k} + \dfrac{1}{(1+k)^2} + \dfrac{1}{(1+k)^3} + \dfrac{1}{(1+k)^4}\right) 8{,}000$

$\dfrac{25}{8} = 3.125 = \left(\dfrac{1}{1+k} + \dfrac{1}{(1+k)^2} + \dfrac{1}{(1+k)^3} + \dfrac{1}{(1+k)^4}\right).$

Looking at Appendix Table 2 (in the row where $n = 4$), we see that k is about 11 percent.

b. $\$30{,}000 = \left(\dfrac{1}{1+k} + \dfrac{1}{(1+k)^2} + \dfrac{1}{(1+k)^3} + \dfrac{1}{(1+k)^4}\right) 8{,}000$

$\dfrac{30{,}000}{8{,}000} = 3.75 = \left(\dfrac{1}{1+k} + \dfrac{1}{(1+k)^2} + \dfrac{1}{(1+k)^3} + \dfrac{1}{(1+k)^4}\right).$

Looking at Appendix Table 2 (in the row where $n = 4$), we see that k is between 2 and 3 percent.

9. a. $.40(.10) + .60(.15) = .13$. Thus, the weighted cost of capital is 13 percent.
   b. $.30(.10) + .70(.15) = .135$. Thus the weighted cost of capital is 13.5 percent.

10. a.

Time (t)	Cash flow (millions of dollars)	$\dfrac{1}{(1+.10)^t}$	$\dfrac{\text{Cash flow}}{(1+.10)^t}$
0	−10	1.0000	−10.0000
1	3	.9091	2.7273
2	4	.8264	3.3056
3	3	.7513	2.2539
4	2	.6830	1.3660
5	1	.6209	0.6209
		Sum	0.2737

The present value of the investment is .2737 millions of dollars.

b.

Time (t)	Cash flow (millions of dollars)	$\dfrac{1}{(1+.12)^t}$	$\dfrac{\text{Cash flow}}{(1+.12)^t}$
0	−10	1.0000	−10.0000
1	3	.8929	2.6787
2	4	.7972	3.1888
3	3	.7118	2.1354
4	2	.6355	1.2710
5	1	.5674	.5674
		Sum	−0.1587

The present value of the investment is −.1587 millions of dollars.

CHAPTER 15

Government and Business

Chapter Profile

Commissions regulating public utilities often set price at a level at which it equals average total cost, including a "fair rate of return" on the firm's investment. One difficulty with this arrangement is that since the firm is guaranteed this rate of return (regardless of how well or poorly it performs), there is no incentive for the firm to increase its efficiency. Although regulatory lag results in some incentives of this sort, they often are relatively weak.

There has been a great deal of controversy over the practices of the regulatory commissions. Many economists have viewed them as lax or ill-conceived. In many areas, like transportation, there has been a movement toward deregulation. In the airline industry, this movement has been particularly dramatic.

The socially optimal level of pollution (holding output constant) is at the point where the marginal cost of pollution equals the marginal cost of pollution control. In general, this will be at a point where a nonzero amount of pollution occurs. To establish incentives that will lead to a more nearly optimal level of pollution, the government can establish effluent fees and enact direct regulations, among other things.

In 1890, the Sherman Act was passed. It outlawed any contract, combination, or conspiracy in restraint of trade and made it illegal to monopolize or attempt to monopolize. In 1914, Congress passed the Clayton Act, and the Federal Trade Commission was created. A more recent antitrust development was the Celler-Kefauver Anti-Merger Act of 1950.

The real impact of the antitrust laws depends on the interpretation placed on these laws by the courts. In its early cases, the Supreme Court put forth and used the famous rule of reason—that only unreasonable combinations in restraint of trade, not all trusts, required conviction under the Sherman Act. The situation changed greatly in the 1940s when the court decided that Alcoa, because it controlled practically all of the nation's aluminum output, was in violation of the antitrust laws. In the early 1980s, two major antitrust cases—against American Telephone and Telegraph and the IBM Corporation—were decided.

The patent laws grant the inventor exclusive control over the use of an invention for 17 years in exchange for his or her making the invention public knowledge. The patent system enables innovators to appropriate a larger portion of the social benefits from their innovations than would be the case without it, but they frequently have only a limited effect on the rate at which imitators appear. Nonetheless, firms continue to make extensive use of the patent system.

In many high-technology industries, there is a widespread feeling among top managers that inadequate protection is being given to intellectual property rights, such as patents and copyrights. The developing countries have particularly weak laws to protect intellectual property rights and less than diligent enforcement of the laws that exist. It is difficult to influence foreign practices of this sort, but U.S. firms and agencies are trying to do so.

Questions

Completion

1. Commissions often set price at the level at which it equals _____, including a fair return.
2. The government (can, cannot) _____ convict firms of violation of the antitrust laws merely by showing that they fixed prices or attempted to do so. The government (does, does not) _____ have to show what the effects were.
3. The Standard Oil case, decided in 1911, resulted in _____. The American Tobacco case, decided in 1911, resulted in _____. The U.S. Steel case, decided in 1920, resulted in _____. All of these cases were tried under Section _____ of the _____.
4. The IBM case alleged that IBM has had monopoly power in the market for _____. This case was tried under Section _____ of the _____.
5. While many economists favor the market _____ approach to antitrust policy, the majority favor the market _____ approach to evaluating undesirable monopolistic characteristics.
6. The market _____ shows the percentage of total sales or production accounted for by the biggest four firms.
7. The _____ outlawed any contract, combination, or conspiracy in restraint of trade and made it illegal to monopolize or attempt to monopolize.
8. At the socially optimal level, the cost of an extra unit of pollution equals the cost of _____ pollution by an extra unit.
9. Patent protection has increased imitation costs by a (larger, smaller) _____ percentage in the pharmaceutical industry than in the electronics industry.

CHAPTER FIFTEEN

True or False

_____ 1. Because price levels have been rising in the past forty years, most regulatory commissions use replacement cost to value a firm's assets.

_____ 2. Regulatory lag results in rewards for efficiency because if a regulated firm is efficient, the lag automatically is reduced and profits increase.

_____ 3. A firm with a 60 percent market share frequently is permitted to go untouched by the antitrust laws, while at the same time two firms with 10 percent of a market sometimes are forbidden to merge.

_____ 4. Whether or not price fixing is illegal depends on the price fixers' share of the market; it their share is small enough, it is not illegal under U.S. law.

_____ 5. If firm A acquires the stock or assets of a competing corporation, this may be illegal based on Section 7 of the Clayton Act, as amended by the Celler-Kefauver Act.

_____ 6. In recent years, horizontal mergers have often been disallowed by the courts, but all vertical mergers have been permitted.

_____ 7. The antitrust laws have as yet had no significant effect on business behavior and markets.

_____ 8. The United States patent laws grant the inventor exclusive control over the use of his or her invention for thirty years.

_____ 9. The patent system and the antitrust laws tend to push in opposite directions.

_____ 10. A firm's size is not necessarily a good indicator of the extent of its monopoly power.

Multiple Choice

1. It is illegal in the United States for rival firms

   a. to agree to fix prices.
   b. to restrict or pool output.
   c. to share markets on a predetermined basis.
   d. all of the above.
   e. only a and b.

2. It is illegal in the United States for a firm

   a. to set its price equal to that of one of its competitors.
   b. to merge with a larger firm.
   c. to charge one customer a different price than another under any circumstances.
   d. to license its patents.
   e. none of the above.

CHAPTER FIFTEEN

3. The most important reason why economists oppose monopoly is that, as compared with perfect competition, monopolies

   a. reap higher profits.
   b. charge higher prices.
   c. result in a misallocation of resources.
   d. are unlikely to be philanthropic.
   e. none of the above.

4. In the United States in 1968, about half of all manufacturing assets were controlled by

   a. 100 corporations.
   b. 500 corporations.
   c. 1,000 corporations
   d. 5,000 corporations.
   e. 10 corporations.

5. If firms enter into exclusive and tying contracts that substantially lessen competition, this is illegal according to the

   a. Sherman Act, Section 1.
   b. Sherman Act, Section 2.
   c. Clayton Act.
   d. Federal Trade Commission Act.
   e. Celler-Kefauver Act.

6. If a firm enters into a contract in restraint of trade, this is illegal based on the

   a. Sherman Act, Section 1.
   b. Sherman Act, Section 2.
   c. Clayton Act.
   d. Federal Trade Commission Act.
   e. Celler-Kefauver Act.

7. In 1958, the Antitrust Division sued Bethlehem Steel and Youngstown Sheet and Tube to stop a proposed merger between them. This case was brought under the

   a. Sherman Act, Section 1.
   b. Sherman Act, Section 2.
   c. Robinson-Patman Act.
   d. Federal Trade Commission Act.
   e. Celler-Kefauver Act.

8. The patent system is defended on the grounds that

   a. it increases the incentive for invention.
   b. it increases the incentive for innovation.
   c. it hastens the disclosure of inventions.
   d. all of the above.
   e. none of the above.

CHAPTER FIFTEEN

Problems

1. Consider an electric power plant that has the marginal cost curve shown below. Suppose that this plant's demand curve varies over time. For simplicity, assume that there is a peak period (when air conditioners are running and lights are on) and an off-peak period (at night). The demand curve during each period is shown below:

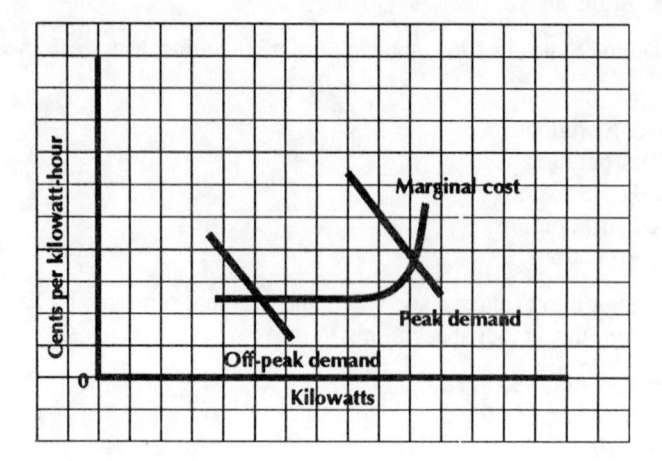

    a. Should the electric power plant charge a higher price during the peak period than during the off-peak period? Why or why not?
    b. In the 1970s, a number of regulatory commissions instituted higher rates for electric utilities during the summer than during the winter. Is this sensible, based on your answer to part a?
    c. In 1978, the Public Utility Regulatory Policy Act required electric utilities to implement time-of-day pricing or to "show cause" why such pricing should not be implemented in their service areas. Time-of-day pricing calls for higher electricity rates during the times of day when the use of electricity is relatively high than during those when it is relatively low. Does time-of-day pricing tend to promote efficiency?

2. In one of the most famous antitrust suits of this century, the government charged Du Pont, the large chemical firm, with "monopolizing, attempting to monopolize and conspiracy to monopolize interstate commerce in cellophane . . . in violation of Section 2 of the Sherman Act." Du Pont produced 75 percent of the cellophane sold in the United States.

    a. Considering Du Pont's share of the cellophane market, was it clear that the company was in violation of Section 2 of the Sherman Act?
    b. The Supreme Court pointed out that "despite cellophane's advantage, it has to meet competition from other materials in every one of its uses. . . . The overall result is that cellophane accounts for 17.9 percent of flexible wrapping materials." How can one tell whether cellophane had to meet competition from other materials, and how stiff this competition was?
    c. The Supreme Court decided that Du Pont was not in violation of the Sherman Act. In reaching this decision, it pointed to the high cross elasticity of demand

existing between cellophane and other flexible packaging materials like Pliofilm. Why is this of relevance?

3. In the early 1960s, the Aluminum Company of America wanted to acquire the Rome Cable Corporation, but this merger was challenged by the government. The 1958 market shares, based on alternative market definitions, are given below:

Definition	Alcoa	Rome
	(percent)	
Bare aluminum conductor wire and cable	32.5	0.3
Insulated aluminum conductor wire and cable	11.6	4.7
Combined aluminum conductor wire and cable	27.8	1.3
All bare conductor wire and cable (aluminum and copper)	10.3	2.0
All insulated conductor wire and cable	0.3	1.3
Combined insulated and bare wire and cable (all metals)	1.8	1.4

Is it obvious that the merger should have been stopped? Do you think that the courts stopped it?

4. In the early 1960s, Continental Can Company wanted to merge with the Hazel-Atlas Glass Company. Continental, the second-largest producer of tin cans in the U.S., sold about one-third of all tin cans. Hazel-Atlas, the third largest bottle maker, sold about one-tenth of all glass bottles.

Do you think that the definition of the relevant line of commerce was important in this case? Do you think that the courts prevented the merger?

5. There are several firms that produce a particular product. Their sales in 1990 are as follows:

Firm	Sales (millions of dollars)
A	100
B	50
C	40
D	30
E	20
F	5
G	5

a. What is the concentration ratio in this industry?
b. Would you regard this industry as oligopolistic? Why or why not?
c. Suppose that firm A merges with firm G. What now will be the concentration ratio in this industry?
d. Suppose that after they merge, firms A and G go out of business. What now will be the concentration ratio in this industry?

6. A producer of table salt does not set the same price for all buyers. Instead, the price varies inversely and substantially with the size of the customer's order. The differences in price are not due to cost differences. The buyers are retail stores, and the large buyers can resell the salt at a lower price than can the small buyers. Is the salt manufacturer's pricing illegal? If so, what law does it violate?

CHAPTER FIFTEEN

7. We list a number of U.S. laws below, after which we list a number of antitrust provisions. In the blank space before each provision, put the letter corresponding to the U.S. law containing this provision.
   A. Sherman Act, Section 1
   B. Sherman Act, Section 2
   C. Clayton Act
   D. Federal Trade Commission Act
   E. Celler-Kafauver Act
   F. Robinson-Patman Act

   _____ a. It is illegal to enter into a contract, combination, or conspiracy in restraint of trade.
   _____ b. It is illegal to discriminate among purchasers to an extent that cannot be justified by a difference in cost.
   _____ c. It is illegal to use unfair methods of competition.
   _____ d. It is illegal to attempt to monopolize trade.
   _____ e. It is illegal to attempt to enter into exclusive and tying contracts.
   _____ f. It is illegal to attempt to discriminate among purchasers, where the effect might be to drive competitors out of business.
   _____ g. It is illegal to attempt to employ unfair or deceptive acts or practices.
   _____ h. It is illegal to attempt to acquire the stock of competing corporations.

8. Some states, such as Oregon and Vermont, have passed laws that all carbonated-beverage containers must carry a minimum refundable deposit.
   a. According to the director of communications services for American Can Company, "What *is* happening in Oregon is that consumers are paying $10 million more a year for beer and soft drinks than they did before the bottle bill became law. Retail price increases . . . have far exceeded those in neighboring states." Why do you think this was true?
   b. According to this executive of American Can Company, "Oregon [and Vermont] consumers are denied their free choice of container." Is this true? According to William Baumol and Wallace Oates, this amounts to "a denial of . . . the freedom to pollute unpenalized." Do you agree?

9. According to one study of the Delaware River, the extra social costs involved in going from one level of pollution abatement to another are shown below. Also shown are the extra benefits to society in going from one level of pollution to another. (All figures are in millions of dollars.)

Transition	Extra cost	Extra benefit
From abatement level 1 to 2	35	200
From abatement level 2 to 3	20	20
From abatement level 3 to 4	130	10
From abatement level 4 to 5	245	25

   a. If abatement level 1 is currently being achieved, is it socially worthwhile to advance to abatement level 2? Why or why not?
   b. Is it socially worthwhile to advance to abatement level 3? Why or why not?
   c. Is it socially worthwhile to advance to abatement level 4? Why or why not?
   d. Is it socially worthwhile to advance to abatement level 5? Why or why not?

10. In 1965, the Ohio Valley Electric Corporation sued Westinghouse and General Electric for damages. According to Ohio Valley Electric, it had been overcharged for electrical equipment it purchased during a period when the electrical equipment producers conspired to raise prices. In the subsequent trial, it built its case in considerable part on the following graph, which shows the relationship between average order prices and book prices during 1948 to 1963.*

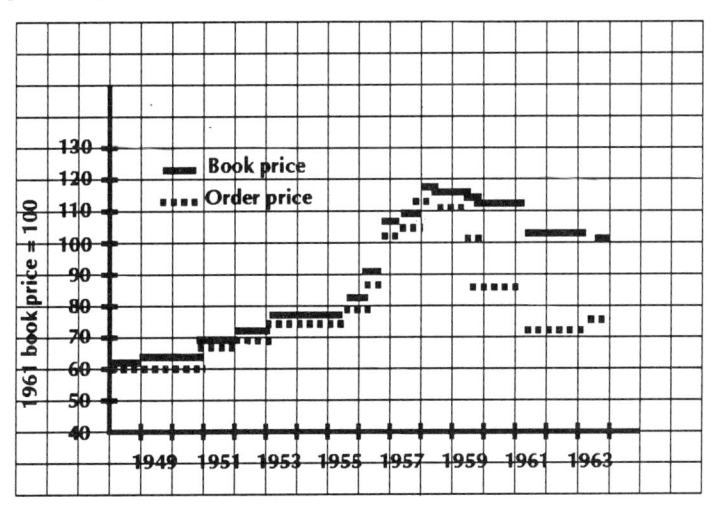

Source: R. Sultan, *Pricing in the electrical Oligopoly* (Boston: Harvard University, 1974).

a. The book price was the published price issued by General Electric and other electrical equipment producers. The average order price was the average price actually negotiated for such equipment. Does it appear that this equipment was frequently sold below its book price?

b. There was evidence that the electrical equipment producers had held meetings to control prices before 1959. Is the relationship between average order price and book price different in the post-1959 period than in the earlier years?

c. According to the Ohio Valley Electric Corporation, in the absence of a conspiracy, the actual order price would have borne the same relationship to the book price in the early 1950s as in the early 1960s. Specifically, it would have been about 75 percent of the book price. Is this necessarily true?

Answers

Completion

1. average total cost 2. can, does not 3. dissolution of Standard Oil, dissolution of American Tobacco, acquittal, 2, Sherman Act 4. electronic computers, 2, Sherman Act 5. performance, structure 6. concentration ratio 7. Sherman Act 8. reducing 9. larger

True or False

1. False 2. False 3. True 4. False 5. True 6. False 7. False 8. False 9. True 10. True

Multiple Choice

1. d 2. e 3. c 4. a 5. c 6. a 7. e 8. d

CHAPTER FIFTEEN

Problems

1. a. Many economists favor such a pricing policy. One advantage is that it would help to even out the amount of electricity utilized at various periods of time.
   b. Yes, if the demand for electric power is greater in the summer than in the winter.
   c. Yes.
2. a. No, because it was not clear that cellophane alone was the relevant line of commerce.
   b. One relevant measure is the cross elasticity of demand between cellophane and other flexible packaging materials.
   c. Because it indicates how closely these other materials can substitute for cellophane.
3. It was not obvious. The Supreme Court ruled against the merger, whereas the district court permitted it.
4. The district court said cans and bottles were separate lines of commerce, but the Supreme Court emphasized the competition between cans and bottles. The Supreme Court ruled against the merger.
5. a. 220/250 = 88 percent.
   b. Yes, because the concentration ratio is so high.
   c. 90 percent.
   d. 140/145 = 97 percent.
6. Yes. The Robinson-Patman Act.
7. a. A.
   b. C.
   c. D.
   d. B.
   e. C.
   f. F.
   g. D.
   h. E.
8. a. Because of increased costs of handling, sorting, washing, returning, and refilling bottles, according to this executive.
   b. The issue is too complex to permit a very brief answer, but many economists would agree with Baumol and Oates.
9. a. Yes, because the benefit exceeds the cost.
   b. No, because the benefit does not exceed the cost.
   c. No, because the benefit does not exceed the cost.
   d. No, because the benefit does not exceed the cost.
10. a. Yes.
    b. Yes.
    c. No. For example, increased competition among electrical equipment producers could result in a decrease in the ratio of actual order price to book price.

Brief Answers to Even-Numbered End-of-Chapter Questions and Problems in the Text

Chapter 1

2. These five basic steps are given in Figure 1.2 of the text. Mr. Eckhardt had to (a) determine what his objectives were, (b) define the problem, (c) identify possible solutions, one of which is to buy IBM's stock, (d) select the best possible solution, which may or may not be to buy IBM's stock, and (e) implement the decision.

4. IBM's research laboratories can affect the firm's total revenues—TR_t in equation (1.2)—by helping to provide the firm's new products, like the IBM Personal Computer (discussed on page 384 of the text). The quality and quantity of such new products can have a big effect on total revenues. Also, the research laboratories can affect the firm's total cost—TC_t in equation (1.2)—by helping to produce the new and improved processes that reduce the firm's costs. Müller's findings probably had an impact on the firm's value, but this impact is very hard to measure.

6. a, b, and c are all true.

8. The answer to all questions is yes.

10. No. Accounting profit generally differs from economic profit.

Chapter 2

2. a. $10 + 10X$.
   b. $8 + 8X^3$.
   c. $[(4 + X^3)3 - 3X(3X^2)] \div (4 + X^3)^2 = [12 - 6X^3] \div (4 + X^3)^2$.
   d. $[(X - 3)4 - 4X] + (X - 3)^2 = -12 + (X - 3)^2$.

4. a. Marginal profit equals $d\pi/dQ$, which is $20 - 6Q$. If $Q = 8$, marginal profit equals $20 - 6(8)$, or -28.
   b. Marginal profit $= 20 - 6Q$.
   c. If $20 - 6Q = 0$, $Q = 20/6$ or $3^1/_3$.

6. a. Since $\dfrac{d\pi}{dQ} = -6 + 11Q - 6Q^2 + Q^3$, it follows that

   $$\dfrac{d\pi}{dQ} = -6 + 11 - 6 + 1 = 0,$$

ANSWERS TO EVEN-NUMBERED QUESTIONS

if $Q = 1$. To tell whether a maximum occurs when $Q = 1$, we find the second derivative which is

$$\frac{d^2\pi}{dQ^2} = 11 - 12Q + 3Q^2.$$

If $Q = 1$,

$$\frac{d^2\pi}{dQ^2} = 11 - 12 + 3 = 2.$$

Since $d^2\pi/dQ^2$ is positive, this is a minimum, not a maximum.

b. If $Q = 2$,

$$\frac{d\pi}{dQ} = -6 + 11(2) - 6(2^2) + 2^3$$

$$= -6 + 22 - 24 + 8 = 0.$$

If $Q = 2$,

$$\frac{d^2\pi}{dQ^2} = 11 - 12(2) + 3(2^2)$$

$$= 11 - 24 + 12 = -1.$$

Since $d^2\pi/dQ^2$ is negative, this is a maximum.

c. The relationship seems questionable. Ordinarily, one expects profit to increase with increases in output up to some point, and then fall.

8. a. $\frac{\partial \pi}{\partial Q_1} = 40 - 10Q_1 - 3Q_2 = 0$

$\frac{\partial \pi}{\partial Q_2} = 30 - 8Q_2 - 3Q_1 = 0.$

Solving these two equations simultaneously,

$$Q_1 = 3.24$$

$$Q_2 = 2.535.$$

b. No, the answer will not change.

10. a. Since $X_1 + X_2 = 10$,

$$C = 7X_1^2 + 9(10 - X_1)^2 - 1.5X_1(10 - X_1)$$

$$= 7X_1^2 + 9\left(100 - 20X_1 + X_1^2\right) - 15X_1 + 1.57X_1^2$$

$$= 900 - 195X_1 + 1.5X_1^2.$$

Thus, if

$$\frac{dC}{dX_1} = -195 + 35X_1 = 0,$$

$$X_1 = 195 \div 35 = 5.57.$$

168

ANSWERS TO EVEN-NUMBERED QUESTIONS

Consequently, she should produce 5.57 cotton rugs per day and 10 − 5.57 = 4.43 wool rugs per day.

b. It would seem more reasonable to maximize profit, rather than minimize cost.
c. She may be able to produce only part of a rug, leaving the rest to be completed on the following day. Thus, 4.43 rugs produced per day may mean producing 443 rugs in 100 days.

12. a. The Lagrangian function is

$$L_{TC} = 7X_1^2 + 9X_2^2 - 1.5X_1X_2 + \lambda(10 - X_1 - X_2).$$

Setting the partial derivatives equal to zero, we have

$$\frac{\partial L_{TC}}{\partial X_1} = 14X_1 - 1.5X_2 - \lambda = 0.$$

$$\frac{\partial L_{TC}}{\partial X_2} = 18X_2 - 1.5X_1 - \lambda = 0.$$

$$\frac{\partial L_{TC}}{\partial \lambda} = 10 - X_1 - X_2 = 0.$$

Solving these equations simultaneously, we find that $X_1 = 5.57$ and $X_2 = 4.43$.

b. Yes.
c. $\lambda = 14X_1 - 1.5X_2 = 14(5.57) - 1.5(4.43) = 77.98 - 6.64 = 71.34.$

This means that if the total rug production increases from 10 to 11 rugs per day, the minimum value of cost will increase by $71.34.

Chapter 3

2. a. $P = 3,000 - 40Q$

$TR = PQ = 3,000Q - 40Q^2$

$MR = \dfrac{dTR}{dQ} = 3,000 - 80Q.$

b. Since $Q = \dfrac{3,000 - P}{40} = 75 - .025P,$

$$\frac{-dQ}{dP} \cdot \frac{P}{Q} = .025 \frac{P}{75 - .025P}.$$

Thus, the price elasticity of demand exceeds 1 if

$$\frac{.025P}{75 - .025P} > 1,$$

or

$.025P > 75 - .025P$

$.05P > 75$

$P > 1,500.$

Thus, demand will be price elastic if price exceeds 1,500.

169

ANSWERS TO EVEN-NUMBERED QUESTIONS

c. To maximize its dollar sales volume, it should set dTR/dQ equal to zero. Thus,

$$3{,}000 - 80Q = 0$$

$$Q = \frac{3{,}000}{80} = 37.5$$

$$P = 3{,}000 - 40(37.5) = 1{,}500.$$

Consequently, price should be set at 1,500.

4. a. If the price elasticity of demand is about 0.5, a price cut will reduce the firm's sales, not increase them.
   b. No.

6. a. If P equals 1, the demand for the firm's product is inelastic. To see that this is the case, note that if $P = 1$, $Q = 5 - 1 = 4$; thus, the firm's total revenue is $4 million per day. If $P = 2$, $Q = 5 - 2 = 3$; thus, the firm's total revenue is $6 million per day. Since an increase in price (from $1 to $2) increases total revenue, demand must be price inelastic. It is unwise for a firm to operate at a point where the demand for its product is price inelastic. By increasing its price, it can increase its total revenue and (because it generally costs less to produce less output) reduce its total cost. Therefore, it can increase its total profit. Thus, Hanover should consider a price hike.
   b. Let's compute the arc elasticity of demand when price is between $1.00 and $1.01. When $P = 1$, $Q = 4$. If $P = 1.01$, $Q = 5 - 1.01 = 3.99$. Thus,

$$\eta = -\frac{(4.00 - 3.99)}{(4.00 + 3.99)/2} \div \frac{(1.00 - 1.01)}{(1.00 + 1.01)/2} = \frac{0.01}{3.995} \div \frac{0.01}{1.005} = 0.25.$$

Therefore, the price elasticity of demand is about 0.25, not 1.0. The marketing specialist is wrong.

8. a. It would fall by about 5 percent.
   b. Because the income elasticity is only .5, according to Sackrin, the quantity demanded of cigarettes would increase by only about 25 percent if income rose by 50 percent.

10. a. Q will increase by 20.
    b. $6.67.
    c. If the demand curve is linear, as in this case, the price elasticity goes up as price increases.

12. a. No, because it does not equal $MC\left(\dfrac{1}{1-1/\eta}\right)$, since η equals 1.5.

b. To maximize profit, price should be set equal to $MC\left(\dfrac{1}{1-1/\eta}\right) =$ $10\left(\dfrac{1}{1-1/1.5}\right) = 10(3) = 30$ dollars.

Chapter 4

2. a. Since each additional dollar of advertising results in 3.1 additional dozens of the product being sold, it results in $31 of additional revenue. Clearly, more should be spent on advertising.

b. $Q = -23 + 4.2(8{,}000) + 3.1(10{,}000) - 4.1P$
$= 64{,}577 - 4.1P.$

Thus,

$$P = \dfrac{64{,}577 - Q}{4.1} = 15{,}750 - .244Q$$

and marginal revenue $= \dfrac{dPQ}{dQ} = 15{,}750 - .488Q.$

c. Since advertising expenditure is fixed, the firm wants to maximize total revenue (in the special situation described here). To do so, it should set

$$\text{marginal revenue} = \dfrac{d(PQ)}{dQ} = 0,$$

Thus, $15{,}750 - .488Q = 0$, and $Q = 32{,}275$.
Since $P = 15{,}750 - .244Q$, $P = 15{,}750 - .244(32{,}275) = \$7{,}875$.

d. Yes. Since $n = 124$ and $k = 3$, the number of degrees of freedom is 120, and the value of $t_{.025}$ is 1.98, as shown in Appendix Table 4. Thus, a 95 percent confidence interval for the coefficient of A is

$3.1 \pm 1.98(2.2)$, or -1.26 to 7.46.

This means that, because of sampling errors, this coefficient could be so small that the firm should not increase its advertising. Although our best estimate is that more advertising would be profitable, it is by no means a certainty.

ANSWERS TO EVEN-NUMBERED QUESTIONS

4. a. Let Y equal shear strength and X equal diameter. If we plot Y against X, we get the following:

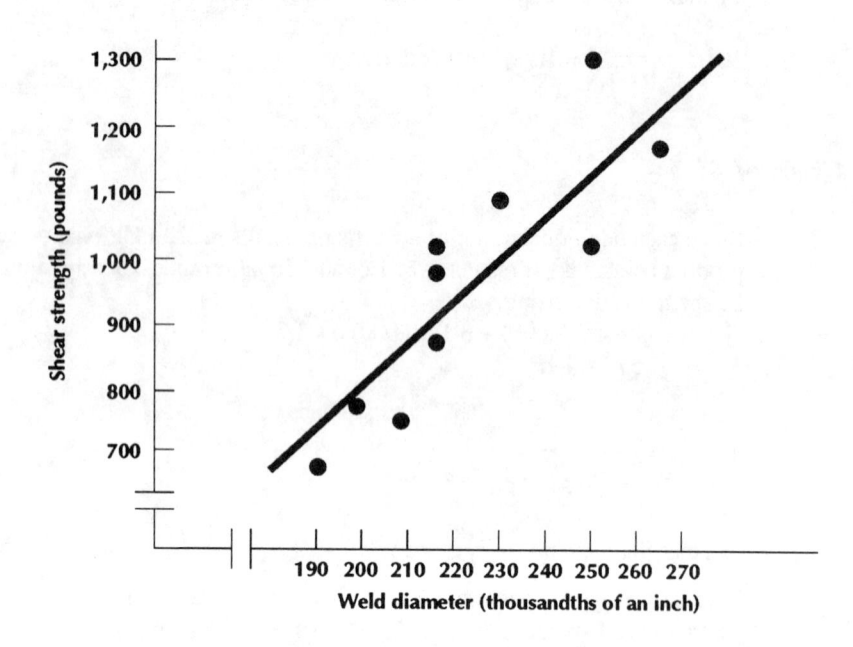

Shear strength (pounds) vs. Weld diameter (thousandths of an inch)

Direct. Yes, since one would expect that a greater weld diameter would be associated with a greater shear strength. It seems so, but with so few points it is hard to tell.

b.

X	Y	X^2	Y^2	XY
190	680	36,100	462,400	129,200
200	800	40,000	640,000	160,000
209	780	43,681	608,400	163,020
215	885	46,225	783,225	190,275
215	975	46,225	950,625	209,625
215	1,025	46,225	1,050,625	220,375
230	1,100	52,900	1,210,000	253,000
250	1,030	62,500	1,060,990	257,500
265	1,175	70,225	1,380,625	311,375
250	1,300	62,500	1,690,000	325,000
Total 2,239	9,750	506,581	9,836,800	2,219,370
Mean 223.9	975.0			

$$b = \frac{(10)(2{,}219{,}370) - (2{,}239)(9{,}750)}{(10)(506{,}581) - (2{,}239)^2} = 6.898.$$

$a = 975 - (6.898)(223.9) = 975 - 1{,}544.46 = -569.46.$

ANSWERS TO EVEN-NUMBERED QUESTIONS

c. The regression line is plotted in the answer to part a.
$-569.46 + 6.898(200) = -569.46 + 1,379.6 = 810.14$ pounds.
$-569.46 + 6.898(250) = -569.46 + 1,724.5 = 1,155.04$ pounds.

6. a. Using the methods described in this chapter, you might see whether there was serial correlation in the error terms. Also, you might see whether there seem to be departures from linearity, and whether the variation in the error terms is the same, regardless of the value of the independent variable.
   b. It might enable the railroad to predict its costs more accurately and to estimate the marginal costs of its switching and delivery services.
   c. It would be important to have R^2, the standard error of estimate, the Durbin-Watson test statistic, and the standard errors of the regression coefficients.
   d. Based on Appendix Table 7, $d_L = 1.35$ and $d_u = 1.48$, if the significance level equals 0.01 (for a one-tailed test). Since, for a two-tailed test, the observed value of d (which is 2.11) lies between d_u and $4 - 4d_u$, there is no reason to reject the null hypothesis that no serial correlation exists.
   e. According to Appendix Table 6, the probability that the F-statistic would equal 4.98 or more is 0.01, if neither independent variable affects the dependent variable. Thus, since the observed value of the F-statistic is 6.92, it seems very unlikely that neither independent variable affects the dependent variable.

8. a. Let Y be the direct measurement, and let X be the indirect measurement.

Y	X	Y^2	X^2	XY
31	6.2	961	38.44	192.2
31	6.2	961	38.44	192.2
21	10.1	441	102.01	212.1
21	8.4	441	70.56	176.4
57	2.9	3,249	8.41	165.3
80	2.9	6,400	8.41	232.0
35	7.4	1,225	54.76	259.0
10	7.3	100	53.29	73.0
0	11.1	0	123.21	0
0	10.7	0	114.49	0
35	4.1	1,225	16.81	143.5
63	3.5	3,969	12.25	220.5
10	5.0	100	25.00	50.0
51	4.5	2,601	20.25	229.5
24	9.5	576	90.25	228.0
15	8.5	225	72.25	127.5
80	2.6	6,400	6.76	208.0
90	2.9	8,100	8.41	261.0
Total 654	113.8	36,974	864.00	2,970.2
Mean 36.3333	6.3222			

Using these calculations, $r^2 = .71$.

ANSWERS TO EVEN-NUMBERED QUESTIONS

b. Based on equations (4.6) and (4.7),

$$b = \frac{-1,164.519}{144.5336} = -8.057$$

$$a = 36.3333 - (-8.057)(6.3222) = 36.333 + 50.937$$
$$= 87.27.$$

Thus, the sample regression line is

$$\hat{Y} = 87.27 - 8.057X.$$

c. The two measures seem to be correlated reasonably well. Variation in the indirect measure can explain about 70 percent of the variation in the direct measure. The relationship between them is inverse, not direct. On the average, the direct measure equals 87.27 minus 8.057 times the indirect measure.

10. a. It is difficult to hold constant other factors, such as changes in the quality of service. Also, it is hard to continue an experiment of this sort long enough to estimate long-run effects.
    b. Approximately 1, since total revenue remained constant in the face of the price cut.

12. a. According to the equation, the price elasticity of demand is 1.2, so a 5 percent price reduction should result in about a 6 percent increase in quantity.
    b. If the t-statistic is only 0.5, the sampling errors in the estimated price elasticity are substantial. The price elasticity could easily be close to zero or above 2.
    c. The firm could increase the sample size.

Chapter 5

2. a. Let $t = 0$ when the year is 1960.

Y	t	Y^2	t^2	Yt
1.5	0	2.25	0	0
1.6	1	2.56	1	1.6
1.6	2	2.56	4	3.2
1.7	3	2.89	9	5.1
1.9	4	3.61	16	7.6
2.1	5	4.41	25	10.5
2.2	6	4.84	36	13.2
2.5	7	6.25	49	17.5
2.7	8	7.29	64	21.6
2.9	9	8.41	81	26.1
3.0	10	9.00	100	30.0
3.0	11	9.00	121	33.0
3.3	12	10.89	144	39.6
3.9	13	15.21	169	50.7
5.3	14	28.09	196	74.2
5.7	15	32.49	225	85.5
Total 44.9	120	149.75	1,240	419.4
Mean 2.806	7.5			

ANSWERS TO EVEN-NUMBERED QUESTIONS

$$b = \frac{16(419.4) - (44.9)(120)}{16(1,240) - 120^2} = .243$$

$a = 2.806 - (.243)(7.5) = 2.806 - 1.823 = 0.983.$

Thus, the equation for the trend line is $Y_t = 0.983 + 0.243t$, where the origin is set at 1960. (Software packages generally provide such results.)

b. Let $t = 0$ when the year is 1960:

Y	$u = \log Y$	t	u^2	t^2	ut
1.5	.1761	0	.0310112	0	0
1.6	.2041	1	.0416568	1	.2041
1.6	.2041	2	.0416568	4	.4082
1.7	.2304	3	.0530842	9	.6912
1.9	.2788	4	.0777294	16	1.1152
2.1	.3222	5	.1038128	25	1.6110
2.2	.3424	6	.1172378	36	2.0544
2.5	.3979	7	.1583244	49	2.7853
2.7	.4314	8	.1861060	64	3.4512
2.9	.4624	9	.2138138	81	4.1616
3.0	.4771	10	.2276244	100	4.7710
3.0	.4771	11	.2276244	121	5.2481
3.3	.5185	12	.2688422	144	6.2220
3.9	.5911	13	.3493992	169	7.6843
5.3	.7243	14	.5246105	196	10.1402
5.7	.7559	15	.5713848	225	11.3385
Total 6.5938		120	3.1939187	1,240	61.8863
Mean .4121		7.5			

$$b = \frac{16(61.8863) - (6.5938)(120)}{16(1,240) - 120^2} = .036567$$

$a = .4121 - (7.5)(.036567) = .4121 - .2743 = .1378.$

Thus, the equation for the trend line is $\log Y_t = .1378 + .03657t$, where the origin is set at 1960. (Software packages generally provide such results.)

c. The one based on the exponential trend line.

d. The one based on the exponential trend line.

ANSWERS TO EVEN-NUMBERED QUESTIONS

4. a.

Month	Forecasted trend value of sales (millions of dollars)	Seasonal index	Forecasted Sales (millions of dollars)
January	114.9	103	118.3
February	116.2	80	93.0
March	117.5	75	88.1
April	118.8	103	122.4
May	120.1	101	121.3
June	121.4	104	126.3
July	122.7	120	147.2
August	124.0	139	172.4
September	125.3	121	151.6
October	126.6	101	127.9
November	127.9	75	95.9
December	129.2	78	100.8

b. To see what sales levels are likely to be, in order to determine what plant capacity, employment, and other inputs should be planned for.

6. a.

Month	Forecasted trend value of sales (millions of dollars)	Seasonal index	Forecasted Sales (millions of dollars)
January	25.24	81	20.44
February	25.56	98	25.05
March	25.88	102	26.40
April	26.20	76	19.91
May	26.52	137	36.33
June	26.84	122	32.74
July	27.16	104	28.25
August	27.48	101	27.75
September	27.80	79	21.96
October	28.12	101	28.40
November	28.44	74	21.05
December	28.76	125	35.95

b. Yes. It is likely to reduce these forecasts.

8. a. The higher the mortgage rate, the more expensive a house. The more pessimistic consumers are concerning the economic future, the less likely they are to buy houses. The lower the level of capacity utilization, the more depressed is the economy, and the less likely are people to buy houses. The higher the occupancy rate, the greater the demand for additional houses. The greater the inflow of deposits into savings intermediaries, the greater the amount of money available for housing.

   b. A host of macroeconomic variables, including GNP, the money supply, and their determinants, are relevant here.

ANSWERS TO EVEN-NUMBERED QUESTIONS

Chapter 6

2. a. From equation (6.4), we know that $MP_L \cdot P$ must equal P_L, where MP_L is the marginal product of labor, P is the price of the product, and P_L is the price of labor. This is because the marginal revenue product of labor equals $MP_L \cdot P$, and the marginal expenditure of labor equals P_L. In accord with pages 214–15 of the text,

    $$MP_L = \frac{\partial Q}{\partial L} = .76 \frac{Q}{L},$$

    where Q is output. Thus,

    $10[.76Q/L] = 30,$

    or

    $$\frac{L}{Q} = \frac{7.6}{30} = .253,$$

    which means that the number of workers per unit of output should be .253.
    b. Since $MP_L = .76Q/L$, it follows from equation (6.4) that $P(.76Q/L) = P_L$.

    Thus,

    $$\frac{P_L L}{PQ} = .76.$$

    Because $P_L L$ is the amount spent on labor and PQ is the firm's revenues, it follows that 76 percent of the firm's revenues will be spent on labor if it maximizes profit.
    c. No. See the answer to part b.

4. a. No. One would expect that other inputs like capital or fuel would have to be used.
    b. No. The marginal product of labor is constant regardless of how much labor is used.
    c. No.

6. a. Yes, since $\alpha + \beta > 1$.
    b. No, since $\alpha + \beta$ would equal 1.
    c. No. Since

    $$\frac{Q}{L} = AL^{\alpha-1}K^\beta,$$

    Q/L depends on A, L, and K, as well as α and β.

8. a. Hughes' hourly profit equals $5Q - 4.5L$. Substituting for Q, the firm's hourly profit is

    $\pi = 5(-0.8 + 4.5L - 0.3L^2) - 4.5L = -4 + 18L - 1.5L^2.$

ANSWERS TO EVEN-NUMBERED QUESTIONS

Thus, setting

$$\frac{d\pi}{dL} = 18 - 3L = 0,$$

we find that $L = 6$, which means that Hughes should employ 6 people.
b. $50.
c. No. If $L = 0$, $Q = -0.8$ according to this equation, which is nonsense. Nonetheless, this equation may be accurate within the relevant range.

10. a. Yes. Output per worker is $5,600/16 = 350$ with the new system, but only $4,100/86 = 47.7$ with the old system.
b. Yes. Output per machine is $5,600/9 = 622$ with the new system, but only $4,100/29 = 141$ with the old system.
c. Yes. Improvements in engineering are an important reason for shifts in the production function.
d. A firm can determine the costs of carrying out such steps and compare them with the benefits. More specifically, a firm can see whether the present value of the extra gross profit from carrying out such steps exceeds the costs of doing so. (Much more will be said on this score in Chapter 14.)

Chapter 7

2. a. Because $dC/dt = -19 + t$, cost must decrease as t increases, so long as $t < 19$. Thus, since only value of t between 1 and 6 are admissible here, cost is lower when $t = 6$ than when it assumes other admissible values.
b. R declines as t increases because the Roosevelt Laboratories is likely to lose some of the market for the new drug to rivals if it is too slow to bring the new drug to the market.
c. As pointed out in equation (7.8), the first-order condition for profit maximization is $dC/dt = dR/dt$. Because

$$\frac{dC}{dt} = -19 + t$$

and

$$\frac{dR}{dt} = -15,$$

this means that $-19 + t = -15$, so $t = 4$.
Thus, the optimal project duration is 4 years.

4. a. According to equation (7.14),

$$P(t) = \frac{m(t)}{n} = \frac{1}{1 + e^{-(A + Bt)}}.$$

Thus,

$$1 - P(t) = \frac{n - m(t)}{n} = \frac{e^{-(A + Bt)}}{1 + e^{-(A + Bt)}}.$$

Consequently,

$$\frac{P(t)}{1 - P(t)} = \frac{m(t)}{n - m(t)} = \frac{1}{e^{-(A + Bt)}},$$

ANSWERS TO EVEN-NUMBERED QUESTIONS

and
$$\ln\left[\frac{m(t)}{n - m(t)}\right] = A + Bt.$$

b. Yes. An estimate of A is -4.0, and an estimate of B is $.22$.

c. In 1995, $t = 15$. Thus,
$$\ln\left[\frac{m(t)}{n - m(t)}\right] = -4.0 + .22(15) = -0.7,$$

and
$$\frac{m(t)}{n - m(t)} = .497,$$

which means that
$$\frac{P(t)}{1 - P(t)} = .497,$$

or
$$1.497 P(t) = .497$$
$$P(t) = .33.$$

About 33 percent of chemical firms will be using the new process in 1995, according to this model.

6 a. A profit-maximizing firm generally will not scrap existing equipment merely because somewhat better equipment is available. The new equipment must be sufficiently better to offset the fact that the old equipment is already paid for, whereas this is not the case for the new.

b. No, since this in general will not maximize profit.

c. No, since this in general will not maximize profit.

8. a. This firm seems to underestimate the cost of its R and D projects. If the cost estimates are biased in this way, the analysis would be biased in favor of carrying out the project in question.

b. One possible way around this problem is to attempt to adjust the firm's cost estimates upward in accord with past experience. But unless one is careful, this may result in still further biases downward, as the R and D personnel adapt to this new environment.

10. a. Since $\frac{1}{1 + e^{(6.1 - .41t)}} = \frac{1}{4}$, it follows that $e^{(6.1 - .41t)} = 3$.

Thus,
$$(6.1 - .41t) = \ln(3) = 1.10,$$

and
$$t = 12,$$

which means that about 25 percent used robots in 1982.

b. Since $\frac{1}{1 + e^{(6.1 - .41t)}} = \frac{1}{2}$, it follows that $e^{(6.1 - .41t)} = 1$.

ANSWERS TO EVEN-NUMBERED QUESTIONS

Thus,

$$6.1 - .41t = 0,$$

and

$$t = 14.9,$$

which means that about 50 percent used robots in 1985.

Chapter 8

2. a. | Output | Average cost |
   |---|---|
   | 100,000 | $5.50 |
   | 200,000 | 4.00 |
   | 300,000 | 4.75 |
   | 400,000 | 4.00 |

   b. | | |
   |---|---|
   | 100,000 | 6.75 |
   | 200,000 | 6.75 |
   | 300,000 | 6.75 |
   | 400,000 | 6.75 |

   c. | | |
   |---|---|
   | 100,000 | 8.00 |
   | 200,000 | 8.00 |
   | 300,000 | 8.00 |
   | 400,000 | 8.00 |

   d.

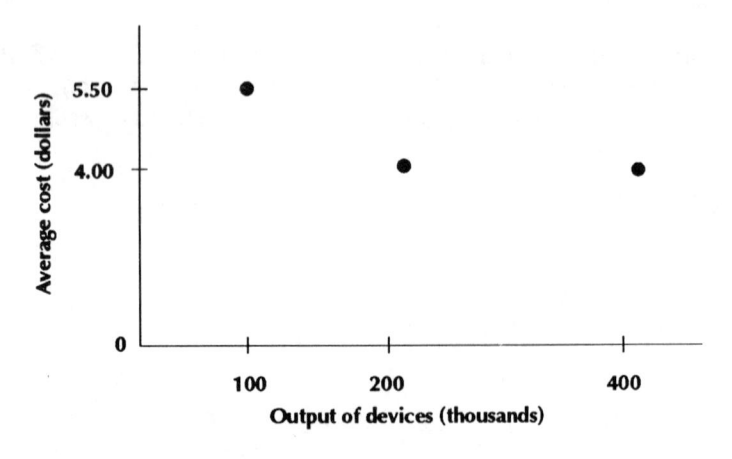

4. a. When $Q = 50$, $TC = 33.905$. When $Q = 51$, $TC = 34.473$. Thus, the increase in fuel cost is 0.568.
   b. This result would be of use in determining whether it would be profitable to increase output.
   c. The marginal (fuel) cost curve is $MC = dTC/dQ = 0.125 + .00878Q$. This curve is useful in indicating whether an increase in output is profitable or not. If the

ANSWERS TO EVEN-NUMBERED QUESTIONS

marginal cost due to an increase in output exceeds the marginal revenue, the increase in output is not profitable.

6. a. Since total cost equals average cost times output, the firm's total cost function is

$$TC = AC \times Q = 3Q + 4Q^2.$$

b. No, since total cost equals zero when $Q = 0$.

c. If the price is $3, total revenue (TR) equals $3Q$. Thus, the firm's profit equals

$$\pi = TR - TC = 3Q - (3Q + 4Q^2) = -4Q^2.$$

If Q is greater than zero, π must be negative, and the firm is incurring losses. If the firm is producing nothing, it is incurring neither profits nor losses. Thus, the firm is better off to produce nothing.

d. $MC = \dfrac{dTC}{dQ} = 3 + 8Q.$

8. a. Yes.
 b. Yes.
 c. One could regress log (C_2/C_1) on log (X_2/X_1), and see whether the regression coefficient is approximately 0.6. In fact, this has been done, and the resulting regression coefficient often is reasonably close to 0.6.

10. a. Yes, since it would bring in $10,000 \times \$25$, or $250,000, in extra revenue, and result in $10,000 \times \$14$, or $140,000, in extra cost.
 b. Yes.
 c. Yes.
 d. $14.

Chapter 9

2. a. Using process A, cost per ton of output is $2(11) + 1(5) + 3(15) = \$72$. Using process B, cost per ton of output is $4(11) + 1(5) + 1(15) = \$64$. Using process C, cost per ton of output is $1(11) + 1(5) + 5(15) = \$91$. Thus, Mr. Chidester should minimize $72A + 64B + 91C$, where A is the number of tons per day produced with process A, B is the number of tons per day produced with process B, and C is the number of tons per day produced with process C.

 b. The constraints are

 $$A + B + C = 100$$

 $$A \geq 0, B \geq 0, C \geq 0.$$

 c. Process B.
 d. It can be regarded as a linear-programming problem, but it can be solved simply by noting that the cost per ton with process B is lower than with processes A or C.

4. a. This means that if the company can hire additional skilled labor for less than $15 per hour, it would be profitable to do so.
 b. Sewing machine time seems to be redundant.

6. a.

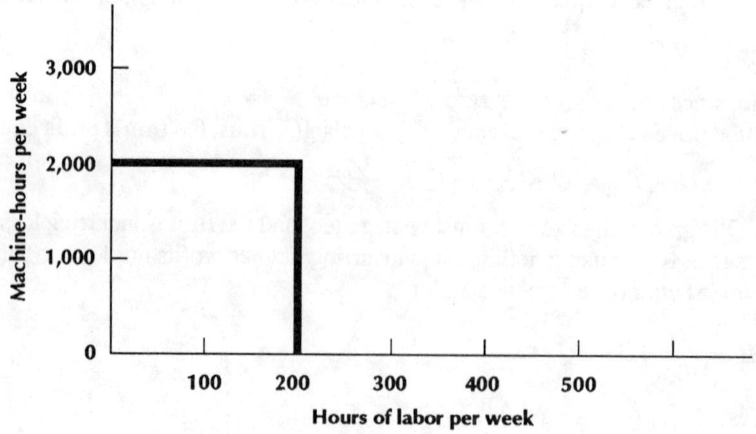
3,000
2,000
1,000
0
Machine-hours per week
100
200
300
400
500
Hours of labor per week

b. The ray is as follows:

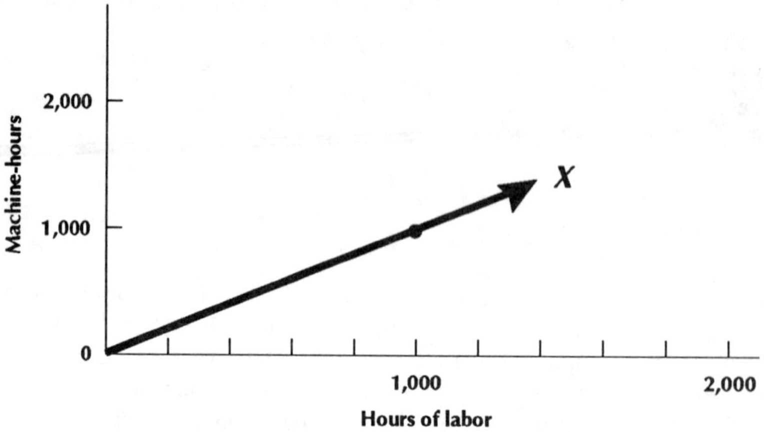
2,000
1,000
0
Machine-hours
X
1,000
2,000
Hours of labor

c. The rays are as follows:

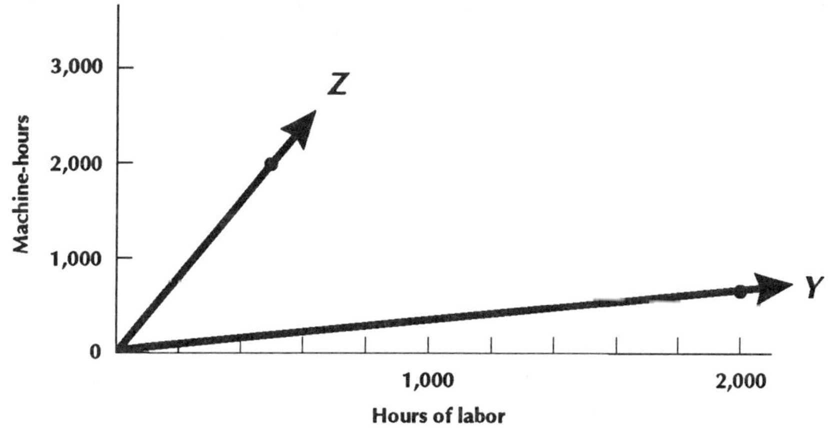

d. The isoquant is as follows:

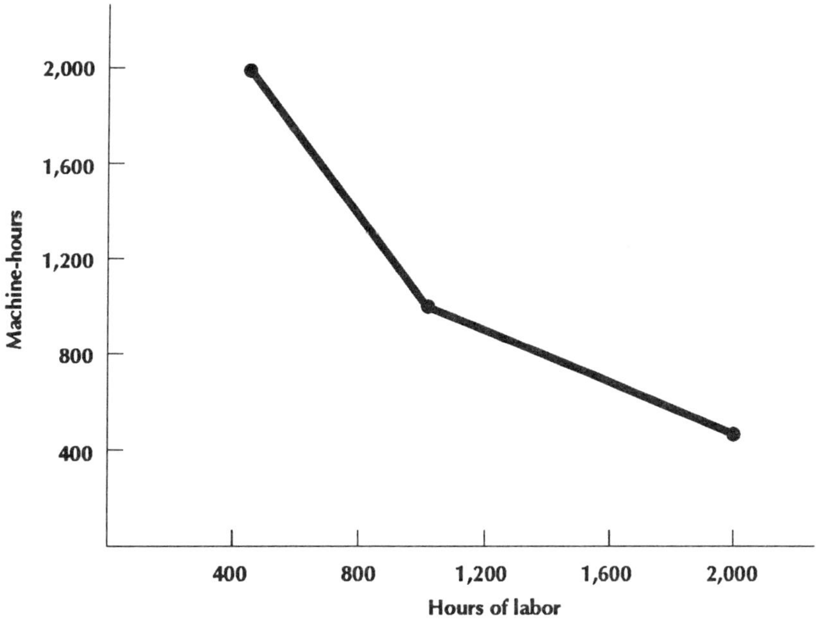

e. It should use the process that uses 1 machine-hour and 1 hour of labor to produce a unit of output. That is, it should use process X.

ANSWERS TO EVEN-NUMBERED QUESTIONS

8. zero, 100, zero.

10. a. Minimize $4A + 6B + 7C + 11D + 7E + 6F$, where A is the number of tons per day shipped from Kentucky to Florida, B is the number of tons per day shipped from Kentucky to Oklahoma, C is the number of tons per day shipped from Kentucky to Arizona, D is the number of tons per day shipped from Oregon to Florida, E is the number of tons per day shipped from Oregon to Oklahoma, and F is the number of tons per day shipped from Oregon to Arizona.

   b. $A + B + C \leq 4,000$
      $D + E + F \leq 5,000$
      $A + D \geq 2,500$
      $B + E \geq 3,500$
      $C + F \geq 3,000$
      $A \geq 0, B \geq 0, C \geq 0, D \geq 0, E \geq 0, F \geq 0.$

   c. The Kentucky plant should ship 2,500 tons to the Florida warehouse, 1,500 tons to the Oklahoma warehouse, and none to the Arizona warehouse. See the printout below.

   d. The Oregon plant should ship none to the Florida warehouse, 2,000 tons to the Oklahoma warehouse, and 3,000 tons to the Arizona warehouse. Using LINDO, the printout is as follows:

```
MIN     4A + 6B + 7C + 11D + 7E + 6F
SUBJECT TO
        2)   A + B + C <=    4000
        3)   D + E + F <=    5000
        4)   A + D >=   2500
        5)   B + E >=   3500
        6)   C + F >=   3000
        7)   A >=  0
        8)   B >=  0
        9)   C >=  0
       10)   D >=  0
       11)   E >=  0
       12)   F >=  0
END

: go
LP OPTIMUM FOUND AT STEP       4
          OBJECTIVE FUNCTION VALUE
   i)            51000.0000

   VARIABLE        VALUE          REDUCED COST
          A      2500.000000         .000000
          B      1500.000000         .000000
          C         .000000         2.000000
          D         .000000         6.000000
          E      2000.000000         .000000
          F      3000.000000         .000000
```

ROW	SLACK OR SURPLUS	DUAL PRICES
2)	.000000	1.000000
3)	.000000	.000000
4)	.000000	-5.000000
5)	.000000	-7.000000
6)	.000000	-6.000000
7)	2500.000000	.000000
8)	1500.000000	.000000
9)	.000000	.000000
10)	.000000	.000000
11)	2000.000000	.000000
12)	3000.000000	.000000

Chapter 10

2. a. If we set $Q_D = Q_S$,

$$140{,}000 - 10{,}000P = 80{,}000 + 5{,}000P$$

$$140{,}000 - 80{,}000 = (5{,}000 + 10{,}000)P$$

$$P = \frac{60{,}000}{15{,}000} = 4.$$

Thus, the equilibrium price equals $4. Since the long-run equilibrium price equals the minimum point on the firms' long-run average cost curves (that is, it equals $4), this is the long-run equilibrium price.

b. When $P = 4$, $Q = 140{,}000 - (10{,}000)(4) = 100{,}000$. Thus, since industry output is 100,000 and the minimum point on each firm's long-run average cost curve occurs at an output of 1,000, there are 100 firms in the industry when each firm operates at the minimum point on its long-run average cost curve.

c. Setting $Q_D = Q_S$, we have

$$150{,}000 - 5{,}000P = 80{,}000 + 5{,}000P$$

$$150{,}000 - 80{,}000 = (5{,}000 + 5{,}000)P$$

$$P = \frac{70{,}000}{10{,}000} = 7$$

$$Q = 150{,}000 - 5{,}000(7) = 115{,}000.$$

Thus, price equals $7 and output equals 115,000.

d. If the industry output is 115,000, if there are 100 firms, and if each firm produces the same amount, the output of each firm is 1,150 boxes per month. It is stated at the outset that a firm producing this amount has a short-run average cost of $5. Since price equals $7, each firm is making profits.

185

ANSWERS TO EVEN-NUMBERED QUESTIONS

4. a.

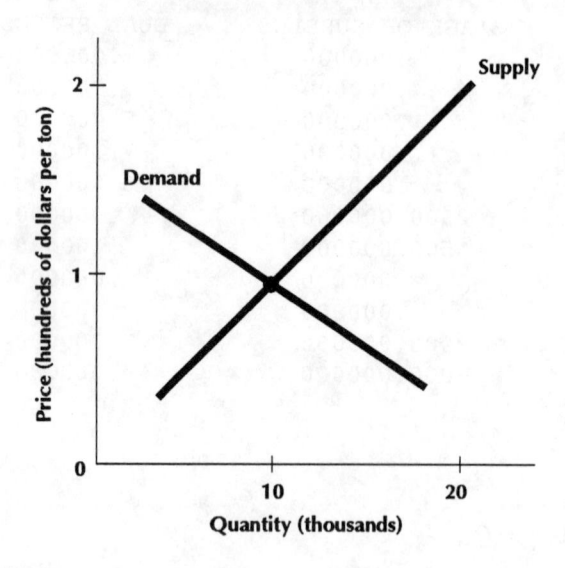

b. $P = 1$, or $100 per ton. (Recall that P is expressed in units of $100 per ton.)
c. 10,000 tons.

6. **a.** Since marginal cost equals $20 + 10Q$, we must set $20 + 10Q$ equal to 50, if price is to equal marginal cost. Thus, $Q = 3$.
   b. $50 \times 3 - [1{,}000 + (20 \times 3) + (5 \times 3^2)] = -955$. Thus, the firm loses $955 per hour.
   c. $368.33.
   d. No, because losses are being incurred.

8. **a.** 2.
   b. No.
   c. Less.

10. **a.** No.
    b. Yes.
    c. No.
    d. Yes. Since $Q = 267.2 - 1.1P$, $P = (267.2 - Q) + 1.1 = 242.9 - .91Q$. Thus,

    $MR = 242.9 - 1.82Q$.

    Since total cost equals

    $TFC + (42 - 8Q + 1.5Q^2)Q = TFC + 42Q - 8Q^2 + 1.5Q^3$,

    $MC = 42 - 16Q + 4.5Q^2$.

    Consequently, if $MR = MC$,

    $242.9 - 1.82Q = 42 - 16Q + 4.5Q^2$,

    or

    $200.9 + 14.18Q - 4.5Q^2 = 0$,

186

which means that
$$Q = \frac{-14.18 \pm \sqrt{14.18^2 + 4(4.5)(200.9)}}{2(4.5)}$$
$$= \frac{-14.18 \pm \sqrt{3,817.27}}{9}.$$
Since $Q > 0$,
$$Q = \frac{-14.18 + 61.78}{9} = 5.29,$$
and
$$P = 242.9 - .91(5.29) = \$238.1.$$

e. No.

12. a. If it sets a price of $10,000, the present value of the firm's profits is
$$\frac{4}{1.10} + \frac{4}{1.10^2} + \frac{1}{1.10^3} + \frac{1}{1.10^4} = \$8.4 \text{ millions.}$$

If it sets a price of $7,000, the present value of the firm's profits is
$$\frac{2.5}{1.10} + \frac{2.5}{1.10^2} + \frac{2.5}{1.10^3} + \frac{2.5}{1.10^4} = \$7.9 \text{ millions.}$$

Thus, based only on the next four years, it should set a price of $10,000.

b. If it sets a price of $10,000, the present value of the firm's profits is
$$\frac{4}{1.08} + \frac{4}{1.08^2} + \frac{1}{1.08^3} + \frac{1}{1.08^4} = \$8.7 \text{ millions.}$$

If it sets a price of $7,000, the present value of the firm's profits is
$$\frac{2.5}{1.08} + \frac{2.5}{1.08^2} + \frac{2.5}{1.08^3} + \frac{2.5}{1.08^4} = \$8.3 \text{ millions.}$$

Thus, based on only the next four years, it should set a price of $10,000.

c. They can estimate what profits will be in the 5th, 6th, . . . , years, and include them in the analysis.

Chapter 11

2. a. Regardless of whether Xenophon engages in a high or low level of advertising, Ulysses will earn greater profits if it chooses a high advertising level than it would if it chose a low advertising level. Thus, Ulysses will engage in a high level of advertising in trade journals.

   b. Regardless of whether Ulysses engages in a high or low level of advertising, Xenophon will earn greater profits if it chooses a low advertising level than it would if it chose a high advertising level. Thus, Xenophon will engage in a low level of advertising in trade journals.

   c. Yes.

ANSWERS TO EVEN-NUMBERED QUESTIONS

4. a. Since marginal cost equals $\frac{dTC}{dq}$, it equals 15 cents. Thus, price must equal 15 cents, which means that industry output equals 100 − 15 = 85 million cans per month.

   b. Let Q be the combined output of the two firms, and π be their combined profit.

   $$\pi = PQ - 4 - 15Q$$
   $$= (100 - Q)Q - 4 - 15Q$$
   $$\frac{\partial \pi}{\partial Q} = 100 - 2Q - 15 = 0.$$

   Thus, Q equals 42.5 million cans per month, and price equals 100 − 42.5 = 57.5 cents.

   c. If $P = 15$, their combined profit is $15(85) - 4 - 15(85) = -4$, which means that they lose $40,000. If $P = 57.5$, their combined profit is $57.5(42.5) - 4 - 15(42.5) = 1802.25$, which means that their combined profit equals $18.0225 million.

6. a. Since $Q = 300 - P$, and the demand for the firm's output is $Q - Q_r$, it follows that Pizzo's firm's demand curve is

   $$Q_b = Q - Q_r = (300 - P) - 49P$$
   $$= 300 - 50P$$

   or

   $$P = 6 - 0.02Q_b.$$

   Thus, his firm's marginal revenue curve is $MR = 6 - 0.04Q_b$. Since its marginal cost curve is $2.96Q_b$,

   $$6 - 0.04Q_b = 2.96Q_b$$
   $$Q_b = 2.$$

   That is, Pizzo's output level should be 2 million barrels per week.

   b. Since $P = 6 - 0.02Q_b$, and $Q_b = 2$, it follows that

   $$P = 6 - 0.02(2) = 5.96.$$

   That is, the price should be $5.96 per barrel.

   c. Since $Q = 300 - P$, and $P = 5.96$, it follows that

   $$Q = 300 - 5.96 = 294.04.$$

   That is, the industry output is 294.04 million barrels per week.

8. a. If it is a one-shot agreement, each is likely to cheat, with the result that each will have a profit of $28 million.
   b. Yes, as stressed on pp. 398–99 of the text.
   c. Yes.

10. a. There could be more than one reason, one possibility being that Radnor feels that if it reduces price, its rivals will match the price cut, whereas if it increases price, they will not raise their prices. However, see the answer below to part c.

b. No.
c. If the firm is operating at the point where there is a kink in the demand curve, price equals $10 and output equals 100. But in this case the firm is not maximizing profit at this point. Since marginal cost equals $5 and marginal revenue equals $20 - 0.2Q$, profits are maximized when $Q = 75$ and $P = \$12.50$.
d. See the answer to part c.

Chapter 12

2. a. In accord with the discussion on page 430 of the text, the ratio of the price in Japan to that in the United States should be $(1 - 1/2) \div (1 - 1/4) = 2/3$, and the ratio of the price in Japan to that in Europe should be $(1 - 3/4) \div (1 - 1/4) = 1/3$. This is contrary to his recommendations.
   b. This seems reasonable. If the price in Japan is $1,000 and the price in Europe is $3,000, the price in the United States should be $1,500, not $2,000, according to the ratios in the answer to part a. The fact that the U.S. price is too high may well account for the quantity sold in the U.S. being "lower than expected."
   c. This satisfies a necessary condition for profit maximization, but it does not insure profit maximization.
   d. No. We do not know that marginal revenue in each area (Japan, Europe, and the United States) equals marginal cost.

4. a. Since marginal revenue equals

   $MR = 100 - .02Q,$

   and marginal cost equals $10 + $4, or $14,

   $Q = (100 - 14) \div .02 = 4,300.$

   b. $P = 100 - .01(4,300) = \$57.$
   c. $10.

6. a. As indicated in equation (12.6), one can obtain the profit-maximizing price by multiplying marginal cost by $\frac{1}{1 - 1/\eta}$. Since $\eta = 2$ in this case, marginal cost should be multiplied by 2, which is essentially what Morrison's president is doing.
   b. He should multiply marginal cost by $\left(\frac{1}{1 - 1/3}\right)$, that is, by 3/2. In other words, he should mark up average variable cost by 50 percent (since average variable cost is approximately equal to marginal cost in this case).

8. a. The production division's marginal cost, which equals

   $MC_1 = 3 + .8Q_1,$

   should be set equal to 20. Thus, $Q_1 = 17 \div .8 = 21.25$ thousands of pounds.
   b. The marketing marginal cost equals 15, so marginal cost equals $15 + 20$, or 35. Thus, the marketing division will choose the output where its marginal revenue equals 35. Since its marginal revenue is

189

ANSWERS TO EVEN-NUMBERED QUESTIONS

$MR = 200 - 6Q_0$,

it chooses an output of $(200 - 35) + 6$, or 27.5 thousands of pounds.
c. $20 per pound.
d. $200 - 3(27.5) = \$117.5$ per pound.

10. a. If the firm accepts the offer, it receives $30,000 for the 6 instruments, but loses $4 \times \$7,200 = \$28,800$. Thus, its total revenues increase by $1,200. However, the extra 2 instruments cost $2 \times \$7,200 + 1.8 = \$8,000$. Thus, the overall effect is to reduce profit by $8,000 - \$1,200$, or $6,800. Thus, the firm should not accept the offer.
   b. Unless the chemical firm pays $6,800—that is, $1,133 per instrument—more for the 6 instruments, Breen will lose money.
   c. If one adheres rigidly to such a policy, it is easy to pass up transactions that would increase profit.

Chapter 13

2. a. 12 percent.
   b. 6 percent.
   c. 18 percent.
   d. 18 percent.

4. a. The firm's annual profit, π, equals $-\$1$ million $+ 20X$, where X is the number of television sets sold. Thus, the expected annual profit equals $-\$1$ million $+ 20E_X$, where E_X is the expected number of television sets sold. Since E_X equals 100,000, the expected annual profit is $-\$1$ million $+ 20(100,000) = \$1$ million.
   b. Since $\pi = -\$1$ million $+ 20X$, the standard deviation of π equals 20 times the standard deviation of X, which is 10,000. Thus, the standard deviation of annual profit is $20(10,000) = \$200,000$.
   c. $\$200,000 + \$1$ million $= 20$ percent.

6. a.

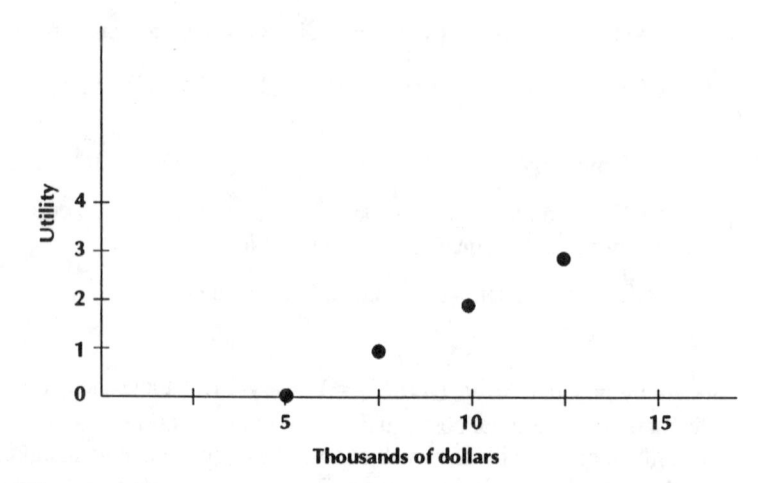

   b. Indifferent to risk.

8. It would have biased the decision in favor of attempting a launch.

10. a.

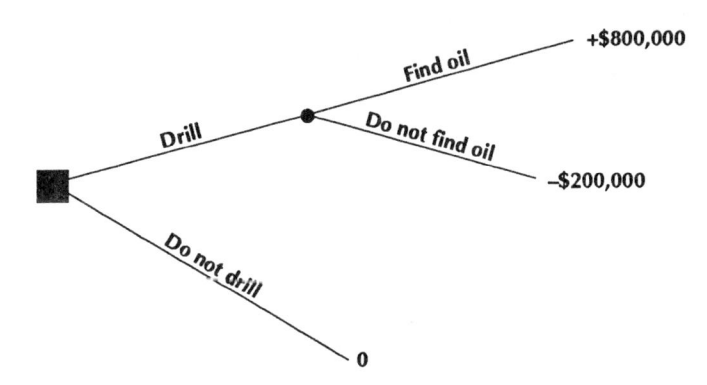

```
                              Find oil
                                        +$800,000
                Drill  ●
                              Do not find oil
                                        −$200,000
        ■
                Do not drill
                                        0
```

b. No, because we do not know the probability of finding oil if he drills a well, and we do not know his utility function.

c. The expected profit, if he drills, is .25($800,000) + .75(−$200,000) = $50,000. If he is a risk lover or indifferent to risk, he should drill, but if he is sufficiently averse to risk, he should not.

d. Yes, because the expected profit if he drills ($50,000) exceeds that if he does not drill (0). Since he prefers risk, he would certainly prefer to drill.

e. Yes, because the expected profit, if he drills, exceeds that if he does not drill.

Chapter 14

2. a. For the investment in his own business, the expected value is 0.1(4,900) + 0.4(5,500) + 0.35(6,500) + .15(7,200) = $6,045. For the investment in another local business, the expected value is 0.2(4,100) + 0.3(5,800) + 0.25(7,000) + 0.25(8,000) = $6,310.

b. The discount rate for the investment in his own business is 15 percent; for the other investment, it is 20 percent. Because of the difference in risk, he uses different discount rates. See pages 479-81 of the text.

c. For the investment in his own business, the risk-adjusted net present value is

$$-\$20,000 + \$6,045 \left\{ \frac{1}{1.15} + \frac{1}{(1.15)^2} + \ldots + \frac{1}{(1.15)^5} \right\}$$

$$= -20,000 + \$6,045(3.3522) = \$264.$$

For the investment in another local business, the risk-adjusted net present value is

$$-\$20,000 + \$6,310 \left\{ \frac{1}{1.20} + \frac{1}{(1.20)^2} + \ldots + \frac{1}{(1.20)^5} \right\}$$

$$= -20,000 + \$6,310(2.9906) = -\$1,129.$$

4. a. The annual saving in labor costs with the type A machine equals 3,000W, where W is the hourly wage rate. If the annual saving in labor costs occurs 1, 2, ..., 6

ANSWERS TO EVEN-NUMBERED QUESTIONS

years hence, and if the extra $30,000 (that must be paid for the type A machine) must be paid now, the extra investment in the type A machine is less than the present value of the labor saving if

$$\$30,000 < 3,000W\left(\frac{1}{1.1} + \frac{1}{1.1^2} + \frac{1}{1.1^3} + \frac{1}{1.1^4} + \frac{1}{1.1^5} + \frac{1}{1.1^6}\right)$$

$$< 3,000(.9091 + .8264 + .7513 + .6830 + .6209 + .5645)W$$

$$< 13,066W,$$

or if $W > \$30,000/13,066 = \$2.30$. Thus, Richmond's president is correct.
   b. No. No data are presented to indicate the profitability of the investment in either machine tool, relative to the profitability of other uses of the funds.
   c. The analysis should be carried out in terms of incremental, after-tax cash flows, not labor savings.

6. a. Since $D_1 = 4$, $W = 75$, and $g = .05$, $k_s = 4/75 + .05 = .103$. Thus, the cost of internal equity capital seems to be about 10.3 percent.
   b. Since $k_s = 4/60 + .05 = .117$, it would be about 11.7 percent.
   c. 12.7 percent.

8. a. The present value (in millions of dollars) was

$$-15 + \frac{2}{1.10} + \frac{2}{1.10^2} + \frac{2}{1.10^3} + \frac{2}{1.10^4} + \frac{2}{1.10^5} + \frac{2}{1.10^6} + \frac{2}{1.10^7} + \frac{2}{1.10^8} + \frac{2}{1.10^9}.$$

This is equal to $-15 + 2(.9091 + .8264 + .7513 + .6830 + .6209 + .5645 + .5132 + .4665 + .4241) = -15 + 2(5.7590) = -3.482$ millions of dollars.
   b. The present value would be

$$-20 + \frac{2}{1.10} + \frac{2}{1.10^2} + \frac{2}{1.10^3} + \frac{2}{1.10^4} + \frac{2}{1.10^5} + \frac{2}{1.10^6} + \frac{2}{1.10^7} + \frac{2}{1.10^8} + \frac{2}{1.10^9}.$$

This is equal to $-20 + 2(.9091 + .8264 + .7513 + .6830 + .6209 + .5645 + .5132 + .4665 + .4241) = -20 + 2(5.7590) = -8.482$ millions of dollars.
   c. Yes. Since its present value was negative, the investment was not worthwhile. The firm's analysts carried out the above calculations and recommended that the project be turned down.[1]

10. a.

	Incremental after-tax cash flow	
Year	Texas	Louisiana
0	−$4,500,000	−$5,000,000
1	$250,000(1 − .3) + $750,000	$321,667(1 − .3) + $833,333
2	$250,000(1 − .3) + $750,000	$321,667(1 − .3) + $833,333
3	$250,000(1 − .3) + $750,000	$321,667(1 − .3) + $833,333
4	$250,000(1 − .3) + $750,000	$321,667(1 − .3) + $833,333
5	$250,000(1 − .3) + $750,000	$321,667(1 − .3) + $833,333
6	$250,000(1 − .3) + $750,000	$321,667(1 − .3) + $833,333

---

[1] While this is an actual case, the numbers have been altered to simplify the calculations. For present purposes, this is of no consequence.

b. $-\$4,500,000 + \$925,000 \left[\dfrac{1}{1.10} + \dfrac{1}{1.10^2} + \cdots + \dfrac{1}{(1.10)^6} \right]$

$= -\$4,500,000 + \$925,000(4.3553) = -\$471,348.$

c. $-\$5,000,000 + \$1,058,500(4.3553) = \$-389,915.$

Chapter 15

2. a. Total cost equals $C = C_p + C_c = 2P + P^2 + 5 - 3P = 5 - P + P^2$.

   Thus, if we set
   $$\dfrac{dC}{dP} = -1 + 2P = 0,$$
   $P = 1/2$. Therefore, the optimal level of pollution is 500 tons.

   b. $\dfrac{dC_p}{dP} = 2 + 2P = 2 + 2\left(\dfrac{1}{2}\right) = 3.$

   Thus, the marginal cost of pollution equals $3 billion per thousand tons.

   c. $\dfrac{dC_c}{dP} = -3.$

   Thus, the marginal cost of pollution control is $3 billion per thousand tons of pollutants cut back.

4. a. The total cost equals $C = C_p + C_c = 3P + 3P^2 + 7 - 5P = 7 - 2P + 3P^2$.

   Thus, if we set
   $$\dfrac{dC}{dP} = -2 + 6P = 0,$$
   $P = 1/3$, which means that the optimal level of P is 1/3. Since
   $$\dfrac{dC_p}{dP} = 3 + 6P,$$
   the marginal cost of an extra thousand tons of pollutants emitted equals $3 + 6(1/3) = \$5$ billion. Similarly, the marginal cost of reducing pollution by an extra thousand tons equals $5 billion. Thus, the effluent fee should be $5 billion per thousand tons—or $5 million per ton.

   b. No.

6. a. No.
   b. It might be charged that Kravis was discriminating to a greater degree than was justified to meet competition.
   c. No. The Celler-Kefauver Act.

8. a. Yes.
   b. It would reduce such incentives greatly.
   c. One important reason was that there would have been a reduction in incentives for innovation if the decision had not been reversed.